The Experience of God

John D. Caputo, *series editor*

PERSPECTIVES IN
CONTINENTAL PHILOSOPHY

Edited by KEVIN HART AND
BARBARA WALL

The Experience of God

A Postmodern Response

FORDHAM UNIVERSITY PRESS

New York ■ 2005

Perspectives in Continental Philosophy Series, No. 48
ISSN 1089-3938

Library of Congress Cataloging-in-Publication Data

The experience of God : a postmodern response / edited by Kevin Hart and
Barbara E. Wall.
    p.   cm. — (Perspectives in continental philosophy ; no. 48)
    Includes bibliographical references and index.
    ISBN 0-8232-2518-6 (hardcover) — ISBN 0-8232-2519-4 (pbk.)
    1. Spirituality.   2. Experience (Religion)   3. Postmodernism.   I. Hart,
Kevin, 1948–   II. Wall, Barbara Eileen, 1943–   .III. Series.
BL624.E955   2005
204'.2—dc22   2005017144

Printed in the United States of America
07 06 05   5 4 3 2 1
First edition

Dedicated to Kail C. Ellis, O.S.A.,
whose leadership and presence have inspired the dialogue of
faith and culture at Villanova University.

Contents

Preface

The essays in this collection had their first life at a conference, "The Experience of God," held at Villanova University in the fall of 2001. The conference took place in the shadow of the 9/11 attacks on the United States. Those events were nothing if not an *experience*, an exposure to peril, and the decision to go ahead with the conference in November on a campus that had been deeply shaken in September was an affirmation of the possibility of another sort of experience, one that can be no less perilous but that is rooted in hope. In taking "the experience of God" as our guiding figure, we invited our speakers to rethink what "experience" might mean when placed near that wild word "God" and to try yet again, after so many earlier attempts by philosophers and theologians, to understand the conjunction of "experience" and "God." That the conjunction crudely bespeaks the impossible is acknowledged: God does not offer Himself to the senses, and the finite cannot experience the infinite. Yet the Bible and the works of many mystics challenge us to make the conjunction speak in a subtler manner, and even to entertain the possibility that an encounter with God discloses itself in counterexperience or nonexperience. Our speakers reflected on the theme by way of their expertise in philosophy, theology, literature, and feminist theory. We are thankful to them for coming to Villanova and for their intellectual generosity while there.

The editors would like to thank Villanova University and, in particular, its Office for Mission Effectiveness for providing the resources for the conference on which this volume is based. Christopher Janosik assisted in the organization of the conference and in the handling of the manuscripts, and Marcella Bray provided logistical support for the conference participants. We are grateful for their assistance. Kevin Hart would like to thank the Department of Philosophy at Villanova University for appointing him to the Visiting Professorship in Christian Philosophy for the Fall 2001 semester in which the conference was held. It is a special pleasure to thank John D. Caputo for all his help with Kevin Hart's stay at Villanova, with the conference, and with the collection.

Kevin Hart
Barbara Wall

The Experience of God

Introduction

KEVIN HART

1

Merely utter the simple expression "the experience of God" and you will divide a room, especially if it happens to be filled with philosophers and theologians. There will always be a group that strenuously objects that the expression makes no sense at all—or, if it does, then it is downright dangerous. "It is the very nature of God not to be experienced by finite beings," someone will offer as a first comment. "And if we do encounter anything that appears divine it would be, at best or worst, an idol." Chances are that another member of this group will quickly add, "You need to realize that 'experience' as you use it is a relatively modern notion, especially when it comes to religion, and besides to yoke 'experience' and 'God' together is to presume the rightness of reducing theology to anthropology." She takes a breath and steadily looks around. "I know that Karl Rahner often talks about experiencing God, and maybe you are quoting him. Let me say that I think that his work is very effective pastoral theology, but his emphasis on turning all theology into theological anthropology can have harmful effects. To speculate theologically on the basis of a philosophical anthropology is to produce at best a stunted doctrine of God and, in the end, a truncated understanding of being human." She stops, but we have not yet finished hearing from this group.

"I don't disagree with what was just said," another person might say, "but there's something else that bothers me." We are all ears. "To view God through the lens of 'experience' is to remain naively within the epoch of the subject; and haven't Martin Heidegger, Jacques Derrida, and Jean-Luc Marion shown us in convincing detail that the modern subject is metaphysical through and through? If you want to avoid perpetuating a metaphysical theology, then rejecting the old *causa sui*, for instance, would be dealing with only the objective dimension of the problem. You also need to examine the subjective dimension, and ensure that you are not erecting a metaphysics there by affirming 'experience' at the heart of your new theology." "Not only that," yet another voice adds, "but the category of experience tends to prize the individual, especially the modern individual, over the entire complex tradition of Christianity. What is important for the believer is to conform to the narratives of faith, hope, and charity that are related in the Bible, which are authoritative archetypes of Christian experience, not to validate what the Bible teaches by reference to events in our own lives."

"Might I read some scripture?" a woman in the other camp asks. She opens a pocket gospel to the twentieth chapter of the fourth gospel. "You all know the context," she says, "the risen Christ has spoken with the disciples who had gathered together for fear of the Jews. The only one of the disciples not there is Thomas. Christ comes into their midst and shows them his hands and his side and then leaves them." She looks about her, testing with her eyes that everyone in the room is taking in the story. "Then Thomas returns and is told what has happened. He says, 'Except I see in his hands the prints of the nails, and put my finger into the print of the nails, and thrust my hand into his side, I will not believe' (John 20:25). Eight days later the resurrected Jesus returns to the disciples, and this time Thomas is with them. Christ invites Thomas to do exactly what he had boasted he would do, and the skeptical disciple responds by saying, 'My Lord and my God' (John 20:28)." She snaps the little book shut. "Now I don't want to get into the details of whether those words are authentic or even how historically reliable the fourth gospel is, I just want to point out that it did not strike the Johannine community as inappropriate to talk about experiencing God."

A hush falls over the room for a moment or two, and then a young man begins to talk. "Those are powerful words, but I want to suggest something quite different," he says. "I want to point out that if we don't have experience of God in some sense then all those beautiful philosophies of religion and sublime theologies we always hear about might be no more than empty structures with nothing but cold air blowing through them. Theology would be vainly seeking to offer us what the philosopher Thomas Nagel calls 'the view from nowhere.'[1] The Bible records stories of the Lord speaking through a burning bush and in the thin silence of the wind; it tells us of prophets who talk intimately with Yahweh and sometimes even dare to argue with Him. Of course, experience of God isn't always the focal point of the Bible, and we are not to expect that we can engage with God as we do created things, but why should we doubt that God has revealed Himself in and through the medium of human experience? Is it possible to think the incarnation without responding to a God who seeks experience and who offers Himself in that realm to us as well?" "Let me add, too"—and here another person takes the floor—"that there is a long and venerable tradition of mystics who encounter God in visions of one species or another: Angela of Foligno, St Theresa of Avila, Jacob Boehme . . ."

"And many others," interrupts an older woman, "but since you have cited two female visionaries I think that I should pose a question. I'm surprised that it hasn't come up before now. It is this: Is experience a gender-neutral category? For my part, I suspect that men and women don't encounter things in quite the same way or, if you prefer, they bring different insights to their communions with God. For one thing, women will use their experience as a resistance to a wholly male theology. And I should point out that if you call God 'He,' as I've heard more than once today, you are talking in the language of experience, and in all likelihood without good reason for doing so."

2

It is true: the word "experience" has a striking ability to divide people when they talk about God, and it has been doing so for centuries. Recall the Spiritualist movement in sixteenth-century Germany. Sebastian Franck was not alone when he emphasized the inner life over the externals of sacraments and scripture. Christianity is at heart an experience of faith, not an affirmation of doctrine, the more extreme Spiritualists insisted. Even those who did not go quite that far, like Valentin Weigel, nonetheless prized experience over tradition. Listen to him speaking in *On the Place of the World* (1576): "For simply turn back inward through Christ, into the inner ground by dying unto yourself, and so on, and you will have to confess that the kingdom of God is within you and all things in Christ, about which it is proper to say no more. Let everyone experience it within himself."[2] Radical words, they go all the way back to a strand of early Christianity. One can hear Augustine in them and, beyond him, Plotinus.[3]

Beginning in the late eighteenth century, many evangelicals believed that reading scripture, fervent prayer, and impassioned preaching could bring about experiences that would lead to conversion or, if the person was already a regenerate, to a deeper relationship with Christ. "Experience" was to be centered on "feeling," and the move was to find theological support in Friedrich Schleiermacher's *On Religion: Speeches to Its Cultured Despisers* (1799). Certainly by the first decades of the nineteenth century it was not uncommon for evangelicals to believe that one's feelings provided reliable evidence of justification. Heard in English pulpits as well in the parishes given to the "German Awakening," this appeal to experience alarmed high churchmen such as John Henry Newman.[4] He objected to a reliance on emotion in Catholic as well as Protestant religious practices. Consider this passage from a sermon before his conversion to the Catholic faith:

> Nothing lasts, nothing keeps incorrupt and pure, which comes of mere feeling; feelings die like spring flowers, and are fit only to be cast into the oven. Persons thus circumstanced will find their religion fail them in time; a revulsion of mind will ensue. They will feel a violent distaste for what pleased them before, a sickness and weariness of mind; or even an enmity towards it; or a great disappointment; or a confusion and perplexity and despondence. They have learned to think religion easier than it is, themselves better than they are; they have drunk their good wine instead of keeping it; and this is the consequence.[5]

Only a religious practice oriented to the creeds and to tradition can keep one from the inevitable sorrows of experience, especially when it is taken in the narrow sense of "feeling."

For some Christians today, the word "experience" still conjures the specter or adventure of theological modernism: Maurice Blondel, Ernesto Buonaiuti, Lucien Laberthonnière, Alfred Loisy, George Tyrrell, and Friedrich von Hügel, all of whom were active in the first decades of the last century. It is hard to generalize about a movement that was organized more by reaction to the rather wooden Thomism of the nineteenth-century manuals of dogmatics than by positive agreements among themselves, and it would be pointless to distinguish modernism in the Catholic faith too sharply from liberalism in the Protestant churches. That said, liberalism and modernism tended to prize religious experience over received doctrine; and within the Catholic Church it was vigorously combated, the major official signals being the decree *Lamentabili sane exitu* (1907) and the encyclical *Pascendi dominici gregis* (1907).[6] With hindsight, it seems as though the decisive Protestant response to modernism was given by Karl Barth in the second edition of his *Epistle to the Romans* (1922), although his *Göttingen Dogmatics*, comprising lectures delivered in the early 1920s, supplies us with a more effective quotation: "The bad thing about the modern theology of experience is that it builds its certainty about God upon something that is given in the human subject when the only thing that is given in this subject, even in the believer, is the question."[7] If Barth rejects theological modernism in those words, he also indicates the limits of Spiritualism and the "German Awakening."[8]

When the word "experience" is pronounced within earshot of philosophers and theologians, disagreements will arise for all sorts of reasons. To talk about the testimony of the New Testament will generate one set of issues, while to consider appeals to experience as justifying theological statements will give rise to another. One way in which a room of philosophers and theologians can divide is over the question of correlation. You simply say "experience of God," and correlationists will band together, leaving noncorrelationists to form a vocal minority opposition. The distinction works at several levels and can be construed in diverse ways. Correlation might involve harmonizing faith and reason, received symbol and modern ontology, the contemporary individual and ecclesial tradition, and so on. But let us stay above these competing ways of going about things. From our vantage point, we can see that, in some respects, the distinction has become more telling for religious life today than the historical and doctrinal ones that separate Catholics, Orthodox, and Protestants.[9] Correlationists might begin by agreeing with Barth that the God-question is given in the subject, but they then seek to find an answer to what has been posed. The existential questions that preoccupy us — Am I free? Why do the innocent suffer? Can there be justice in this world? Is death the end of life? — are held to be answered satisfactorily in Christianity. Correlational theologies do not say that experience is the *source* of our apprehension of God but rather that it is the *medium* through which we encounter the deity.[10] If correlational theologies turn around the word "dialogue" or "mediation," noncorrelational theologies orient themselves with reference to the word "declaration" or "interruption." The progenitor of all modern mediating theologies is of course G. W. F. Hegel, although his intellectual children have inherited from him in diverse ways. Karl Rahner widely differs from Paul Tillich in doctrinal and methodological issues, for example, while Jürgen Moltmann and David Tracy would disagree as often as they would agree.

Where these mediating theologians are mistaken, the noncorrelationalists insist, is that they prize revealability over revelation and, in doing so, tacitly grant a methodological priority to the human over the divine. So correlation never actually happens, they think: the divine Word is interpreted in advance so that it might fit a modern, secular worldview and in the process its divinity is annulled. What occurs under the sign of "correlation" is something else: reductionism. Who are these noncorrelationists? Karl Barth is the best known, to be sure, and his many followers popularized the position. The Jean-Luc Marion of *God Without Being* is the most philosophically incisive representative of the view today, and John Milbank reminds us that it is possible to develop a noncorrelational theology while not aligning oneself with neo-orthodoxy.[11] Yet nowhere is the objection to correlation put more succinctly and more pungently than in these remarks by Eberhard Jüngel:

> The scandal which the word of the cross is for the wisdom of the world is not to be found in the fact that it is not reasonable enough. That explains why I regard the question-answer model in which man is asserted to be the question to which talk about God is supposed to answer as inappropriate. This model fails to recognize the center of the Christian faith whose necessity it still wants to prove, namely that God has spoken definitively, that God has become man—and what is there the answer and the question? If that is supposed to be capable of seriously being believed, then any rational grounding which precedes faith arrives too late and in a fashion which disqualifies the entire undertaking.[12]

Deus dixit! God has spoken: His Word has interrupted our worldly discourse, and it is the Christian's task to declare that Word to all generations, not conceding anything to contemporary pressures.

Immediately after this vigorous rejection of the *Frage-Antwort-Modell*, Jüngel lets us glimpse his counterstrategy:

In a colloquium with my Catholic colleague in Tübingen, Walter Kasper, and his colleagues, we agreed that theological thinking lives both materially and formally out of the past statements of the New Testament which bear the future within themselves and thus are neither capable of nor require any rational grounding. (xiv)

To which a theologian of mediation might respond by asking a couple of rather pointed questions. Is not this antifoundationalist fideism itself a reaction to a limp liberalism that precedes it, along with a culture that sustained belief in progress and individuality? Is it not at heart a correlation with a very deep cultural presupposition, namely the impulse to recover a past authenticity in danger of being lost? And yet, for all his fierce rejection of a philosophical grounding of theology, Jüngel does not follow Barth in rejecting experience as a category. On the contrary, he explores what he calls an "experience with experience" (*eine Erfahrung mit der Erfahrung*), a reevaluation of all experience in the dark light of nonbeing which results in a grateful acknowledgment that one has been brought out of nothingness and is preserved from it. This consciousness is an event that cannot be deduced from previous episodes in life, one that Jüngel does not hesitate to call "the *revelation of God*" (33).

God takes shape as a question in human experience, not as an answer, yet God as answer—the divine "Yes"—which we never experience as such is infinitely more significant than any question about God that we might ask. Such is the young Barth's response to the theology of Friedrich Schleiermacher and all the liberals who followed him.[13] The eminent Reformed churchman had no taste for the mystics, but maybe they offer a counterexample to his general position. After all, one might think, if anyone has been touched by God it would be the mystics, whether in the prayer of quiet or in moments of rapture. Yet there is little talk of experiencing God, at least in the Latin Church, until the twelfth century; and even thereafter the great mystics express considerable caution with regard to the idea. St. John of the Cross offers this caveat in *The Spiritual Canticle*: "However surely it may seem that you find, experience, and understand God, you must, because He is inaccessible and concealed, always regard Him as hidden, and serve Him Who is hidden in a secret way."[14] Nonetheless all mystics, and surely the bulk of believers as well, sense that an exposure to God—even if it be merely an inchoate awareness of a presence or a trace—forms itself as a question that sets us on a quest for union with the deity. Severe as he can be, St. John of the Cross also tells us in *The Dark Night* that the soul could not endure the terrible absence of God without first having had "the experience of sweet and delightful communion with Him" (333).

A path has opened before us, and we can pass further more quickly along it by recalling T. S. Eliot's *Four Quartets* (1943). What became the first poem of the sequence, "Burnt Norton" (1935), begins with the speaker evoking a moment of transcendence that occurred when visiting a rose garden outside a manor house in Gloucestershire; it marks for the speaker a precious state of elevated calm that offers profound consolation for the past but that devalues the future. For that too now seems to him no more than "waste sad time." The remaining three poems, from "East Coker" (1940) to "Little Gidding" (1942), partly reflect on that occurrence, test it, find it wanting in essential respects, and eventually place it in a broader context in which personal illumination counts for comparatively little in the spiritual life as a whole. "We had the experience but missed the meaning," the speaker tells us in "The Dry Salvages" (1941), and later in the same poem reflects on the elusive relation of event and meaning:

> For most of us, there is only the unattended
> Moment, the moment in and out of time,
> The distraction fit, lost in a shaft of sunlight,
> The wild thyme unseen, or the winter lightning
> Or the waterfall, or music heard so deeply
> That it is not heard at all, but you are the music
> While the music lasts. These are only hints and guesses,
> Hints followed by guesses; and the rest
> Is prayer, observance, discipline, thought and action.[15]

What Eliot calls "the rest" is by far the larger part of a Christian life, and although prayer, observance, discipline, thought and action are experiential only the first has any claim to be counted as an experience of God, and even then it calls for many reservations and caveats. To attend mass, to take on the rigors of meditation and mortification, to think theologically and to act so that the kingdom might come: all these, for Eliot, are impelled or bolstered by a fleeting experience that lifts us out of time and that is perhaps an insight into the divine.

Perhaps. That is the most one can say, unless one has been given a special charism like the man, presumably himself, whom St. Paul recalls when writing to the church at Corinth. This person "was caught up into paradise, and heard unspeakable words, which it is not lawful for a man to utter" (2 Cor. 12:4). The experience of God, if the expression can be trusted, does not turn on yielding positive knowledge of God. The event is *lived*—and three shadings of the verb need to be identified. First, the encounter is something that is passed through, enjoyed, or suffered, even if it cannot be neatly internalized like commonplace events. It is this inability to appropriate the event, to fold it into one's sense of self, which makes it insuperably hard for a recipient of a special charism to distinguish experience from nonexperience. Second, it is an encounter in which we are involved both before and after it occurs. Before a Christian has anything that might possibly count as experience of God, he or she has usually anticipated it in Christian categories and in all likelihood will continue to interpret it in the same way. Sometimes the experience requires inherited concepts to be refigured or adjusted; sometimes it calls for them to be enforced all the more strictly; and sometimes it calls for a long negotiation of event and concept: the speaker's apprehension in "Burnt Norton," for instance, was of a lotus slowly rising in an empty pool, and much meditation on the event was required before it could be folded into a trinitarian perspective in "Little Gidding."

The third shading of "lived" is the lightest and most important. If God is encountered, the blessed soul comes to grasp "experience" differently: you are reoriented, you take your bearings from a point that transcends the world. It is not enough to say that one is now guided by love and that love does not belong to theoretical consciousness, for the very meaning of "love" has both deepened and ramified. For the Christian, it will not have anything to do with any *égoïsme à deux*, even if the two are God and the soul, but will reveal itself in a radical self-emptying. Humility is endless, Eliot wearily assures us in *Four Quartets*. We can make sense of this erasure of all limitation by acknowledging the absolute asymmetry between the created soul and the Creator, and we can think it also by coming to terms with a love that embraces unmerited suffering, on the one hand, and that affirms itself as the most innocent play, on the other; and for us that is an infinite task.

Taken as a whole, Eliot's *Four Quartets* suggest that the distinction between the mystical life and normal Christian existence is less sharp than it might at first appear. The distinction can be questioned from both sides. Thus Karl Rahner regards the borderline as divided when he approaches it from the perspective of Ignatian spirituality. He talks of a "mysticism of everyday life."[16] On his account, common human phenomena such as love and hope, disappointment and despair, contain a vague and unthematized reference to the deity.[17] We are perpetually drawn toward the withdrawing horizon of the Holy Mystery, and the pull occurs in and through our relations with one another where God makes Himself felt though not known. Here, Ignatian spirituality properly grounds a vision in which the difference between mystics and typical believers is of degree, not kind. Experience of God is not to be sought solely in the cloister or in extraordinary graces; it is also freely offered in the ordinary events of our daily lives. Can one see the border between the mystical and the quotidian as divided from the perspective of the quotidian?

Yes, says Jean Moureaux. He ends his long meditation on Christian life by saying that "Christ is the traveler's bread; and the Christian experience is a little of this bread, which he gives to his own, to prevent them from falling by the wayside."[18] It is in our belonging to the Church, in our living in the Spirit, and in our acts of selfless love that we can lay claim to "Christian experience." We are not usually given visions of the deity, but we should usually partake of the Eucharist, and it is in a life devoted to the sacraments that we can truly believe we have received Christ. By "Christian experience," Moureaux asks us not to conceive a path to truth, which is precisely what Rahner does, but "the possession, the consciousness of, the deepening insight into, a structured reality" (ix).

It will surely be objected here that Moureaux is not talking of "experience of God" but "experience of faith," which is quite a different matter. The claim is interesting, but is it valid? Realists about God will say it is, since for them the deity's being is ultimately independent of our relations with Him. Theology should seek to be founded in a doctrine of God, they maintain, not in an analysis of faith. They therefore differ strongly from the young Heidegger, who argued in his 1927 lecture "Phenomenology and Theology" that "Theology is the science of faith," by which they meant that it is "the science of that which is disclosed in faith," "the science of the very comportment of believing," "the science that faith of itself motivates and justifies," and, finally, the science of cultivating "faithfulness itself."[19] The slide from theology to philosophical anthropology that realists find in Heidegger and his followers doubtless represents a complex danger for modern theology, not the least element of which is the construction of a God who, even in our encounters with Him, remains external to us. Yet theological realism must distance itself from philosophical realism if it is to avoid an even worse danger. It is one thing to distinguish "theology" from "economy," as the Orthodox do, and affirm that the immanent Trinity is not grounded in the economic Trinity. In Himself, God would be God without the world. However, it is a quite different thing to conceive God as a "given" in reality. To do so would be to bypass the essential truth that God reveals and conceals Himself as judge and redeemer.[20] There is no acknowledgment of God outside the sphere of grace, and faith belongs to that sphere. With that in mind, we can rightly say that to speak of the experience of faith can be an indirect and prudent way of evoking the experience of God.[21]

Moureaux indirectly teaches us that each and every Christian life is extraordinary, not because of any special actions that may be performed or any charisms that are given, whether ecstasy or the gift of tongues or the grace of working miracles, but because even the slightest action performed in a state of grace is already marked by the life of the triune God. And here we might benefit by remembering a passage by a poet of a quite different stripe than Eliot: Gerard Manley Hopkins. "The Principle or Foundation" is not a poem but an address based on the opening of St. Ignatius Loyola's *Spiritual Exercises*. The final paragraph considers the meaning of being in a state of grace, and here are its closing sentences:

> When a man is in God's grace and free from mortal sin, then everything that he does, so long as there is no sin in it, gives God glory and what does not give him glory has some, however little, sin in it. It is not only prayer that gives God glory but work. Smiting on an anvil, sawing a beam, whitewashing a wall, driving horses, sweeping, scouring, everything gives God some glory if being in his grace you do it as your duty. To go to communion worthily gives God great glory, but to take food in thankfulness and temperance gives him glory too. To lift up the hands in prayer gives God glory, but a man with a dungfork in his hand, a woman with a sloppail, give him glory too.[22]

For Hopkins, Christian experience would not commonly be centered on "experience of God" but rather on praise of God. What is important is to live *coram deo*, and this can be and should be done without any hope or expectation of having one's devotion to the deity confirmed by special events.

Yet we can turn this sentiment around, and view it from the side: our experience of God will characteristically occur liturgically, whether inside our outside a particular building or even a service. Here the believer is not passive but turned toward his or her Creator. Here the believer is not alone, even if he or she prays in solitude: any prayer, no matter how secret, joins one to the whole Church, past, present, and to come. As one of Hopkins's most ardent admirers puts it: "By being dynamically inhabited by God, man is brought to attunement (*Stimmen*) by God: he possesses a voice (*Stimme*), and the right voice at that. He does not stammer and babble; he speaks with God."[23] In no sense is this attunement an immediate apprehension of the deity, a notion that annuls "experience" in any case. Rather, attunement to God is achieved in and through human acts that have been inspired by the God who became human. Let us listen to Hans Urs von Balthasar yet again: "If experience . . . even in a worldly sense is not a state but an event . . . it follows that it is not man's entry (*Einfahren*) into himself, into his best and highest possibilities, which can become an experience (*Erfahrung*), but, rather, it is his act of entering into the Son of God, Christ Jesus, who is naturally inaccessible to him, which becomes the experience that alone can claim for itself his undivided obedience."[24] If we strive to live *coram dei*, we do indeed experience God, though indirectly, by registering profound changes in ourselves. By following the exemplary Christ in our days and years, we come to a radical kenosis. That emptiness, that suffering, that lightness, that joy, that vulnerability, that loss of self, is, we believe, the experience of God acting upon ourselves.

3

We begin with John D. Caputo's reflections on the impossible as the proper modality for approaching the idea of the experience of God. There have been philosophers and theologians aplenty who have declared that "experience of God" is strictly impossible on logical grounds: we cannot experience what by definition transcends phenomena. Caputo turns the table on this argument. The experience of God is fitted, he says, to the God of experience. In other words, our problem is not the impossibility (and the impiety) of adjusting the concept of God to the finite categories of human understanding. Rather, we need to rethink "experience" other than as determined by Kant and refined by Husserl. Experience always involves a reference to its Greek root —*peira*, danger —and consequently we have experience only when we pass the limit of the possible, of what has become acceptable. Experience of God is not impossible, but, like any experience worthy of the name, it must always pass through the figure of the impossible. It must negotiate one or more aporias, places where our road is blocked or simply peters out. Caputo attempts to outline a way of talking about our encounters with God that remains answerable to phenomenology and scripture. If he differs from Husserl's insistence that "there is no difference between the experience [*erlebten*] or conscious content and the experience itself [*Erlebnis selbst*]," he does so only because he affirms a sense of experience as risk that is more deeply phenomenological than that given by the intentional structure of consciousness.[25] And if he departs from an understanding that the Bible records God's experiences of us, rather than vice versa, he does so only because of a deep conviction that the people of both Testaments encounter the divine in ways that are unforeseeable and life changing, for themselves and for those who read about them.

Experience has been an important yet uneasy category in feminist theologies, as Kristine Culp reminds us in her essay, "'A World Split Open.'" On one hand, a feminist theology should recognize, reclaim, and honor the great wealth of female experiences; on the other hand, it should be wary about prizing "experience" over the templates of meaning and power that have structured oppression and that require close analysis if things are to change. Can an appeal to female experience produce the appropriate affective and cognitive material for a viable feminist theology? No: feminist theologies need more than an appeal to experience. And yet the category of experience should not be jettisoned. It recalls us to grounds we should not forget: that theology must be engaged with life in all its ambiguities, and that feminist theology gains an impetus from female resistance and protest. So we need to retain the category of experience while closely attending to how we reconstruct and interpret it. To that end, Culp relates the story of her visit to Lourdes and reflects on the differences between "having" experience and reconstructing it after the fact. When does an experience begin, occur, and end? The question is less easy to answer than to pose. In her reflections on that question, Culp also invites us to ponder what experience can offer to us. Not a firm ground on which to base our spirituality or our theology, but a capacity to disrupt our habits of perception, even when (and especially when) we find that they easily cohere with our politics or our theology.

Disruption is one of the themes of Kevin Hart's contribution to the discussion: he begins by pondering a man knocking on your door and saying, simply, "I have experienced God." What could this mean? At the least, it signals that, if we are to encounter God in any way or to any extent, we must do so in the medium of experience. It does not follow, however, that the divine must present itself as an item of experience, whether that be *Erlebnis* or *Erfahrung*. Hart seeks to determine the figure that "God and experience" cuts against the ground of the New Testament. Accordingly, he grants a privilege to prayer, and notes that all prayer, no matter of what sort, is a response to a prior call. In prayer we encounter God as absolute subject, and never as intentional object. That is, God is disclosed only in the dimension of faith. So, strictly speaking, we cannot talk of experiencing God. Instead, we must invoke a different figure, one that bespeaks both faith and response, namely "counterexperience." In prayer there passes through our lives a disturbance that we do not inaugurate and that we cannot control, either intellectually or affectively. Counterexperience unsettles us, invites us to stand only in the ground and abyss of faith and there to see our experiences from the perspective of divine love. Taking the prayer for the Kingdom to come as his model, Hart resets the question of experiencing God so that it concerns the experience of the Kingdom of God. It is in our complex experience of the Kingdom, as here yet still to come, that we encounter the triune God, not as an item of experience but as a trace that passes through our experience of divine love.

Prayer is also Jean-Yves Lacoste's point of entry to his reflections on our experience of God in the liturgy. Like Caputo and Hart, Lacoste was schooled in phenomenology, and his essay, "Liturgy and Coaffection," works closely with Heidegger's revision of Husserlian phenomenology. Rather than take as his model the sole person in prayer, Lacoste focuses on the liturgy. At mass we sing "almighty God and Father, we worship you, we give you thanks, we praise you for your glory"; we solemnly say, "We believe in one God" and "We believe in one Lord, Jesus Christ" and "Give us this day our daily bread." Yet who is this "we"? It is the congregation and it is the Church. Lacoste invites us to look for a philosophically deeper answer, to take part in a phenomenological investigation of the "we." The aim: to draw closer to the reality of the "we," to offer a more precise description of what occurs in the liturgy, and to determine the extent to which the "we" of the liturgy refers to coaffective experience. In *Being and Time* (§29) Heidegger examines *Befindlichkeit*, which might be translated "state of mind" or, with less of an analytical flavor, "already having found-itself there-ness."[26] *Befindlichkeit* is an ontological attunement to the affective order, a structural trait of *Dasein* that is prior to any and all ontic states (or "moods"). What intrigues Lacoste is the "we"-dimension of this attunement, *Mitbefin-dlichkeit*; it belongs to a well-known series in Heidegger that includes *Mitwelt*, *Mitsein*, and *Mitdasein*. The other person is always and already there with me, not as an intentional object but before any questions of knowledge even arise for me. Liturgical experience occurs at a level before any distinctions can be drawn between subject and object. We stand before God as brothers and sisters, not as a collection of separate Cartesian subjects, and we do not necessarily experience either God or each other at the level of feeling. The "with" of "being with" takes hold at a deeper level. Liturgy presumes a certain distancing that serves as a critique of the feeling that subtends Schleiermacher's theology and all the sacramental theologies that draw from it.

Prayer is attunement to the God who has already crossed the gulf from divinity to humanity. While prayer must occur in the realm of experience, it seldom gives rise to particular experiences; and when it does, the believer will find that the great mystics, like St. John of the Cross and St. Teresa of Avila, counsel him or her to treat them very circumspectly. For God does not usually present Himself as an object to be experienced. Far more common, for mystics as well as for the faithful in general, is a complete lack of experience in prayer. We sense nothing, we feel nothing, and we wonder if any contact is made with the deity. In time we accept that this absence of affect is the condition of a mature life of prayer, and we link it with a wider theology of God. Luther underlined that when talking about God we are constrained by our fidelity to scripture to speak in two registers at the same time. We affirm *deus revelatus*, the revealed God, yet at the same time we must also acknowledge *deus absconditus*, the hidden God. Christianity does not teach that God first hid Himself and then revealed Himself fully in Jesus Christ. Not at all: the revelation of God irreducibly involves a reveiling of God. God is revealed *sub contrario*; majesty is manifest in Christ's abject suffering on the Cross. Such is the dark ground that Michael Purcell explores in his essay, though he orients himself by the Psalms instead of the Gospels and takes Emmanuel Levinas rather than Martin Luther as his guide. Once again, then, phenomenology is brought into conversation with scripture and faith; and, since Purcell follows Levinas in prizing ethics over theory, once again we are placed in the midst of prayer for the Kingdom.

The essays by Caputo, Culp, Hart, Lacoste, and Purcell were given as plenary papers at a conference hosted by the Office for Mission Effectiveness at Villanova University in November 2001. "The Experience of God" brought together philosophers and theologians to examine once again the simple, seductive, and dangerous expression that we took to name the concerns we wished to discuss. Each plenary paper was followed by a response, and these are included in this volume. Michael Scanlon, Renee McKenzie, James Smith, Jeffrey Bloechl, and Kevin Hughes probe each paper sharply and sensitively, and the editors have thought it important to keep alive the rich sense of intellectual debate that characterized the conference. Other, shorter papers were also presented at "The Experience of God," and we have included a selection of these, not as secondary pieces but as lively contributions to the original discussion that amplify or extend the insights offered there.

Experience of God is leagued with idolatry: such is one of the main themes of this collection in both its philosophical and theological parts. Yet, with equal insistence, we have heard that we can encounter God only in the dimension of human experience. That is a given for those, like Michael Purcell, who are committed to a theological anthropology as well as those, like Kevin Hart, who regard revelation as supplying its own conditions of possibility. Can one refigure "experience" so that we can speak of God without reducing divinity to the categories of human understanding? That is a question coiled in all the essays collected here. Interruption and the impossible are two words that have been spoken more than once in these papers. Jeffrey Bloechl, who also looks to phenomenology and scripture as his touchstones, investigates the possibility of an ego that is dislodged from its presumed central point in the philosophy or theology of experience. Only such a displaced ego, Bloechl argues, could possibly receive divinity without claiming to comprehend it. If the ego spreads a light of understanding on all that it encounters, the condition of being approached by the divine would be the dimming of that light. There are several paths that lead from the light of intelligibility to the darkness of unknowing—Nietzsche's and Levinas's, as well as those trodden by the mystics—and Bloechl explores them with care. In the end, it is a mistake to think that we are to be approached by God, as though He were outside us. Christianity teaches that we already live in the divine presence. There are no conditions that must be met before we can encounter God in the realm of experience, not even humility and hope. God does not wait for us to establish conditions of possibility: He is already here, waiting for us. We should not speak of the experience *of* God but of experience *with* God.

That the concept of experience weighs heavily on the modern mind is acknowledged in a variety of ways by the contributors to this volume, regardless of whether or not they ground theology in experience. This is not to say, of course, that the faithful did not encounter God in earlier times, or that they did not reflect on such events. St. Augustine's remarkable ascent to the deity while conversing with his mother at Ostia, as described in *Confessions* IX. x. 23–26, is the best known of such occurrences in patristic times. Yet while Augustine developed a powerful theology of desire, one that is announced at the very start of his most popular work ("Your heart is restless until it rests in you," *Confessions*, I.i.1), he cued it into what became for him and the tradition he partly generated a broader theology of faith and reason. *Nisi credideritis, non intellegetis* ("If you do not believe, you will not understand"): Augustine was fond of quoting Isaiah 7:9, and in *De Trinitate* he rephrased scripture, saying *Fides quaerit, intellectus invenit* ("Faith seeks, understanding finds").[27] This linking of faith and understanding was to be taken up by St. Anselm and St. Thomas Aquinas. In addition, it was to be asterisked for attention by the Vatican at the beginning and the end of the period when theologians were the most interested in the category of experience. In *Aeterni patris* (1879) Leo XIII called for theology to be centered in the summae of Aquinas, while in *Fides et ratio* (1998) John Paul II drew renewed attention to the value of the Thomist synthesis of supernatural faith and natural reason. For the Vatican, modern theologies of experience, whether modernist or Rahnerian, must be set within a wider context before they can function properly.

Michael Andrews follows in the wake of Augustine and Anselm in taking up the theme of "faith seeking understanding." The central figure for him, however, is Edith Stein, the most important woman of the phenomenological movement and a writer whose works are only now becoming available in English. Like Lacoste, Stein is interested in the "we" behind the "I"; it is at the base of her philosophy of empathy. And like all phenomenologists, she responds to the questions folded in "the experience of God" not as difficult equations to the solved but as a field of tensions where we must live. Because experience of God does not translate readily into knowledge of God, it does not follow that the expression has no meaning. Rather, as Andrews brings out in his reading of Stein, we must recognize that in our encounters with God, nonexperience can have the same traits as experience. Indeed, we cannot find God unless we first lose Him—as a concept, as a source of psychological consolation, and as a ground. All this has long been known by the great mystics, beginning with the Pseudo-Dionysius, although Stein's emphasis on empathy is original and helpful. As Andrews puts it, "Through empathy, I feel into [*Einfühlung*] what is structurally absent." Perhaps here we find a way in which Schleiermacher's theology of feeling can be rethought on a firmer phenomenological base.

As the collection draws near its end, it makes a half twist back toward its beginning. Crystal Lucky develops themes struck by Kristine Culp while extending them in a new direction: the experience of black women. There is also a new concern: the shaping that occurs in and through oral narrative. We read that Culp's experience of Lourdes was interpreted and adjusted by way of Ruth Harris's *Lourdes: Body and Spirit in the Secular Age* (1999). Lucky's interest is in those women who for the most part lived and worked outside the realm of the printed page, the black female preachers of nineteenth-century America. Like Culp, they were also prompted by an autobiographical passion, and their sermons presented a unique inflection of the more familiar Protestant spiritual narrative. We come to know the curves of this inflection by following one of these black preachers, Mrs. Julia A. J. Foote.

The literary concerns that come to the fore in Lucky's consideration of sermons have not been wholly absent in earlier essays. The psalms are poems, needless to say, and the liturgy is public drama; we have heard lines from T. S. Eliot and Muriel Rukeyser; and we have been referred to prayers mimed by Yves Bonnefoy and A. R. Ammons. It is only in our concluding essay, though, that literature is primarily addressed. Kim Paffenroth leaps across centuries and cultures in order to link together Blaise Pascal's *Pensées*, conceived in the years before his death in 1662 and first edited as late as 1844, and Herman Melville's *Moby-Dick* (1851) by way of the theme of the "wisdom of the heart." Our everyday experience is thoroughly mediated by the Bible. We refer ourselves and others to biblical characters, try to live up to them or react against them, while our deeds are oriented to scriptural injunctions, models, and even hermeneutical templates such as allegory and typology. Pascal's experience of God is firmly shaped by the scriptures, while the Bible is in turn marked by the ways in which he frames it. And we can read an entire theology condensed in the pages of *Moby-Dick*, one whose sense and function are quite different from the orthodoxy that animates Pascal.

The experience of God: there are many ways in which it occurs, many ways in which the divine offers itself to us. If not one of the contributors represented here suggests that finite creatures can grasp the infinite Creator as an intentional object, not one of them denies that credible witnesses have spoken of encountering God. To experience God requires that we reflect on "experience" with all the literary, philosophical, and theological sophistication at our disposal. For some, experience can be retained in its ordinary sense, and we must rethink how the deity relates to it: we can talk of experience *with* God but not, strictly speaking, *of* God. For others, experience is to be rethought by way of the impossible: it is closer to peril than possibility, and consequently the thought "experiencing God" tells us more about experience than does an ordinary event such as picking up an apple and turning it over in the hand. And for yet others, the very category is to be treated with extreme caution lest it lead the faithful into idolatry. The conversation continues and shows no sign of concluding anytime soon.

The Experience of God and the Axiology of the Impossible

JOHN D. CAPUTO

Who would not want to have an experience of God? But if no one has seen God and lived, who would want to risk it? Would this experience be some very extraordinary and death-defying event, like landing on the moon or being abducted by aliens? Or would it rather be a much calmer, cooler, and more calculating affair, like trying to read extremely complex computer data from the Galileo telescope that only a few highly trained experts can understand? What would "experience" mean if one had an experience of God? For that matter, what would "God" mean if God could be experienced?

Rather than engage in any speculative adventure, I will keep close to the phenomenological ground, for phenomenology, which is nothing but the cartography of experience, is what for me comes "after ontotheology."[1] Although I will speak of a certain leap, what I offer here is a careful explication of what is going on here below, in experience. On that basis, then, let me pose a risky hypothesis: I will venture the idea that the very idea of "experience" drives us to the idea of God—which may sound at first a little bit like the dream of an "absolute empiricism" that Derrida discusses at the end of his essay "Violence and Metaphysics"—and, in a strictly parallel way, that the very idea of "God" is of something that (or of someone who) sustains and sharpens what we mean by experience, with the result that the "experience of God" requires a "God of experience." On this hypothesis, then, "God" and "experience" are intersecting, prefitted notions that fit together hand in glove. This is all possible, I will hypothesize, only in virtue of the impossible, of what I call, after Derrida, "the impossible." The impossible will be the bridge, the crucial middle term in my logic, that links "God" and "experience."

I will pursue the hypothesis that the experience of the impossible makes the experience of God possible, or, to put it slightly differently, that we love God because we cannot help but love the impossible. But by "the impossible," I hasten to add, I do not mean a simple contradiction, the simple logical negation of the possible, like (p and -p), which is a cornerstone of the old ontotheology,[2] but something phenomenological, viz., that which shatters the horizon of expectation and foreseeability. For if every experience occurs within a horizon of possibility, the experience of the impossible is the experience of the shattering of this horizon. I am resisting all a priori logical and ontotheological constraints about the possible and the impossible in order to work my way back into the texture of the phenomenological structure of experience.

The Impossible

Let us assume as an axiom that only the impossible will do, that anything less will produce what the noted Danish phenomenologist Johannes Climacus calls a "mediocre fellow." Climacus is speaking about the phenomenon of the paradox: "But one must not think ill of the paradox, for the paradox is the passion of thought, and the thinker without the paradox is like the lover without passion: a mediocre fellow. But the ultimate potentiation of every passion is to will its own downfall, and so it is also the ultimate passion of the understanding to will the collision, although in one way or another the collision must become its downfall. This, then, is the ultimate paradox of thought: to want to discover something that thought itself cannot think."[3]

On Climacus's hypothesis, the highest passion of thought is to think something that cannot be thought. To think something less, to confine oneself to thinking within the horizon of what it is possible to think, is to fail to extend thinking beyond itself or push it beyond its normal range. Thinking within the horizon of the possible has all the makings of mediocrity, of that measured, moderate middle ground that wants to minimize risk and maintain present boundaries.

Mediocrity confines itself to practicing the art of the possible. What Climacus here calls the ultimate "potentiation" of a passion, which means raising it to its highest pitch, means at the same time reaching a point of impotency and impossibility (which are at root the same word, *adynaton*) in a kind of phenomenological *coincidentia oppositorum*. The full intensity of experience, the fullest passion, is attained only in extremis, only when a power—which here is "thinking"—is pushed to its limits, indeed beyond its limits, to the breaking point, to the point where it breaks open by colliding against what is beyond its power.

Clearly we can extend Climacus's hypothesis to other passions and other powers and formulate a kind of general theory of impossibility, turning on a certain axiom of impossibility, which might represent a kind of Aristotelianism—a theory of potencies and powers—gone mad, but with a divine madness. Thus the ultimate potentiation of desire would be to discover something that exceeds desire, that desire cannot desire, in a desire beyond desire; to desire something that it is impossible to desire because it is beyond desire's reach. Desire thus is fully extended and reaches its apex only when desire wills or desires its own downfall. When we confine our desire within the horizon of the possible, of the realistically attainable, will that not always result in something less than we truly desire? What can arouse desire more than to be told we cannot have the object of our desire, that it is forbidden or unattainable? Rather than extinguishing desire, does not the very impossibility fire and provoke the desire all the more? Desire is really desire when we desire beyond desire, when the desire of desire is in collision with itself. The highest potentiation of a passion and a power is reached when that power is brought face to face with its own impotency. The impotency and the impossibility provide the condition of possibility of the potentiation. The very condition that blocks the expenditure is what intensifies it. Anything less than the impossible just will not do; anything less will leave the power intact, still standing within the horizon of the same, and will not push it beyond itself or force it to another register. So to put our axiom very precisely we can say that for any x, where x is a power, like thinking or desiring, x reaches its highest potentiation only when it is impossible for x to act. Thus a power is most intensely itself only when it is brought to a standstill, brought to the point that it breaks up or breaks open and is forced beyond itself; it reaches its highest potentiation only when by a kind of discontinuous leap it moves, or is moved, to another sphere or register, beyond its own proper potency.

Experience

The axiom of impossibility, the law of the highest potentiation, goes to the heart of what I mean by experience, by the passion and intensity of experience, for an experience must have passion to be worthy of the name. To have an experience is to have a taste for adventure, for venturing and risk, which is meaning of the root *peira*. Thus to be a real "empiricist" means not to sniff along the ground of experience like a hound dog but to search for opportunities, even perilous ones, like piracy (all of which have the same etymology).[4] So experience in the positive and maximal sense, experience that is really worth its salt—and salt is my criterion of experience—is not for mediocre fellows. The easy humdrum drift of everydayness is experience only in the minimal and negative sense that we are not stone dead, fast asleep, dead drunk, or completely unconscious, although sometimes, it seems, we might just as well be. Experience is really experience when we venture where we cannot or should not go; experience happens only if we take a chance, only if we risk going where we cannot go, only if we have the nerve to step where angels fear to tread, precisely where taking another step farther is impossible. (Since the condition of its possibility is its impossibility.)

Having, or rather venturing, an experience, involves a double operation: first we understand full well that it is impossible to go, that we are blocked from moving ahead, that we cannot take another step, that we have reached the limit: then we go. We venture out and take the risk, perilous as it may be. First immobilization, then movement. The movement is mobilized by the immobilization. We take the Kierkegaardian leap into the rush of existence, come what may. First we are frozen with fear and immobility; then we leap. When we go where we cannot go, then we are really moving and something is really happening, over and above the routinized flow of tick-tock time that runs on automatic pilot. The immobilization belongs more to the cognitive domain: we know this can't be done; we have been instructed by the understanding about the limits of what it possible. But then we go. Thus the movement is carried out by a shift to the sphere of praxis and the pragmatic order (which is also related to *peira*), to a certain noncognitive leap that overcomes the hesitations of the understanding; that is what Augustine calls doing the truth, *facere veritatem*. We know better but we do it anyway against our knowledge, or—to give this a sharper edge—we do it for just that reason. Experience is for leapers and risk takers, for venturers and adventurers, while mediocre fellows would rather stay home and let the clock run out on life, preferring the safety and security of their living rooms to the leap. The impossible is what gives experience its bite, its kick, and draws us out of the circle of sameness, safety, ease, and familiarity.

Seen from a modernist and Kantian point of view, I am adopting a perverse and quite contrarian position. According to my axiom of impossibility, whatever conforms to what Kant calls the "conditions of possibility of experience" is precisely not what I mean by experience, while the mark of experience in the highest sense, *sensu eminentiore*, is the impossible, which defies and exceeds Kant's conditions. Experience has to do precisely with what is not possible, with what violates or breaches the conditions of possibility that have been set forth by the understanding. Seen from a Lyotardian point of view, experience does not mean merely to make a new move in an old game, but to invent a new game altogether. An experience does not move about safely within fixed limits, abiding within prescribed conditions of possibility, playing the game by the existing rules; rather, it ventures forth and crosses the borders, transgressing and trespassing the limits laid down by the understanding, the limits of the possible, of the safe and sane and the "same."

God

By "God," I mean the possibility of the impossible, a sense that is both scriptural and phenomenological. I am not speculating about this name[5] in the manner of an ontotheology, but consulting one of its oldest and most venerable uses in the biblical tradition. When the angel Gabriel visits the virgin Mary and gives her the startling news, Mary first remarks upon the great unlikelihood that the angel is right, to which Gabriel replies with angelic imperturbability not to fear, "for nothing will be impossible with God" (Lk. 1). When Jesus heals the epileptic boy, the disciples wonder why they could not do the same, and Jesus tells them that it is because they have too little faith. "For truly I tell you, if you have faith the size of a mustard seed, you will say to this mountain, 'Move from here to there,' and it will move; and nothing will be impossible for you" (Mt. 17:20–21). Nothing is impossible for God, or for those who being faced squarely with the impossible put their faith in God and let God do the heavy lifting. When Jesus tells the rich man to sell everything he has and give it to the poor, and then adds that it will be harder for a rich man to gain entrance to the kingdom of God than for a camel to pass through the eye of a needle, the disciples are thrown into despair, for who then can be saved? They have reached the point of the impossible; they see there is no way to take a single step forward. Then, having been driven to that point, Jesus says, "For human beings it is impossible, but for God all things are possible" (Mt. 19:26). Including the impossible. What is impossible for us (*para anthropois*) is God's business, for with God (*para theo*) nothing is impossible. That is why Nicholas of Cusa says, and this is another axiom to add to our axiology of the impossible, "since nothing is impossible for God, we should look for Him (in whom impossibility is necessity) in those things which are impossible in this world."[6] Wherever the impossible happens, there is God. The impossible (*adynaton*), then, is a sign of God, like a marker in the road that points us toward God, *à Dieu*, where the road swings off, occasioning a shift from our powers and our possibilities to the powers and possibilities of God, where we pass from the sphere of human rule to the sphere where God rules, which is what the scriptures call the kingdom of God (*basileia tou theou*). The mark of God's kingdom is that there *imposse* becomes *posse*, the *adynaton* becomes *dynaton*. The impossible draws us out of the sphere of the sane and the same, of the "human," into another sphere, where a divine madness rules, which is the rule of God.

It follows that the "experience of God" is closely tied to the "God of experience" and that the love of God is tied to our love of the impossible. "Experience" is the sort of thing that calls for God and the name of "God" is the sort of thing that raises experience to its highest pitch. Anything that falls short of God will not have the bite of experience. By the same token, anything that eludes or has nothing to do with charging experience to the utmost will not be God. In the experience of God, "experience" and "God" are keyed to each other in such an intimate way that experience enters into what we mean by God. To which I should hasten to add, what we mean by God and what we mean by experience, for by tracking experience phenomenologists are always tracking someone's experience, not some transcendental, transhistorical "essence" in the manner of classical Husserlian phenomenology; in that sense, phenomenology is ineluctably hermeneutical, probing the structure of an historical experience.[7] So I am trying to get a sense of what we Westerners mean, we who have a specific scriptural and historical tradition behind us, where there is a taste for time and history, for freedom and decision, in a word, for "experience," for what we mean by experience. The experience of God always comes down to our experience, and our experience is of a God of experience, a God who lends himself to experience.

The Experts of the Possible

We can put a sharper point on what we mean by this experience of the impossible by contrasting it with what I will call here the experts of the possible, the master practitioners of the art of the possible. The experts of the possible practice what was called by the medieval theologians the "cardinal" virtues, which would be precisely those virtues that are possible "for humans" (*para anthropois*), as Matthew has Jesus say, viz., those virtues that remain within the horizon of the powers of human beings. The cardinal virtues are, as the image goes, the "hinges" (*cardo*) upon which a hale and whole human life swings, if we have a door hinge in mind. But since there are in fact four cardinal virtues — practical wisdom, justice, courage, and moderation — the metaphor seems to suggest the hinges by which the four legs of a table are attached to the tabletop, hence the hinges upon which our moral life is stabilized and firmly planted on the floor. Either way, the cardinal virtues, which go back to Plato and Aristotle, have to do with the life of *arete*, of human excellence. They turn on the figure of what Aristotle called the *phronimos*, the man of "practical wisdom," or "prudent" man (*phronesis* was translated as *prudentia* in the Middle Ages).

Aristotle was the master of those who know what is what about the possible and the actual, the master theoretician of potencies and possibilities, and he thought you could explain anything in those terms, so long as you saw that the actual moved about within the horizon fixed by the potential and stayed as far away as possible from the impossible. That is the central thesis of ontotheology, which tended to keep a metaphysical lid on experience in a way that I am resisting. The *phronimos* is a well-bred, well-educated, well-trained, and in general well-hinged fellow who knows how to conduct the business of life amid its shifting circumstances. He is a man of good habits and insight, the noble, aristocratic sort of fellow who shows up all the time in the novels of Jane Austen and Anthony Trollope. We need not strain to use gender-neutral language here because Aristotle was only talking about men; it did not hit him that women (or slaves) could hit the mark of *arete* just as regularly as men do (which was not true of Austen and Trollope).

The *phronimos* does the good so regularly that it comes to be a kind of second nature for him, a stratum of virtuous conduct layered over his basic human nature so thickly that doing the right thing comes almost as naturally as breathing. The facility in virtuous conduct comes to him by dint of practice, and the practice breeds the "habit," the *hexis*, the natural possession, of hitting the mark, like the skill acquired by an archer who practices every day for many hours. All this practice sharpens his eye so that he can easily sight the mark and hit it. The exact mark is the middle of the target, neither too high nor too low, neither too much nor too little. The mark is the median point of moderation, the well-measured middle mark, right in the center. This moderation does not produce mediocrity but excellence (*arete*), because finding the right mark is rare and hard to do and most people miss it, which is where the mediocrity would lie for Aristotle.

For example, the *phronimos* knows that "courage" does not consist in being stupid, in putting one's body in front of a six-axle truck that is roaring down a street out of control in order to stop it from plowing into a crowd. He also knows that courage does not mean being cowardly under the cover of caution, avoiding a situation we should confront, failing to speak up when a word is required of us. Now this can be very hard to determine and sometimes requires exquisite judgment. When Pius XII held his tongue about Nazi atrocities during World War II, his defenders said he was being prudent and his critics said he was being cowardly. The *phronimos* avoids excess (*hyperbole*), overshooting the mark, and defect (*elipsis*), undershooting the mark. He regularly sees and does what is just right. But this is not a fixed but a moving target, a floating mark that bobs up and down in the flux of changing circumstances, and it takes a practiced eye to spot it, what defines the *phronimos*.

Now when the *phronimos* runs into trouble, that is, when he hits an idiosyncratic and anomalous situation, then far from falling apart, far from willing his own downfall, far from breaking up from the force of the collision, this well-hinged fellow hits full stride and comes into his own precisely as the prudent man that he is. For the *phronimos* has so sharp and practiced an eye, an eye that so regularly sizes up what is to be done and what is not to be done in most situations, that when he hits an irregular and incommensurable circumstance, he has the insight to make a good judgment, to adjudicate just what is demanded here and now by this particular situation, in just these singular circumstances. He is not bowled over by the oddity of the situation but he gets on top of it and reaches a judicious and equitable judgment about just what is demanded, about just what justice requires, or courage. The oddity of the situation does not knock him off his hinges but he stands firm like a table with all four feet firmly fixed on the ground.

From our point of view, the *phronimos* is a self-possessed fellow who does not lose it, whose highest potentiation is to maintain the calm possession of his powers. He is smart enough to know not to tamper with what lies outside his domain of his own possibilities. He wisely remains within the realm of things over which he retains the powers of disposition, over which he rules with a seasoned eye and practiced self-control. He is, in a word, a master of his powers, an expert of the possible. He undertakes the risky business of the hitting the mark in unforeseen circumstances, which is why we admire his expertise, but he does not dare venture out into that abyss where he does not rule. The latter is the place where there are no experts, where, according to the scriptures, God rules, with whom all things are possible, including the impossible, where the experts of the possible are forced to yield to the experience of the impossible.

Faith and the Unbelievable

The expert of the possible is a well-hinged fellow, and who can fail to admire such excellence? He knows what is what and remains in control. But the requirement of a genuine experience involves taking a greater risk than that, venturing into the domain where our powers of self-possession slip away and we are exposed to risk on every side. So in contradistinction to the four virtues of the well-hinged, let us offer the three "virtues" of the unhinged—if that phallocentrism is a word we still want to use at this point (virtues suggest something virile). In the interest of coming up with something that comes after ontotheology, let us propose three cases of the frame of mind of those who will the ultimate potentiation of their powers right on up to the point of the impossible, where the highest potentiation of one's powers lies in willing their downfall.

The *phronimos* is a prudent man, and he does not do foolish things. He knows what his chances are and he carefully deliberates about when a risk is worth taking. This is the sort of fellow one wants as an investment counselor. So when he believes something we can be assured that he has good reasons for believing it, that it is eminently believable. What he believes is credible and his credulity is warranted. His idea is the moderation not the ultimate potentiation of belief, not to believe too much too easily or to believe too little with too much resistance. For he believes in things just insofar as they are warranted and reasonable. But that is to believe something just so far as he can see that it is likely to be so, just where the evidence is the greatest and the amount of actual faith required is the least. Inasmuch as his beliefs are organized around the principle of the possible, which is here the probable or likely, he always prefers the situation that requires the least faith and the most evidence possible. Once the scale of probabilities tips against him, he will abandon his belief and put his confidence elsewhere. So it is not faith that has won the heart of the *phronimos* but evidence, seeing, where faith is a kind of tentative supplement or prosthesis that he employs while waiting for all the evidence to arrive to support his primary thetic act. But clearly this is a fellow with only a moderate faith in faith, with only a moderate heart for the ultimate potentiation of belief, for is not faith most required when things start to look a little unbelievable? Is not faith really faith just insofar as it tends to be impossible to believe? We need faith precisely when the odds are against us, when everyone else thinks it mad to go on, when it starts to look incredible. Faith is faith not in the reasonable and likely, which is less a matter of faith and more a calculus of probabilities; faith is faith in the incredible. That's when we need faith to go on just in order to keep on going.

Let us take the case of an innocent man who has been unjustly accused of wrongdoing. At first his friends believe in his innocence and rally around him in support, especially early on, when they do not know the whole story and the facts are on his side. But as the tide of evidence shifts against the fellow, the more fainthearted among his friends fade away and the crowd of his supporters thins. For they, alas, are disciples of the principle of the possible, and they shy away from the axiom of the impossible. They believe things only insofar as they are believable, that is, reasonable, which is to believe something only insofar as it requires a minimum of belief. That is what Johannes Climacus would call the faith of a mediocre fellow who tries to stick to the golden middle where all the evidence is clustered. But this poor fellow under unjust accusation needs friends precisely at the extreme point, which requires a maximum of belief, where all the evidence is against him, in that darkest midnight hour in which he is condemned as a guilty man by all the world. To go on believing in this fellow then, when in all likelihood he is a guilty man, at that point when it seems unbelievable, that is faith, the ultimate potentiation of the faith one has in a friend, a faith tried and tested in the fire of the impossible. The rest is just happy-hour companionship, the vacillating support of a hail-fellow-well-met who heads for the door at the first sound of trouble.

Faith does not come down to believing things just insofar as they are believable, but believing in what has become unbelievable, when it has become impossible to believe. Only the impossible will do to fire the steel of faith. At that most extreme point, at that darkest hour, when we have run up against the impossibility of believing and going on, just then, we believe. Before that, it was just a poker game and we were playing the odds.

At that point, we reach one of the edges of our experience, a boundary or limit case where our own powers and potentialities reach a breaking point and we realize that we have entered a domain where we have no control, where we do not rule, and we put our faith in God—or something, God knows what, since it is out of our hands. That is one of the ways that the name of "God" enters our "experience." For God to gain admission, for the name of God to come into play, the walls of the possible must be razed and the experts of the possible must have fled the scene. For God is given in the experience of the impossible, when we have reached our limits and conceded that we do not know what to do.

"I believe you, I believe in you, I will stand by you no matter what, even if for all the world you are condemned as guilty. I will believe the unbelievable, right on up to the end. And I commend you to God. I will pray for you and ask God to watch over you. For with God all things are possible, even the impossible." For us, for our limited powers, it is impossible, but it is possible for God. For God makes the crooked straight and makes the lamb to lie down with the lion. God watches over the little ones and sets his heart not on the ninety-nine who are in the fold but on the one who is lost, the odd one out. The name of God is the name of one who can make this possible, even if it is impossible. For God is the giver of all good gifts, above all if they are impossible. That is what we mean by God, what the name of God means, and it is this sort of limit-experience—a term that is in a certain sense redundant, that gives the name of God meaning, what we might call its phenomenological content, which is in the truest sense of the word experiential. For to have an experience is to take a risk, to brave the stormy seas of the impossible, to venture out where common sense tells us to stick close to the land and keep the shoreline in sight, to expose ourselves where the odds are against us. We look for God, as Cusa says, where the impossible happens.

The experience of God is to "see" the hand of God in the course that things take, to take the course of experience as guided by God, to find a loving hand, a providential care where others see chance, so that when things happen they happen as a gift, not fortuitously but gratuitously. But the gift is not a gift of chance, a bit of fortuitousness, but a gratuity that is marked by a divine graciousness.

Of course, we must concede that this will always include the possibility that the outcome will be a disaster, that God will have permitted a disaster, God knows why. As Qoheleth points out, God also makes his sun to shine upon the wicked and the just so we none of us know how this will turn out. The disaster may strengthen the hand of those who say our lives are held not in the palm of God's hand but exposed to chance and the play of forces. That is true, but only on the basis of the logic or onto logic of the possible. For the disaster also strengthens the hand of those who believe in God, because faith is faith in the face of the impossible, in the midnight hour where night is its element and it has become impossible to believe, according not to the logic of the possible but to the axiom of the impossible. I will come back to this complication about chance.

Hoping Against Hope

The experts of the possible have reasonable hopes. Their hope is well founded on the facts so that they can have every reasonable expectation that things will turn out well. The physician says the disease has been caught in its earliest stages and he expects a full recovery. He has treated many such cases before and the outcome is almost always favorable. The future has all the weight of the past behind it; the course of events seems almost inevitable. That is hope with a minimum of hope and a maximum of reasonable expectation.

That is hope in a "future-present," a future I can almost see and taste on the basis of the present, a future that is so strongly predictable that it has practically happened already. I have done everything that is possible, everything that is in my power, to make the future happen just as I planned. One is reminded of the "future" for stockbrokers who bid up the price of stocks on the basis of the expectation of good news—like the expectation that the Federal Reserve Board will lower interest rates—so that when the expected action by the

Board in fact takes place, nothing happens to the stocks; the future event was already built into the price.

But in the experience of the impossible, all such reasonable calculation breaks down and things look hopeless: the disease has spread too far and has not been caught in time and there is no hope for the patient. But are not those bleak and hopeless times just when hope is required? Is not hope really hope only when things begin to look hopeless and it is mad to hope? Is that not when we need to brave the stormy waters of hope, undertake the risk of hope, which is, we recall, what having an experience means? That at least is the opinion not of the stockbrokers or of Aristotle but of the Apostle Paul, whose favorite example is not the *phronimos* but Abraham, the father of us all. Abraham is remembered not as the father of the stock market or of the *phronimoi* but as the father of faith and hope. Abraham trusted in the promise of the Lord that he would be the father of many generations just when it was hopeless, when his body was as good as dead, and he was nearly a hundred years old, and Sarah's body was barren. Being fully convinced that it was impossible, Abraham continued to hope, even to the point of what Paul calls "hoping against hope" (Rom. 4:18), which is, it seems to me an exquisite formulation of the axiom of impossibility. Hope is hope only when one hopes against hope, only when the situation is hopeless. Hope has the full force of hope only when we have first been led to the point where it is impossible to hope—and then we hope against hope, even as faith is faith in the face of the incredible. Hope is hope when I all I can do is to try to keep hope alive even though there is no hope. There is no hope, I know that and I am convinced of that, but still I hope. Only the impossible will do for the highest potentiation of faith and hope. The experts of the possible will have long since slipped out the back door.

But why did Abraham continue to hope even when it was hopeless? Because "God was able to do what he had promised" (Rom. 4:21). For the name of God is the name of the possibility of the impossible. We invoke the name of God in order to "keep hope alive," as Jesse Jackson says—the name of God is the name of hope for Jackson and for Martin Luther King, for Gandhi and Dietrich Bonhoeffer, for Nelson Mandela and Bishop Tutu—to keep the future open, even when every door has been closed. We need hope when we see no way out, no way to go, when we are blocked on every side in an aporia more complete and encompassing than Aristotle ever imagined. The name of God is the name of our hope, the power that steps in for our weakness and hopelessness. For "if God is for us, who is against us?" (Rom 8:31) Nothing at all—"neither death nor life, nor angels, nor rulers, nor things present, nor things to come, nor powers, nor height nor depth, nor anything else in all creation" will be able to stand between us and our hope (Rom. 8:38–39).

Paul says that "hope that is seen is not hope. For who hopes for what is seen? But if we hope for what we do not see, we wait in patience" (Rom. 8:24–25). If hope has to do precisely with the unseen then, in its highest potentiation, it is concerned not with the unseen but foreseeable, but with the absolutely unforeseeable, which constitute a more radical and "absolute" future than the "future present" of the stockbrokers.

When the future is more or less planned and foreseeable, time becomes a certain approximation process that gradually edges closer and closer to the hoped-for point in the future, making asymptotic progress toward the goal. Then we are filled with rising expectations. But hope that has pushed to its highest potentiation is blinder than that, more open-ended than that, and cannot see its way. Hope cannot imagine what the future holds, or how things will turn around, and when the unexpected happens we are left wondering how that was possible, given that it was impossible. So insofar as the name of God is linked to the experience of the impossible, it also opens up another experience of time and a certain phenomenology of an absolute future.

The name of God is the name of a horizon of absolute expectation, of unconditional hope. More precisely, the name of God is not the horizon but rather the hope that lies beyond the horizon when there is no hope in sight, no hope on the horizon. The name of God opens closed horizons, interrupts the predictability of the future. When we are surrounded on every side by an encompassing horizon that encloses us within hopelessness, when we see nowhere to turn, then we turn to God. When every possibility has been dashed, then the way has been made clear for God, for with God everything is possible, including the impossible. When we reach the limits of our power to hope, then the power of God steps in to lift us out of despair.

What I am suggesting on purely phenomenological grounds is an important part of what we mean by God and hope, what *we* mean, as I have said, we in the West, where there is a taste for time and history, in a word, for "experience." Our experience of God is very much tied to a God of experience where experience has the sense of venture and adventure, of risk and exposure to the future. I do not deny that this experience of God is our experience, and our idea of

God, whoever we are, we who are an ambiguous mix of Greek and Jew, who live in the difference between the two.

Love Is Without Why

Let there be no mistake, the *phronimos* has friends and is an advocate of *philia*. He thinks that when it comes to friendship the best should stick with the best and that true *philia* is possible only among those of equal station, where it can be properly reciprocated, so that men may love women, slaves, and animals only in an increasingly weak and proportionate extension of the term. You need friends to be happy because no mere mortal can make it alone. You need a talent for friendship and you need the good fortune not to be born mean, repulsive, and curmudgeonly so that you drive people away from you. Having a closed circle of friends, of people who mutually will the good of one another and support each other when times are tough, belongs to the circle of good that one draws around oneself in order to be happy. A good wine, a good job, a good investment counselor, and good friends are all part of the good life.

Now of all the "virtues" that least lend themselves to the *phronimos*'s idea of measured moderation, love leads the list, for the only measure of love is love without measure. The fellow who says he loves something—be it a woman or a cause or even his cat—just so far and but too far, neither too little nor too much, all within the limits of reason and moderation, since one never wants to go overboard, is a lover without passion, the very idea of what Climacus means by a mediocre fellow. If upon being pressed whether he loves his spouse or fiancée, this fellow says, after a certain amount of deliberation, "yes, in certain respects, and up to a certain point, very definitely— but you always have to watch out for number one," then whatever it is the poor fellow feels, it is not love. For love is measured by its measureless expenditure, its unconditionality, its no-holds-barred, until-death-us-do-part commitment and giving.

Love does not calculate the return for its expenditure; it is perfectly true that one loves and desires the return of love for love, but the return is not the condition or precondition of the expenditure. Love is a gift that is given unconditionally.

Love, too, perhaps love above all, is governed by this axiom of the impossible, is potentiated or raised to its highest potentiation by the impossible. For, after all, what is easier than to love those who love us, who sing our praises, who stick by us, who think well of us, and return our love with love? Is that not even a common practice among the Mafia, an organization not widely known for love? Loving those who are lovable and who return our love with love—is that not possible, all too entirely possible? Does it not rank high among the achievement of the experts of the possible?

But does not love begin to reach its higher registers only when it starts to become a little madder, a little more impossible, which would mean when what we love is not so lovable and tends not to return our love? Like loving an aged parent who no longer even knows our name or recognizes us? Or loving an ungrateful child who has no appreciation of the genuine bond that unites children with their parents? Or an ungrateful friend who only shows up when he needs a handout and never shows the least bit of gratitude for all we do for him? We are beginning to move into a space where love is tested and fired by the increasing heat of—what else?—the impossible. We start to hit a point where it is not possible to love these people, where the understanding says, "these people do not deserve our love," which of course an eminently reasonable thing to say. But then again, must love be deserved—or is love a gift? If love must be deserved or earned, then it is something we owe to the one who earned it, and then it is more like wages for labor than a gift we give without condition.

Is love given unconditionally or do you have to meet certain conditions in order to earn it? Does love always have to have be reasonable, to have a logos, a why, a reason—or is love without why?

But let us raise the stakes still higher, and push love to its highest potentiation. Consider the following hymn to the impossible:

> But I say to you that listen, love your enemies, do good to those who hate you, bless those who curse you, pray for those who abuse you.
>
> If you love those who love you, what credit is it to you? For even sinners love those who love them? If you do good to those who do good to you, what credit is that to you? For even sinners do the same. If you lend to those from whom you hope to receive, what credit is that to you? Even sinners lend to sinners, to receive as much again. But love your enemies, do good, and lend, expecting nothing in return. Your reward will be great and you will children of the Most High; for he is kind to the ungrateful and the wicked. Be merciful, just as your Father is merciful. (Luke 6:27–28, 32–36)

These sayings are predicated directly on the axiom of impossibility, turning on the idea that nothing short of the impossible will do, that the impossible makes for the highest potentiation of love, for here we are asked to love the completely unlovable, and to love those who return love with hate.

But that is impossible. To be sure. It is mad; yes, indeed. That is why this love is what it is and why we love this love so much, or at least recognize in it love's highest potentiation, even if we keep a safe distance from it ourselves and would not blame someone who avoided it. Just as thought desires to think what cannot be thought, and faith is asked to believe what is most unbelievable, and hope is called for when it is hopeless, so love is love when love is faced with the most loveless and unlovable hate, when it is mad to love. When your love is like that, then this text from Matthew says you are the children of love, or of God, for God is love: Beloved, let us love one another, because love is from God; everyone who loves is born of God and knows God. Whoever does not love does not know God, for God is love. . . . God is love and those who abide in love abide in God and God abides in them" (1 John 4:7–8, 16).

There is no name more closely associated in the Christian scriptures with "God" than love.[8] That is what God is, and this comes as close as the New Testament comes to a "definition" of God, as opposed to defining God ontotheologically in terms of possibility and actuality, essence and existence. Even so, it would be at best a quasi-definition because in saying that God is love one is not defining God in the sense of setting forth God's limits and boundaries, but saying that God is unbounded and unlimited and unconditional excess, for love is love only in excess and overflow not in moderation.

So the experience of God is given in the experience of love. But love is perfect not when love is drawn around a closed circle of friends and intimates, which makes perfect sense and is perfectly possible, but precisely when love is stretched to the breaking point of loving when love is mad and impossible. The God of love and the God of the impossible seem like a nice fit, a kind of prefit.

Thanking Our Lucky Stars

Thus to the well-hinged experts of the possible, sane and moderate fellows that they are, whose acts are always well ordered within the horizon of the possible and properly proportioned to their potencies, we oppose the experience of the impossible, which is a kind of divine madness that is intoxicated with excess and the impossible, that does not get going unless it is provoked by the impossible, which is when or where God rules.

God—or perhaps just chance? Now we come back to a point I intimated earlier. With the experience of the impossible, we cannot avoid feeling a little like June bugs with whom children play of a summer's night, or like fish caught in a cosmic net, twisting and flipping about until the air gives out. Here, at this limit point, in extremis, when we are or when someone we love is struck by a potentially fatal disease, a qualitative shift takes place in our experience and we enter another domain where things slip out of our control. Speaking in strictly phenomenological terms, the things that are not under our control, where we have run up against the limits of our powers, are the raw materials of religion, the stuff of which it is made, the occasion upon which the name of God makes its entry.

We would do well to make it clear that in this confrontation with the impossible we are not praying for a magical divine intervention on the course of nature. For a God who, upon being pressed by our prayers, alters natural processes is every bit as ontotheological as the *causa sui* of metaphysical theology, constituting a kind of divine supercause who produces effects that are beyond our human powers. For even after the event, after the death of the beloved, when history or nature has taken its deadly course and God has not intervened to stop the disaster or the disease in its tracks, we are still praying.

For our prayer is a way to affirm that there is meaning in our lives, that behind the meaninglessness and tragic course that is taken by our lives, both personal and collective, there is a mysterious love not blind chance, that our lives have meaning for God in the midst of this tragedy. The impossible is not that, against all the odds, there will be a miraculous intervention from on high, but that there is a meaning here, in this impossible situation, that a meaning is possible where it is impossible that this death or illness, this tragedy or misfortune, could have any meaning, for with God all things are possible.

The prayer of Jesus in Gethsemane is paradigmatic in this regard. Foreseeing the sufferings that lay ahead, he "threw himself on the ground and prayed, that if it were possible [*dynaton estin*], the hour might pass." Then he said, "Abba, Father, for you all things are possible [*panta dynata soi*]; remove this cup from me; yet, not what I want, but what you want" (Mark 14:35–36). First we pray for a specific outcome, for what I want, for with God, all things are possible. Then, in a second motion, we amend that prayer and pray for what

God wants, that we will have the strength to believe and hope and love that, come what may, God's mysterious love is unfolding in our lives. We do not pray that God rethink the matter and alter his present plans, but that what is happening in our lives, which it is impossible to comprehend, is sustained by incomprehensible love.

Still, the question persists, do these limit situations necessarily present us with "God" or with what we sometimes call "the gods," by which we just mean chance? At these limit points in our experience, have we come face to face with the gift of God's grace? Or with a fortuitous turn of events? Might the impossible be a mark not of the "kingdom of God" but of the domain of fortune and chance, not of love but of luck?⁹ Indeed, if we treat life itself as a gift, is it a gift of God?

Or is it not just the effect of a quirky molecular mutation taken in some far off corner of the universe, just an idiosyncratic turn of events in the great cosmic stupidity as it hurdles its way into entropic dissipation? Here we touch upon the question of the gift and its enigmatic hermeneutic.

In terms of the specific problematic of the impossible, the question is this: Can one desire to think what cannot be thought, or to hope against hope, without implicating oneself in God or religion? With God, nothing is impossible, but might the impossible be possible without God? Is the "highest potentiation" of our powers an independent phenomenological structure that stands with or without God, with or without religion? By confining ourselves to a rigorously phenomenological ground, have we actually pulled the rug out from under religion? Even if the name of God is the name of the possibility of the impossible, might "the possibility of the impossible" go under another name than "God?" Might the name of God be an incognito under which the possibility of the impossible travels? Might the impossible still be possible, even without the God of the Jewish and Christian scriptures, with whom nothing is impossible? Might there be an experience of the impossible that would belong to a certain religion that we can call a religion without religion, which gets along without what the scriptures call a loving father? Might the work that is performed by (in) the "name of God" be carried out in other ways and under other names? Might a certain "religion" survive as a residue of biblical religion in the phenomenological structures it leaves behind (if biblical religion has been left behind, which I doubt)? Are not these structures inscribed deep within our "experience," which is the experience of us Westerners who have been shaped by (among other things) these very scriptures, like it or not?

We concede that our lives are tossed about by the winds of chance and there is no benign design behind it all. We hang on to such happiness as we have by a tenuous gossamer thread, knowing full well that it can be extinguished by the slightest shift in the cosmic winds. Johannes de Silentio said that without faith in God, with whom all things are possible, we can only get as far as infinite resignation; we need faith in God to believe that we will get Isaac back, that there will be a repetition, for after having given Isaac up one would actually be embarrassed to get him back. For faith is not just believing something in "childlike and naive innocence," which though it is a beautiful thing that can "bring the very stones to tears . . . does not dare, in the pain of resignation, to look the impossibility in the eye." That is true, and far be it for me to take on as redoubtable a phenomenologist as Johannes de Silentio. But since I take the results achieved by Johannes Climacus and Johannes de Silentio to be phenomenological, I can conclude that one might use the name of God as a kind of "placeholder" or "incognito" for our hope against hope.

After all, the name of God means the possibility of the impossible. I did not invent that and it is not up to me to ban that linguistic usage, to try to outlaw it. The name of God is the name of one who can make the impossible possible; the impossible is where we look for God. That is a large part of what the name of God signifies in the biblical tradition, which I am treating here as its phenomenological content, its detachable phenomenological content. For the phenomenon stands with or without the historical religions. Constituting a certain religion with or without the historical religions. (The next question is this: is "the possibility of the impossible" a kind of free-standing phenomenological unit that sometimes goes under the name of "God" in religion? Or is it radically parasitic upon the historical scriptural traditions, from whom we learned it in the first place?)

Things happen in this sphere beyond our control "gratuitously," like a grace, but the gift may well be a gift of chance, a bit of fortuitousness, not the gratuity of a divine graciousness. We believed against all the odds and kept the faith in order to keep the future open but we were prepared for the worst, prepared to go under. Still, we caught a break and our faith and hope were "rewarded." The impersonal course of things took a fortuitous turn. If there is a "gift" here, the gift is not the doing of anyone's generosity and there is no one to thank; if we express our gratitude to the stars we are engaged in a monologue and we are simply purging ourselves of a need to express our gratitude. We thank our lucky stars but the stars, alas, do not know we are here.

The phenomenological structure of ineradicable faith, hope, and love, the phenomenological structure of this passion for the impossible, remains in place, but without the historical religions, constituting the structure of what Derrida calls a religion without religion. By this Derrida means, and I am following him here, a passion for the experience of the impossible, which is a passion that outstrips the conditions of possibility imposed upon experience by modernist criticism. Modernity is marked by a needless and distortive secularization of our experience, which is why it has come under increasing fire ever since Kierkegaard first gave it a piece of his formidable mind.

There is an ineradicable undecidability here between "God" and "the gods," the gift of God and the gift of chance, mysterious love and blind chance, between two different ways to regard the gift and to treat the course of events, whose discernment constitutes the stuff of what I like to call a "more radical hermeneutics." One might well think that a repetition, however impossible, is just the sort of thing that might be brought about by the shifting tides of time and chance, which could bring Isaac back just as easily as they snatched him away, just so long as we do not give up, which is what the scriptural traditions call God.

We got lucky, the gods smiled upon us—or we were blessed by God—and the impossible happened. To be sure, no such hermeneutics, radical or more radical, will be able to provide a general formula for resolving the difference, for there is no higher axiom in virtue of which one could name, identify, or resolve the irresoluble fluctuation in the experience of the impossible. Making a move in this impossible situation is what I mean by radical hermeneutics, which does not set out to resolve this conflict but to identify the precise point of fluctuation at which a resolution, if there is one, would be carried out.

I can—indeed, I would say as a phenomenological matter, I must—love the impossible and think that anything is possible, even the impossible, for only the impossible will do. And if the impossible happens, I thank God, or my lucky stars. I love God because I love the impossible, but I love the impossible in any case. When the impossible happens, I thank what the great patristic phenomenologist Augustine of Hippo called in the most intimate and the most powerful phenomenological terms *"ðeus meus,"* "my God." Speaking strictly as a phenomenologist, I would say that I thank God because with

God nothing is impossible, but the question is, as Augustine also said, "what do I love when I love my God?"

Now, by way of a parting gesture, a concluding impudent post-script, let us thicken the plot and complicate the paradox with a final twist that would call for another and extended analysis: suppose one said that nothing turns on how one resolves this fluctuation, that as a phenomenological matter faith is faith, hope is hope, and love is love, so long as each is fired by the experience of the impossible, so that it does not matter whether one makes use of the name of God at all?

Then what difference would there be between standing by the be-loved until the end, even though the situation is impossible, in the name of God, for with God nothing is impossible, and standing by the beloved until the end, tout court? I have been arguing that the "experience of the impossible" is the way in which the "experience of God" is given. But might the "experience of God" be no more than a name we have for the experience of the impossible, and the "love of God" be no more than a name we have for our love of the impossi-ble? Perhaps. But now we ask, as long as one hopes against hope and loves beyond love, does that matter? Recalling that the *peira* of experience and praxis share a common root, does not a certain trans-formation into praxis occur at this point in virtue of which the experi-ence of God and the experience of the impossible are caught up in a cognitive fluctuation that is resolved in the doing, in loving God in spirit and in truth, in spending oneself on behalf of the democracy to come? *Facere veritatem.* Could it be that the experience of God is given in an experience in which the name of God never comes up? Unlike landing on the moon, might one undergo an experience of God and never even know that that is what happened? Would that not corre-spond rather nicely to what Derrida calls a "gift," where no one sus-pects that anyone gave anyone anything? Again, would it not correspond to what theology calls God's kenosis, where God slips out of sight in order to let the world come into view, where God with-draws in order to make things possible, all things, including the im-possible, for with God nothing is impossible?

2

Experience of God
A Response to John D. Caputo

MICHAEL J. SCANLON, O.S.A.

In the seventh chapter of his epistle to the Romans, St. Paul tells us how he wants to do good—how he wants to follow Christ, but confesses that it is impossible for him to do so. Then comes the eighth chapter, and he finds himself able to do the impossible, and now he writes that he has been empowered by the divine Dynamis,[1] the Spirit of God, the Spirit of Christ, to do the impossible. What was impossible for Paul while he lived *kata sarka* (in the blood, that is, on his own) is now more than possible because he lives *kata pneuma* (in the Spirit). What an exhilarating experience as Paul proclaims us freed by the Spirit from sin, death, and the Law.

This Pauline experience of liberation from impotency is repeated, of course, by Augustine, who never tires of telling us that we cannot—we cannot even will, never mind do the good without grace. Augustine would interpret Paul's "I want to do what is good" in Romans 7:21 as a mere velleity, a totally inefficacious, half-hearted bit of conation that we often refer to with a "that would be nice" sigh. For Augustine, as long as we live "on our own" the *posse* (the ability), the *velle* (the willing), and the *agere* (the doing) are impossible.[2] This is a summary of the Augustinian theology of grace (*gratia operans*, or operating grace, "what God does in us without us"), which became church doctrine (doctrines always begin as somebody's theology) when it was received against the Pelagians by the Council of Carthage in 418 with subsequent papal approval. In many ways this is "good news"—it tells us that God saves us. A later Augustinian theologian, Martin Luther, was so delighted with this good news that he added another *sola* to his list of *solas* (God alone, Christ alone, grace alone. . .): *"experientia sola facit theologum."* Not only the Christian but also the theologian must experience this liberating delivery from being "on his own." Luther no longer needed the extra "work" of being an Augustinian friar; he was freed from the burdens of "the religious life" (the "higher way") to join his fellow Christians in their freedom in "the congregation of the faithful."

But shortly after the time of Augustine, some monks in Provence were dissatisfied with the Augustinian form of the good news. Here they were, trying to live the life of asceticism, and there seemed to be no way to give a positive theological evaluation to human works. Yes, Augustine had provided another description of grace as *gratia cooperans* ("what God does in us with us"), but it was his teaching on *gratia operans* that had received doctrinal status. So some of these monks modified this doctrine to find some place for what we do for our salvation,[3] and they came up with the heresy we now call "Semipelagianism," a heresy attacked vigorously by some Augustinian theologians who had it condemned by the Council of Orange in 529, again with papal approval.[4] Augustine himself had anticipated this new Pelagian heresy in his theology of "prevenient grace," which provided the orthodox answer Orange used against Semipelagianism. The lesson taught by Orange is clear—divine efficacy and human efficacy are never to be placed on the same level; divine primary causality is always the ground of creaturely secondary causality. However, the development of the notion of "cooperating grace," which is based on this distinction, had to wait for another day. That day came centuries later with the theology of St. Thomas Aquinas.

Commenting on Israel's discovery of history in relation to the faith of Abraham, Mircea Eliade claimed that "it must not be forgotten that, if Abraham's faith can be defined as 'for God everything is possible,' the faith of Christianity implies that everything is possible for man."[5] Caputo quoted the New Testament text that gives a solemn pledge to this impossible possibility: "For truly I say to you, if you have faith the size of a mustard seed, you will say to this mountain, 'Move from here to there,' and it will move; nothing will be impossible for you" (Mt 17:20–21). In the Catholic tradition (and Eliade was an Eastern Catholic) the Reformation's "either / or" (either God or the human being) does not resonate—the Catholic position is always "both / and" (both God and the human being). St. Thomas Aquinas is the perfect illustration of this Catholic stance.

I cite just one rather famous passage: "To detract from the perfection of creatures is to detract from the perfection of the divine power. But if no creature has any action in the production of any effect, much is detracted from the perfection of the creature: for it marks the abundance of perfection to be able to communicate to another the perfection which one has oneself."[6] Some saints are identified through their distinctive emphasis; e.g., St. John of the Cross, St. Theresa of the Child Jesus. An apposite reference for Aquinas would be St. Thomas of the Creature. According to Josef Pieper, the marriage of faith and reason proposed by Aquinas in his great synthesis of a "theologically founded worldliness" was not merely one solution among many, but the great principle expressing the essence of the Christian West.

Concurring with the teaching of Augustine, the Doctor Gratiae, that we need grace because we are sinners, Aquinas goes further, declaring that we need grace because we are creatures. We cannot experience God as Gift without becoming a new creation. God must overcome the infinite distance between Creator and creature by making us friends of God, by raising us to parity with God (for all friends are equal) through a grace that he calls "elevating."[7] Thomas's "elevating" metaphor recalls the pre-Augustinian theology of deification among the Greek Fathers whose theology of Adamic inheritance was not as radical as that of the Augustinian West. For the Greeks, death, not guilt, was our inheritance from Adam.[8]

St. Thomas's "grace optimism" continues throughout the history of Catholic theology. His twentieth-century disciple, Karl Rahner, sounds very "Thomistic" in a speech given on the occasion of his eightieth birthday: "Let it be admitted here, even if with some anxiety, that in my theology the topic of sin and the forgiveness of sins stands, in what is certainly a problematic way, somewhat in the background in comparison with the topic of the self-communication of God."[9] Against a common neoscholastic opinion that grace, while really, there is not ordinarily experienced in this life, Rahner claimed that grace is habitually experienced but not focally as grace; it is the tacit dimension in all human experience. In line with St. Thomas, who taught that grace is a habitual elevation of human nature, Rahner modernized this teaching by translating it into the language of experience—grace is a habitual change in human consciousness. In his later writings, Rahner concurred with the political and liberation theologies that, given a radical historical consciousness, grace must now be understood as the divine empowerment to change the concrete socio-economic-political circumstances whence consciousness arises. Again, like St. Thomas, Rahner finds the extraordinary in the ordinary—in the mysticism of everyday life.[10]

John Caputo reminds us that the impossible immobilizes us on the cognitive level, but then we shift to the conative, to the sphere of praxis and the pragmatic order. And this is where St. Thomas developed his theology of grace even to the point of a theology of "merit," wherein our grace-enabled praxis creates our eternal destiny. As Caputo might put it, we experience the impossible by doing it (*facere veritatem*). And we do not want to be overly aware of this doing lest on the day of judgment we be not surprised to find ourselves with the sheep "on the right side." For Aquinas merit is not a psychological category of motivation—it is grace realism in the pragmatic order. Thomas developed his theology of merit within his theology of grace, elaborated in the philosophical categories of Aristotle. He spoke of "human nature," which is the essence of the human being as source of human activity unto a human end. Since his faith instructed Aquinas that there is no "connatural" human end on the level of nature, he elevated this nature to the "supernatural." God raised human nature to a divine level so that, thus raised by grace, the human being could work toward his or her only end, the vision of God. Again, using Aristotelian anthropological categories, Aquinas portrayed grace as a "new nature," with new powers—intellect becomes faith, will becomes hope and charity. Thus, grace for Thomas is most often "created grace" or the new human being transformed by the Uncreated Grace of the Holy Spirit. In this form of Christian anthropocentrism the human being becomes her or his grace, thoroughly recreated by the divine Dynamis, so that life eternal is gained by what Aquinas called "condign" merit, a merit based on justice and not merely on "fittingness." Given our current historical consciousness, the awareness that human beings create history, the Thomistic doctrine of merit is eminently retrievable. Christian freedom (2 Cor. 3:17) becomes our grace empowered ability to create our eternity out of our time. Eternity becomes the fruit, the issue of time.

Experience is a modern word. It presupposes the modern "turn to the subject." It is interesting to note the work of theologian Johannes Metz here. In his doctoral thesis under the direction of Karl Rahner, Metz presented the work of Thomas Aquinas as a turning point in the history of Western thought.[11] In his theocentric anthropocentrism

Aquinas initiated the characteristically modern exploration of human subjectivity within a Christian framework wherein God is not to be understood as an object but as the transcendent ground and horizon of human subjectivity and freedom.

As part of the modern vocabulary, the term *experience* fell under the suspicion of the Vatican, which delayed the development of any modern Catholic theology. Today postmodern philosophy and theology question subjectivity together with the objectivity of metaphysical language as appropriate loci for talk about God. In fidelity to its emphasis on the communal over the individual, Catholicism seeks to express its experience of God through that intersubjectivity of a community that celebrates its liturgy with critical attention to the culture of which it is a part. By now it must be obvious that no liturgical reform can be successful without efforts to reform the culture in which it is embedded. Worship and witness go together, and whatever success we have in reforming both are partial, fragile, and provisional in dependence on the Impossible Who renders possible our cooperation with the Gift that becomes our responsibility. In and through each other we may experience the Impossible Who graciously becomes possibility for us. St. Thomas Aquinas remains the prototypical Catholic theologian. He is the "sapiential" theologian whose faith seeking understanding participates in the Divine Wisdom to such an extent that he is able to give us in all humility a "God's eye view" of things. He recedes behind his exposition of divine revelation in order to focus attention to God's self-disclosure. In his essay "The Importance of Thomas Aquinas," Karl Rahner goes as far as to claim that "Thomas has acquired the status of a Father of the Church."[12] His respect for the relative autonomy of God's creation in his theology of secondary causes, his realism in his theology of grace, his sacramental principle—all of these emphases are continuing lessons for theologians today.

3

"A World Split Open"?

Experience and Feminist Theologies

KRISTINE A. CULP

If a woman told the truth about her life, "the world would split open," the poet Muriel Rukeyser observed.[1] This was gospel for the earliest feminist theologians. Mary Daly gave this now classic explanation, "In hearing and naming ourselves out of the depths, women are naming toward God."[2] Or, to paraphrase the playwright Ntozake Shange, as feminist theologians working in the late 1970s and '80s sometimes did, women found God in themselves and "loved her fiercely."[3] When women told what they had undergone, what had sustained them, oppressed them, and set them free, how they had endured and survived, what they told opened rifts in what had been taken for granted.[4] In those fissures, from those rifts, emerged new understandings of selves, world, and God.[5]

The clarion call of "women's experience" was not as simple as it sometimes seemed. Its clear demand at times belied the complex negotiations it assumed. As used in early feminist theologies, "women's experience" usually signified not only what women had undergone but also acts of "naming" or interpretation. Through these acts, often

I am grateful to Barbara E. Wall, O.P., and Kevin Hart for organizing the Experience of God conference and allowing me the latitude to revisit not only central assumptions in feminist theologies, but also, as it were, Lourdes. I am indebted to the conference participants and to Kay Bessler Northcutt and William Schweiker for conversations and comments that have greatly enriched this essay.

referred to as processes of consciousness-raising, women engaged various gender, political, and cultural critiques to help render meaning from the immediacies of their lives.[6] Thus, "women's experience" in early feminist theologies often assumed the retrieval and reconstruction of what women had undergone in relation to critical constructs of gender, liberation, and oppression, among other things. In addition, whether as immediate or as reconstructed, it was a social account of experience. That is, "experience" entailed an interaction with the stuff of persons, history, cultures, and the like, and not merely a private, essentially passive, sensory reception or apprehension.[7]

Finally, feminist theologians didn't merely interpret experience and theorize about the conditions of women's lives; they felt compelled to "use" it, to make something of it. These theologians found in experience both source and authority for telling truths that could alter basic understandings of reality (that is, that "split worlds"), reconstrue personal and social existence ("name toward selves, world, and God"), and reorder affections and values ("love fiercely" the God who was disclosed in a woman's life).

Those days of heady, ready confidence in the gospel of women's experience are gone. Diverse theologies—among them womanist and mujerista, African, Asian, Latin American, lesbian, and working class women's theologies—rightly exposed early feminist theologies as themselves being based primarily in the experiences of white, privileged, albeit radicalized, women.[8] Later generations of feminist theologians came to distrust appeals to women's experience as masking the messy, contending, shifting differences among actual women and as insufficiently attentive to grids of meaning and power that produce gendered, sexed, racialized, and class-based experiences. Additionally, they questioned the adequacy of appeals to the "evidence" of experience as the basis for theology.[9]

Such decentering and epistemic challenges have, in the last fifteen years or so, made feminist theologians skittish of invoking experience at all, let alone of making claims about the experience of God. We recognized blindness, naivete, and overambition in feminist theological projects, and moved to correct these problems. (Although, as I have already alluded, the first generation of white U.S. feminist theologians, certainly Rosemary Radford Ruether, Letty Russell, and Beverly Harrison among others, worked with a more nuanced construal of "women's experience" than they are usually given credit for—but that is a matter for another essay.)[10] We filled the space opened by questions about experience with productive work on metaphor, discourse, interpretation, practices, strategies, power, and difference as well as with a rich diversity of theological vantage points and proposals.

This skittishness also resulted from a relative remove from the struggles for liberation and life that so informed the first generation of U.S. feminist theologians.[11] Distanced from the fiercest struggles and epistemologically challenged in speaking of "women" or "experience" or "God," we have evaded claims about truths that rend the world and instead have narrated multiple worlds and theorized split truths. Our primary interlocutors have often become theorists rather than change agents and literary evocations of women's lives rather than understandings formed in shared struggles—not that I want to distinguish too sharply between academic or intellectual struggles and more overtly political ones. We have been susceptible to cooptation by the interests of particular theories and doctrines, and to evasions of broader truths while in service of theory's narrower claims.

Nevertheless, there are good reasons to reconsider the use of experience in feminist theologies. Chief among them are (1) the need for theology to engage richly with the ambiguous—wonderful, terrible, odd, tragic—stuff of life and (2) the importance of experience as a root of protest and resistance. First, we must examine what we undergo and how we reconstruct and interpret it, and do so in relation to history, culture, and meaning. Elsewise, we surrender possibilities for both complex individuality and profound connectedness as well as for a richer understanding of life.

If we are working with a social account, experience can offer a lens or opening to a broader world and to the "big questions" of survival and flourishing, perishing and tragedy, evil and God. But to use experience in this way will be in contrast to American tendencies to fetishize "experience": that is, to fashion experience for high rituals of consumption by psychologizing and even politicizing it. Such fetishized experience feeds narcissism. It can't be lived through; it closes off the world and history rather than opening onto them. Second, we need to reconsider experience because a rich, living engagement with the world provides the basis for questioning false authority and dogma.[12] Consider the potential power of the seemingly simple observation, "that's not my experience . . . I see it differently," when uttered against the grain of presumption. Experience has been the root of protest and resistance, of the power to overturn ideas, ideologies, disciplines, religions, republics. Feminists especially dare not sever this root, and feminist theologians ought to be doubly cautious because theology itself cannot flourish apart from idolatry critique.

This essay cannot take up a full reconsideration of the use of experience(s) in feminist theologies. Rather, I propose a modest and somewhat indirect foray into the topic. I want to consider the circulation of experience in our lives, and, by implication, in theology. I will explore the threefold move that I noted earlier: from undergoing, to reconstructing experience, to using experience to say something about God. To these three, I add a fourth movement that completes—and begins again—the circulation: I refer to it as living through experience. By this I mean not only being accountable for understanding what we undergo, but also being accountable to other persons, history, and God for using well the knowledge and power that we gain through experience. I will not attempt to elaborate how other feminist theologians have considered the circulation of experience or what it might mean for them to do so, I leave that conversation implicit and as the background. Instead, I begin with a narration of a quirky experience of my own, and move from a description of what I underwent through my own processes of interpreting it, and then to some observations about what experience entrusts.[13]

Finally, I will indicate the dangers of refusing to struggle with and take responsibility for the ambiguities and power of what we undergo. I hope that by the end it will be clear that there are indeed good reasons to reconsider the use of experience(s) in feminist theologies, and that chief among them are those I noted above: one, the need for theology to engage richly with the ambiguous stuff of life and, two, the importance of experience as a root of protest and resistance.

Undergoing Lourdes: The Flow of Experience

How do we get from the quirky experiences of our strange lives to saying anything about God? I approach this question through a narrative of what I underwent one morning. While narrating the flow of events certainly involves interpretation, I will reserve reflections on interpretive processes until later. In this section, I begin by describing what I saw and sensed.

This story takes place in a small town in the French Pyrénées. After a short morning drive, my friend and I parked our car below the rocky outcrop with its ancient fortress. The haze and fog were too thick to burn off in the summer sun. The distant mountains were hidden; the fortress above stood out against the sky's gloomy cloak.

We were in Lourdes. One hundred and forty years before, an impoverished, asthmatic fourteen-year-old named Bernadette Soubirous had a series of apparitions in a riverside grotto on the outskirts of town. The small female being who appeared to her revealed a spring, requested a procession and a chapel, and finally explained, "I am the Immaculate Conception." Today, an estimated four to six million pilgrims go to Lourdes every year, where they seek healing from the spring and the Virgin's beneficence, and where they find more tourist accommodations than in any French city except Paris.

Lourdes was, for me, a day excursion on a trip whose real destinations were the soaring simplicity of Romanesque cathedrals and the delights of French food. I had seen eleventh- and twelfth-century churches at Tournus and Vézelay and found them to be luminous in the full Rahnerian sense. I sought the soul-satisfying delight of spaces that were filled with earth and sky and centuries of Christian life and worship, that opened my imagination to the fullness of life and God.

At Lourdes I saw ranks of six-foot-high candles and a late-nineteenth-century "Romanesque-Byzantine" style basilica that featured an awkward tympanum of Jesus standing on his mother's lap teaching and holding, together with her, an enormous rosary. Pilgrims drank from, washed in, and filled every manner of container at the holy water faucets nearby. What I didn't see was the spring itself or where Bernadette had been when the woman in her vision directed her to find it. I didn't see them because I couldn't bear to.

I had expected—anticipated with a mixture of curiosity and dread—the kitschy spectacle of Lourdes. The gauntlet of shops along the way to the shrine didn't disappoint. There was the Immaculate Conception souvenir shop, the Rosary Palace with its department-store-sized selection of religious supplies, and a bonanza of water bottles for sale, including multiple sizes of blue and white plastic ones shaped after Bernadette's vision, supposedly approved for delivery by the French post office.

I already had a modest-sized, mailable Mary bottle in hand when I ducked into a small shop on the way to the grotto. A television set in the corner fixed the shopkeeper's attention, while a hushed voice intoned details. A funeral cortege passed throngs of mourners; the camera cut away to a vast sea of flowers.

Unbelievable: we had traipsed into Lourdes on the morning of Lady Di's funeral, oblivious to an event that fixed the attention of millions. It was going on just across the English Channel, but it seemed worlds away.

Out in front of the store, a different sort of procession was passing by. It was no less somber than the televised one. A man with a flag led a proud but weary band of pilgrims toward the grotto. Theirs wasn't the weariness of a long journey that would be shrugged off at destination's end. Rather, their bodies were worn by lifetimes of hard work and harsh conditions. Perhaps they had traveled from the eastern edges of Europe; quite likely it took years of saving to be able to make the journey.

The clash of pieties—devotion to a princess and devotion to Our Lady, both evoking religious consumption on wide scale—gave a surreal cast to the day. My traveling companion and I had taken a break from medieval churches and pieties, including dubious relics of sometimes dubious saints, to find the end of the millennium at least as odd.

We followed the direction where the band of pilgrims had disappeared. Toward the shrine, the crowd thickened as wimple-wearing attendants steered the wheelchair-bound into its midst. We headed up the promenade toward the ugly basilica. There, a larger-than-life statue, clad in white and sashed with blue, proclaimed, "I am the Immaculate Conception." The wire fence around her gathered bouquet after bouquet from her admirers. A beaming woman paused to be photographed before leaving her own tribute. I discretely snapped my own photo. Unlike the other places we had visited, I had seen few cameras at Lourdes. Unlike me, I surmised, these were pilgrims, not tourists.

I was touched and slightly alarmed by these pilgrims, some proud and beaming, others weak and wobbly. To be honest, I had hoped merely to be amused by the wacky, tacky religiosity of Lourdes and unaffected by others who traveled there. Warily, I crossed into the basilica under Mary, Jesus, and the giant rosary. As I circled the aisles, the excess of gilded paintings and the beseeching throng overwhelmed me. The walls started to close in; there was no place for God or senses to soar.

I fled outside where the churning in my stomach said, this is wrong, wrong, wrong. My ears pounded: superstition, magic, deception of innocent sufferers . . . "God and no other." Did I ever feel Protestant! Martin Luther might as well have been perched at my ear. Yet it wasn't so much Luther hammering these phrases in my ear as it was a surge of sensibilities from deep within me—but they were perhaps kindred sensibilities to the ones that gave rise to his theology. It didn't help that the plaza in front of the basilica where I had fled was lined with rows of benches reserved for "malades," the sick and suffering. Fortunately, they weren't occupied that day; but, in the streets and in the basilica, I had seen the pleading faces of those who had already waited in other places for miracles and favor. There was desperation under the spectacle of Lourdes.

We hadn't been to Bernadette's grotto yet, but I wanted to leave immediately. I couldn't be a mere tourist at a place like Lourdes. It was too overwhelming, too unrelenting, and its pilgrims were too earnest to allow one to stand in its midst as other than a participant. Lourdes demanded my consent at the same time that its pilgrims deserved their dignity. No ironic, bemused distance was possible, only participation or separation. And if I participated in the spectacle of Lourdes I would be complicit in what I judged to be idolatry, deception. If I separated myself from all claims that Lourdes made and merely observed, I would be a voyeur of earnest, suffering souls. I could not remain at Lourdes.

I divested myself of my souvenir blue and white Virgin Mary plastic holy water bottle then and there. My friend went on to the grotto. She was on a pilgrimage of her own that day, not for miraculous intervention or consolation, but on a vicarious journey for her mother-in-law who had always wanted to go to Lourdes the way I had always wanted to go to France. I stood apart from the spectacle. When my friend returned, she said that she felt a kinship of suffering supplicants. By then I had calmed down a little, but was still anxious to leave. It was after we left that my Protestant panic attack finally ceased: a stop along the road had brought us to an ancient Cistercian abbey, and I was standing in the remains of its cloister.

"Having" and Reconstructing Experience

That morning I experienced a more demanding truth than most of my days yield. I would not call it an experience of God—it was more opaque than that. But neither would I say it was a lesser experience. I sensed that I had traipsed into perilous territory—though to what extent I was on holy ground with inappropriate footwear and to what extent I was trespassing on other persons' hopes and dignity, I could not have told you. I knew that something was profoundly amiss and that it wasn't just me. I surged with protest against ugliness, against deception, against idolatry, against suffering. Or rather, protest surged through me, for it moved through me like a current.

Only later could I begin to make sense of what happened that morning. In this section of the essay, I turn to that process. To do that, I rely on a contrast between experiencing or undergoing as an immediate, ongoing activity and experience as a completed event or interaction.

To have an experience, an event has to be completed, a thing has to have been lived through or met with. If the former flows, the latter is congealed, a clot. To render meaning from experience and make it both more fully our own and more communicable, we assume the former flowing kind of experience but turn to the latter kind of experience, the clotted kind.[14] When demarcated as "an experience" with a designated beginning and ending point, we can get hold of it and endeavor to make sense of it in a way that is not possible in the immediacy of undergoing.

There was a center to what I underwent at Lourdes, a period of intensity around which a clot formed. At its center was my revulsion and protest, when my ears pounded and my stomach churned, when ugly excess became unbearable, when the palpable despair grew insufferable, when innocuous pretensions cumulated to thoroughgoing falsehood. But there were no sharply distinguished beginning and ending points. In order to interpret what I had undergone, which is to say, in order even to "have" it, to get hold of it and to begin to make something of it, I circumscribed it by time—a morning—and location—Lourdes. I marked off the edges and fashioned "an experience."[15]

To interpret and reconstruct experience, we rely on the mediation of memory. For example, when I sat down to write about what happened, I first remembered the feeling of panic and the sheer oddity of seeing scenes of Lady Di's funeral in the midst of Lourdes. When I pulled them out of my memory, as it were, other fragments followed. Memory not only retained much of the flow of experience, but it also afforded a certain critical distance from it. Distance allowed reflexivity: I could query my memories for the glint of truthfulness in a way that immediacy, by definition, could not allow.

I moved back and forth through thoughts and memory, considering events, sensibilities, and context. The center became a point of orientation for interpreting and reconstructing experience. I set aside details that drew me away from, or did not help clarify, the intense center. For example, how did Lady Di's funeral fit into the whole—

was it extraneous? An odd coincidence that generally confirmed the quirkiness of my experience? Or did it open a connection between the pieties cultivated at Lourdes and other popular yearnings and devotions? With these queries, I began to retrieve and maneuver the ambiguous mass of experience—or at least some salient fragments and images that my memory held.[16]

What I am referring to as reconstructed experience, then, involves both evaluating memories of what was undergone and fashioning a recognizable whole from them. Some things that were part of that morning's events proved insignificant to my reconstruction—for example, how the shopkeeper interacted with me. Other things that I was only vaguely aware of at the time, if at all, became crucial to the reconstruction—for example, the lasting effects of that morning's events. Part of my reconstruction involved identifying what I brought with me to Lourdes and how it shaped what I experienced. For example, Lourdes felt suffocating in contrast to the luminous places of worship I knew. As I excavated and evaluated, I became more aware of the suspicions and generosities I brought, and also of what inattentions and glosses to suspect myself. But the purpose of identifying such preunderstandings and predispositions was neither to sift them out and somehow refine "pure experience" nor to seize upon them and somehow explain away all experience as suggestion or illusion. Rather, I first wanted to understand how preunderstanding and postures became pressed together and reconfigured with all sorts of sensibilities, interpretations, apprehensions, and interactions. All of these were bound together in the clot of experience—as were deceptions and profundities, pretensions and disclosures.

I don't for a minute assume that I encountered the whole truth and nothing but the truth that morning. I am aware of the limits of my engagement and understanding. My friend (and her mother-in-law) have different stories to tell. Then, too, that band of pilgrims would have truths of its own to tell. Moreover, all of our truths are a little suspect. I suspect myself of elitism and of the extent to which I've merely embraced Western skepticism in the name of iconoclasm (though arguably skepticism itself, healthy and not, descends from religious iconoclasm). I suspect my friend of a sort of postmodern romanticism. The pilgrim band I suspect of some desperation—even as I imagine, in my own suspiciously postmodern romantic sort of way, the resilience and resourcefulness of their pieties.

Moreover, when I compare my photographs of Lourdes to the images of Lourdes in my memory, I find discrepancies. For instance, that weary band of pilgrims looks more prosperous in the photographs than I remember. How do I explain these discrepancies? Do I say that my memory is distorted or that my experience was distorted? No doubt my skepticism, my Protestantism, my tourism, and all manner of other "isms" simultaneously shaped and distorted my experience, my memory, and my interpretations (photographic, narrative, and reflective). Or do I say that the photograph did not capture what I remember I sensed? Indeed, what I remember as the morning's insistence of the dignity of suffering humanity seems truer than what my photographs convey—than what most photographs could ever convey.

Experience, at least the kind of experience to which theologians might refer in attempting to speak of God, is dense, even opaque, hardly clean-edged, ambiguous, and demanding.

The clot of experience will not yield an unambiguous touchpoint of the holy, somehow unattached from language and culture, somehow loosed from memory and expectation. But it can yield fresh and compelling understanding of the humanly profound and the holy if we are willing to clarify its ambiguities and struggle with its significance.

Author Patricia Hampl says that "we do not, after all, simply have experience, we are entrusted with it. We must do something—make something with it."[17] At the most basic level, to "make something" of experience is to give its relative shapelessness a more definite form. That is what a writer does in telling experience as a story. In her marvelous collection of essays entitled *I Could Tell You Stories: Sojourns in the Land of Memory*, Hampl explores the relation of experience, image, and memory in an Augustinian sort of way. Our memories store images—a woman on a bus and a childhood piano lesson are images that she plumbs from her own memories, but it might as well have been a wearied band of pilgrims or a garden with a pear tree. Telling the story that we recognize as somehow attached to these images, that is, recreating experience in narrative, creates a place for wrestling with what Hampl refers to as "the big words," a habitation for speaking of love, meaning, history, sin, grace. The measure of what is "made" from experience is, then, greater than its adequacy to the particularities of an individual life or self. Rather, to tell a true story about one's experience is to wrestle with the more expansive questions that a life touches.[18]

In his *Confessions*, Augustine explores the vast field of his remembered experiences and of his experience of memory—that is, memory's capaciousness and limits — in search of God. Although God is not always easily found, Augustine's problem is not finally the knowability of God, but the difficulties of his own searching. "O Lord," he confessed, "I am working hard in this field, and the field of my labors is my own self. I have become a problem to myself, like land which a farmer works only with difficulty and at the cost of much sweat."[19] He is confounded by his own experiences and memory. In part, what Augustine confesses is the contrast between the greatness of God and the difficulty of working the field of his own experiences, capacities, and memory.

I have reframed Augustine's classic question slightly in this essay. I have been asking how we get from the quirky experiences of our strange lives, and from our capacities and incapacities, to knowing or saying anything about God. Like Augustine, I approach this question through my own quirky experience, and like him I find the terrain somewhat confounding. The terrain of experience confounds at several levels: first, what we undergo, the flow of experience, itself can seem opaque; second, the processes of interpreting or reconstructing what we have undergone, the clots of experience as I have referred to them, are acts of artistry more than extraction and involve all sorts of choices and ambiguity; third, even idiosyncratic experiences open out onto vast regions of culture, history, and meaning.

Perhaps the most confounding aspects of the terrain of experience are to try to understand what experience entrusts to us, to use Hampl's phrase, and what, if anything, experience's trust enables us to know or say about God. To consider these questions requires working not only fields of experiences and memories, but also fields of scripture and accumulated human understanding for greater truths. I turn now to consider what experience entrusts to us, and what, if anything, experience's trust enables us to know or say about God.

To Be Entrusted with Experience

After I fashioned my narration, I knew that I was not quite done with the Lourdes experience. There was more to tell. I had told what had happened, but I hadn't fully wrestled with its significance. What did that experience demand of me? What had I been entrusted with in it? How did it connect with a broader world and more expansive truths?

As I noted earlier, I was not inclined to call it an experience of God — it was more opaque than that. But neither would I say it was a lesser experience. Like Jacob in the book of Genesis, I was struggling with a stranger—in this case, a strange place and a strange set of events—who might reveal the face of God. Jacob struggled through the night with the stranger at the ford of the Jabbock and did not leave the mysterious encounter unscathed. If we do not merely accumulate strange life adventures, but rather wrestle with what we are entrusted in them, we will be changed, even wounded by what we undergo. Jacob won a blessing from his nightlong struggle, his life was preserved, and he gained a new name, a new existence, but he was left limping for the rest of his days. What blessing do we seek? What mercies do we receive? Perhaps like Jacob, life itself, understanding and truth, and authorization for a new existence, an existence shaped against the grain of presumption.

That morning conflicting sensibilities and claims pressed upon me. On the one hand, I was repelled by imagery and piety that filled up the space before God with so much clutter, pleading, and busyness. I was repelled by trust in processions, prayers, rituals so superfluous as to suggest either belief in supernatural magic or else presumption about redirecting the will of the deity. But mostly, I was repelled by the religious establishment of Lourdes, which seemed to have positioned itself as some sort of broker between God and human need.

On the other hand, my touristic complacency was shaken as I found myself both repelled and compelled by the human drama before me. Persons scrounged for healing and wholeness, perhaps were willing to secure them at the price of deception. And yet, their earnestness and suffering were real; they were fellow souls who deserved sympathy, not disdain. Even as they sought favor and entertained deceit, they bore the undeniable dignity of fellow creatures. On the one hand, I was confronted with the claim of the inviolability of God, on the other, with that of the inviolability of human dignity.

The claims of the inviolability of God and of human dignity were not obviously conjoined that morning, and yet they refused to be sundered. If I could have chosen iconoclasm over sympathy or sympathy over iconoclasm, I might have found a way to remain in Lourdes—either raging against what I saw before me or embracing it in prayer. This was the wrestling match that took place in me. Both sensibilities took hold with such tenacity that it was as if they split the world part way open between them. Nonetheless, somewhere deep in the rift they met. That they met was as undeniable as anything that morning. Only now, though, do I imagine their raw, shining point of convergence, a point where the deepest protests and deepest sympathies converge toward God and all of suffering humanity. I construe this meeting point just beyond my experience as a place where divine glory and human dignity are bound together, where protest and sympathy kindle each other.

This, then, is what I have come to say: that the world split partway open that morning, and the straight edge of that split offered something against which to adjust the alignment of my life. I have come to name those aligning edges, the truths that were demanded, as the inviolability of God and the inviolability of human dignity. We must live in a way that resists false pretension to deity and that expands our sympathy to all of suffering humanity. These were hardly new truths, but they were compelled of me anew. They were, in fact, older than the protests of Martin Luther, as old as the two tables of the commandments, as old as the teaching of Jesus.

I settled on the metaphors of world split partway open and of aligning edges fairly early in my struggle to reconstruct and interpret the Lourdes experience. Or rather, it seemed, they settled on me. In many ways, these two metaphors came closer to expressing what I experienced than did my narrative. In fact, I narrated toward these metaphors. Although this essay has presented a somewhat linear movement from undergoing, to reconstructing, and then pursuing further implications, the actual movement involves constant circulation. I gauged the adequacy of my narration not only in relation to what I could retrieve from my memory, but also by whether it helped me to understand what gave rise to these metaphoric expressions. Moreover, the purpose of narrating was not only to reconstruct experience, but also to help "unpack" the meaning and significance of the metaphors of world split partway open and of aligning edges. These metaphors offered important indicators of what had been entrusted in the Lourdes experience; they pointed the way from the immediacy of personal and idiosyncratic experience to a broader world and more expansive truths.

Indeed, this essay itself was shaped in relation to an allusion offered by the metaphor of a world split part way open. This allusion, at first unrecognized by me, was of course to Muriel Rukeyser's observation that if a woman told the truth about her life, the world would split open. When I first narrated the experience for others, long before I wrote this, I didn't really consider rending worlds with what I had to tell. Rather, I affixed the metaphors as a crown, as a way of topping off a gloriously odd and even ironic experience:

"Tourist ventures to an over-the-top Catholic pilgrimage site on no less a day than Lady Di's funeral and discovers how truly Protestant she is—it is as if the world splits part way open. . . ." With all due respect to the poet Rukeyser, and to women whose struggles give them more to tell than I, I couldn't split the world by telling about my Lourdes experience. More to the point, I had traipsed into the middle of truths that already had sundered worlds. It was my world that was split, my life that needed realignment. I was the one judged for my nonchalance and convicted of a more demanding truth and sympathy.

But as time and space separated me from the immediacy of that morning, I continued to be compelled by the truths of which I had so powerfully been reminded. The Lourdes experience gave new impetus to my pursuit of long-standing intellectual interests in the "protest" in Protestantism and in the "catholic," the world-embracing and sacramental, as crucial theological insights and moral commitments, not just as sociological or ecclesial descriptions. More than that, it pressed upon me the vital necessity of holding together protest and sympathy in a time when they are often disjoined. In the midst of the blasphemous fundamentalisms and consumptive greed of our time, my experience at Lourdes insisted on the inseparable inviolability of God and of human dignity—and on the necessity of giving that articulation in word and deed.

Being Accountable for Experience

What Rukeyser meant by telling the truth about our lives cannot be a matter of taking ourselves too seriously, but rather of taking ourselves seriously enough. Seriously enough, that is, to struggle with and take responsibility for the ambiguities and power of what we undergo in life. To tell the truth about our lives, then, does not mean endless personal confession of what we felt, saw, did, thought, perceived. The point of telling is not therapy for ourselves. Rather it entails being accountable for understanding what we undergo and being accountable to other persons, history, and God for using well the knowledge and power that we gain. If we refuse to "do something" or "make something" with experience, to receive its trust and render meaning from it, Hampl cautions, someone else will. If we do not struggle with experience, we reject a rich engagement with the flow of life and history, we fail to render meaning from it, and we surrender the root of our ability to question false authority and to be agents of mercy and transformation. To forget what we have under-gone—as persons, cultures, and human beings—is to surrender polit-ical, moral, and spiritual power. If we do not struggle with experience, some political regime, some cultural flow, some dogma-tism, some marketing strategy will step in to tell us what we have undergone, to tell us what to do with it.

We can learn this lesson from Lourdes as well. For the story of Lourdes in part is about how experience's power to inspire and mo-bilize was usurped and fanned by religiously, politically, and cultur-ally reactionary forces. In her superb book, *Lourdes: Body and Spirit in the Secular Age*, Ruth Harris traces the rise of the phenomenon of Lourdes. "[Bernadette's] appeal was non-verbal and non-literate," Harris explains, "not unlike the apparitions themselves, in which her bodily comportment was more important than language, except for the brief messages conveyed to the priests. Her spirituality was in-vested in a mission accomplished, in which she was hidden behind the enormity of her encounter."[20] As ecclesiastical and civil powers certified Bernadette's experiences, built the shrine, and organized pilgrimages, authority was transferred from her experience to their dogmas, organizations, and agendas.

Bernadette herself receded, first entering a cloistered order nearby, then moving to the motherhouse across the country. Harris observes that "by keeping herself always slightly hidden, Bernadette protected her visions and her integrity, able to resist the pressure of photographers, priests, and pilgrims alike."[21] She died in 1879 at the relatively young age of thirty-five, ill from asthma and tuberculosis.

Meanwhile, Lourdes came to bolster Pius IX's promulgation of the dogma of the Immaculate Conception (decreed just four years before Bernadette's apparitions) and his stand against modernism. The advancement of Lourdes served also to advance ultramontanist doctrine with its central tenet of papal infallibility. Later, the promo-tion of national pilgrimages to Lourdes became entwined with a French antirepublican, antihumanist agenda of restoring both the Bourbon monarchy and so-called traditional Catholic values to soci-ety. Included with these agendas was the reinforcement of a gender-stratified social order and the promotion of a "feminized" piety.

When Leo XIII broke with his predecessor's intransigence toward the modern world, the Assumptionist order, promoters of the na-tional pilgrimages, did not. Instead, they moved farther to the right and their fears of "degeneracy" found expression in the virulent anti-Semitic hatreds of the Dreyfus Affair. The order was expelled from

France in 1900 for plotting against the republic. The Lourdes estab-lishment itself was somewhat reshaped under the French anticlerical laws that soon followed; however, it was not purged of anti-Semi-tism. Harris notes that in 1940, "Lourdes came to symbolize the part-nership between the Catholic Church and the new Vichy regime, which reasserted the phantom of conspiratorial links between Jews, Freemasons and republicans."[22]

Reactionary religious and political forces were able to usurp the power of Bernadette's experiences and the appeal of Lourdes to fur-ther their ends. Indeed, the widespread appeal of Lourdes is due in large part to their promotion. I do not want to imply, however, that Bernadette alone could have closed off these reactionary forces if only she had been less naive and more articulate. In fact, Harris con-cludes that her simplicity made her "immune from co-optation as a symbol of resurgent Catholicism"[23] even while religious organiza-tions associated with Lourdes fostered the worst of it. Bernadette's simplicity contrasted with and thereby highlighted "the enormity of her encounter," and in turn provided a defining, and in some sense, delimiting, expression.[24] These simple delimitations, though, were not enough to resist cultural, religious, and political forces that were able to deploy the surplus of meaning in Bernadette's encounter to insidious ends. No matter its "enormity," experience is not able to remain innocent of history. If we do not struggle with experience as a connection to the broader world and more expansive truths, some political regime, some cultural flow, some dogmatism, some market-ing strategy will step in to tell us what we have undergone, to tell us what to do with it.

As one might suspect, the story of Lourdes is yet more complex than a tale of how naive experience was taken over and reengineered into a propaganda machine for the extreme right. Even while the anti-Semitic collaborations with the Vichy regime were emerging, a Jewish-Viennese novelist, Franz Werfel, found refuge in Lourdes as he was fleeing to America. He wrote a book about his experience, *The Song of Bernadette*, later made into a Hollywood movie, in which he explained that the shrine enabled him to "magnify the divine mys-tery and the holiness of man—careless of a period which has turned away with scorn and rage and indifference from these ultimate values of our mortal lot."[25]

Harris suggests that "Bernadette's enigmatic figure perhaps partly explains the sanctuary's capacity to attract so many people of diver-gent spiritual inclinations, for on her frail form could be projected the many different longings of different eras."[26] Many interests, organizations, and ideologies attempted to define a proper interpretation and response to what Bernadette underwent in that grotto. At the same time, innumerable pilgrims themselves interpreted and responded to what Lourdes offered and represented to them. For example, the poor and the sick were drawn by the simplicity of Bernadette's message and character. At Lourdes, Harris explains, "the sick and dying, usually relegated to the unseen margins of society, took centre stage."[27] Upper-class women and women religious who organized to aid the suffering found measures of autonomy and religious freedom that were unusual in their day. Then, too, it offered women and sometimes men the ability "to encounter Mary and Jesus sometimes without mediation, to use the imaginative resources that their religious universe afforded without recourse to hierarchy."[28] For these masses, indeed for many of the millions who still come every year, Lourdes offered possibilities of healing and wholeness, a new vision of body and spirit, changed social relations, and revitalized pieties. Yet, away from Lourdes, these temporary inversions of poor and rich, weak and strong, women and men, laity and hierarchy, often served to reinforce social hierarchies.[29]

Ruth Harris concludes her study with this observation: "For, despite the attempts by some to romanticize, by others to politicize and by still more to medicalize, throughout the history of Lourdes there has always remained one fixed point: the essential image of a young, poverty-stricken and sickly girl kneeling in ecstasy in a muddy grotto."[30]

The theologian, however, must tarry a bit longer. Bernadette was an icon of an ecstatic, all-encompassing encounter with divinity, if not of a world saturated by the divine. She was so in a time when that worldview was increasingly challenged, even attacked. To moderns, by contrast, Lourdes was an icon of antimodernity, of ignorant belief in miracles and the supernatural. No modern asserted the absence of divinity in the world or the illusory character of religion itself more forcefully than the French novelist, and later defender of Dreyfus, Émile Zola. "Lourdes," he contended, "the Grotto, the cures, the miracles, are, indeed, the creation of that need of the Lie, that necessity for credulity, which is a characteristic of human nature." He continued, "At first, when little Bernadette came with her strange story of what she had witnessed, everybody was against her. . . . But Lourdes grew up in spite of all opposition, just as the Christian religion did, because suffering humanity in its despair must cling to something, must have some hope: and, on the other hand, because humanity thirsts after illusions. In a word, it is the story of the foundation of all religions."[31] To postmoderns, Zola's words themselves seem overly simple, naive. Postmodernity, at least some strains of it, would have us celebrate the enigma and fluidity of religious experience and to consider again the impossible possibility of mystical encounters and a world saturated with God.

However, we cannot evade the ambiguity of our lives, of what we undergo, of what we hold on to as "experience," or of what we are entrusted with. Our lives are neither flooded with the divine nor is the divine flushed from them. Perhaps a more modest—and apt— way to characterize our situation at the end of high modernity is to say that we live between saturation and absence. We hover over life and lurch through history with truth and meaning sometimes evading us, while at other times, truth is told and the world splits open.

The theologian's work cannot be simply to put suspicions into play and narrate partial truths, but somehow to speak of and live before "God," that which defies our presumptions while yet circulating in all that we undergo. We theologians must keep our suspicions engaged, knowing that we humans have the capacity to deceive ourselves, even at what we take to be our best moments. This protesting hermeneutic is informed by the iconoclasm of Jewish and Christian scriptures. We must also keep our generosity and sympathy engaged, knowing that our perspectives will always be partial and shifting, knowing that we always have more to understand, much of it from unexpected persons and places—which is also to say that we are given, surprisingly, the capacity to surpass ourselves. This embracing, even sacramental, hermeneutic is informed by the struggles of the ages to live in faith, hope, and love, and to receive life itself as a merciful gift.

Our task, as theologians and human beings, is to engage deeply and richly with the messy—wonderful, terrible, odd, tragic—stuff of life, to attend to the blooming, buzzing confusion of what we undergo, to piece it together and struggle to make sense of it, to struggle to understand and articulate how we are connected through it to the rest of suffering humanity and even God, and to be accountable to others, history, and God for how we use, live through, experience. Experience will confound us. It will not offer us unambiguous perceptions, whole truths, or pure touchpoints of the holy. Nonetheless, it can disrupt what we have taken for granted about our selves, world, and God; it can cause us to realign our affections and values; and it can enable us to speak truths that may even split worlds.

4

A Womanist Experience
A Response to Kristine Culp

RENEE MCKENZIE

Kristine Culp has taken us on an interesting ride. We have experienced with her memories of her visit to Lourdes, and we have shared with her a partial yield of her reflection. We have discovered that she, unlike some postmodern feminists, wants to reclaim, at least for feminist theology, the intrinsic and extrinsic value of experience in saying something meaningful to ourselves and others about God and our self. This work is intriguing even with the recognition of its being read with the eyes of one who, in great similarity to Culp's experience at Lourdes, could neither fully participate in what she recounted nor separate from it for fear of trivializing or denigrating the reality to be conveyed. If there is no middle ground between participation and separation, how do we engage any experience not our own? How is one to read this essay, to attempt to live in this moment, as limited as that possibility might be, to grasp as fully as possible the reality of which it speaks? How is that accomplished if the two options, separation and/or participation, effectively leaves one without any option at all?

Culp's dilemma was a pull between the either/or options of participation or separation on her trip to Lourdes. She could not fully embrace either position. She could not participate in the pilgrimage she saw acted out around her because her religious and spiritual sensibilities found that particular religious expression idolatrous. Neither could she separate completely from the experience she saw, because the draw to the human suffering on display necessitated a response. To separate from the reality of that suffering while still remaining visually engaged with it was to take on the role of voyeur. In separating, she would be turning a blind eye to human suffering and the loss of human dignity. In participating, she would be assenting to a view of the divine contrary to her own. These two seemingly polar opposite impulses of participation and separation met within her, and this meeting allowed her to conclude that one could remain free of religious or spiritual pretenses even as one experiences great sympathy for the suffering of others. In effect, her choice was not to choose but to mediate.

As I reflect on the nature of the experience useful for theological reflection as shared by Culp in this essay, a few observations seem warranted. The first observation is this: experience, as she describes it, is individual and unique. It is always my experience made available for my reflection. Given the anti-essentialist critique of the universalizing of feminist experience considered as effectively co-opting the breadth of women's experiences into the specificity of the particular, it would seem that Culp operated from the perspective that the most one can say about experience is that it is mine, singular and individual. Perhaps this position attempts to avoid falling into the trap of universalization. A problem with this line of thinking is revealed in the observation that any reflection upon the reality of the other acted out before me is done from the limitations of my experience. As I reflect upon what I see of the other's reality, I may very well find myself projecting upon the other's reality rather than engaging with it.

Culp saw people with physical and perhaps mental maladies. These people appeared to have been suffering. Clearly they came to Lourdes for a healing that is frequently defined as an end to suffering. Without having directly engaged one or more of the pilgrims, one can never know exactly what their experience is or has been. To the outside observer of these others, one might infer that suffering was taking place and, with this suffering, the loss of human dignity. The reflection of the observer, which in many ways amounts to speculation, becomes a reflection on the observers' perception of the experience of the other. This reflection is shaped out of the experience of the observer and used to serve a theological end. In this case, the reality of the other has been subsumed. Perhaps one could even say that the particular experience of the observer resulted in a universalization of that experience, because rather than yielding space to the experience of the other, the projection of the observer was applied to the other. The particular took on the projection of a universal. Situating experience as singular and individual, therefore, does not shield one from the possibility of universalization.

This question of how experience might be useful as a method for avoiding essentialism is of particular interest to many scholars, womanist scholars in particular.[1] In the endeavor to self-name, self-define, and self-identify, the womanist scholar must navigate that sometimes narrow space of saying something about who she is, or who her community of women are, but doing so without making generalist observations and essentialist claims. Some feminists may deny that one can speak legitimately of a thing called "women's experience" as a nontotalization or universality, but, according to bell hooks, it is via experience that the essentialist label can be avoided. While denying any idea of a black essence, hooks affirms the authority of experience in shaping African American identity. To speak of the African American experience is not to talk of a singular experience that would be common to all black Americans. Rather, it is to recognize that the African American experience is as individual and unique as each individual particular intersectionality or race, class, gender, sexual orientation, family, and community, and other identifiers may be. "There is a radical difference between a repudiation of the idea that there is a black "essence" and recognition of the way black identity has been specifically constituted in the experience of exile and struggle."[2] Hooks is not alone among scholars who speak of black identity as if it is the product of exile and struggle alone. But to limit the shaping of black identity to this is insufficient. The bitter fruit of oppression is but one factor in the shaping of an African American identity that is also shaped by the context and the quality of the positive and negative intragroup dynamics within the community.

Experience thought of in this way, as arising out of the context of being in community, is as uniquely individual as it is not. It starts not from the location of an individuated "I" but rather from the position of an "I" in community, which is to say a "social I" or a "social self." From the vantage point of the social self, one can readily move into speaking of the individuated experience of the "I," but doing so from within the historically situated group. Individual experience in the group is not prescribed in a group dynamics but takes on shifting meanings in the differing contexts in which it emerges.

Experience, considered in this way, is not situated as only past event, or a clotted experience, as Culp so richly names it. There is a quality of the collective experience as having both past and present components. The idea of speaking of experience as being either flowing or clotted, as one thinks with relationship to blood, is intriguing nonetheless. The image of a clot of experience provides a useful vantage point upon which to reflect and to scrutinize an experience for the purpose of discovering ways in which this experience can add to the self-view by revealing something new. The clot is the center from which interpretation both flow toward and flow away from. The congealed nature of the clot does, so to speak, give one something to hold on to. It is something of substance even if only relatively so.

A clot also suggests something else. It speaks of relative impermeability, of stasis, of an external border that rarely undergoes substantive change without significant transformation. A clot has a tendency to remain in its essential form without marked change minus the imposition of a significant internal or external event. Is this consistent, one might ask, with how one normally thinks of experience, even when considering an event closed through the passage of time and inherent unrepeatability? Does not the simple reliance upon memory in experience formation, re-creation, and apprehension suggest something less static and more dynamic as each reencounter with the experience through memory occurs from a slightly altered perspective?

For Culp, a congealed experience is held together through the imposition of time as both a limiting and fixating factor. In circumscribing the experience, time claims limits in an attempt to lock the event into place. Unlike an historically constituted experience seen as representative of a collective experience and composed of both a historical and a present component, within the framework of a clotted experience, a present or ongoing component seems to be reckoned inconsequential, as if the memory and interpretation of the moment is fixed in the mind as it would be by the pen or the word processor.

That caveat aside, the clot remains a useful way of thinking about a particular experience self-limited by its nature to a time and place but not so limited in reflection, apprehension, and mediation. For one who shares in the commonality of experiences of oppression in hierarchical power relations of race, class, and gender, it is difficult to move comfortably into the realm of speaking of an experience as individual and closed, because from this starting point experience rarely is that. Each potentially individuated experience is seen as layered upon the collective experience that forms the group cultural identity also shaping and informing. Experience rarely if ever reaches congealed state, for it is always in the flow of being connected in some way to the whole of being.

For Culp, the experience in Lourdes was an occasion when the world split partway open, and in this splitting she was moved beyond herself to engage the larger world; she was called to see the larger world in a new or renewed way. It is through engagements with this type of truth that one can become compelled to see the world in terms much more expansive than "my world" and "my existence." It becomes a moment when truth invades our lives and we see with an insight or clarity not normally a part of who we are. Having the world split apart by the brilliance of truth as described in this essay seems to be a moment of moving into community, of finding the points of connections between my limited world and the expansiveness of the world that is beyond my existence.

Rather than visualize the moment of insight that makes available the reality of the larger world lived in the specific experience of some other as being a time when the world splits apart, one approaching it from a different starting point may be inclined to name it differently. The violence of the metaphor of the world splitting partway open lends itself more readily to a time when violence is experienced with something far less than a positive and redeeming outcome, as Culp suggests. The world splits apart for some whenever one is confronted with an experience of reality that seeks to impose a view of the world desiring to alienate one from full humanity, that seeks to limit the ability to self-define and self-name, that seeks to divest of human agency. This is the world splitting apart even if such splitting occurs only by degrees. The violence of the metaphor is reinforced by the violence of the intended result.

When the epiphany of an experience yields a vision of the world beyond my own reality, when forced or privileged by such an access to truth that moves toward community, this is experienced as a coming together rather than a splitting apart. In the coming together, the wholeness of being is accentuated and resituated so that the sense of community that informs my experiential starting point in engaging the world can itself be broadened or simply reinforced.

In the end I must agree with Kristine Culp when she writes, "If we do not struggle with experience some political regime, some cultural flow, some dogmatism, some marketing strategy will step in to tell what we have undergone, to tell us what to do with it." For an experience to be ours, however negative or positive, we must name and define it. But there is also a sense in which our experience is always more than that which belongs solely to the individual. In sharing it, and sometimes also just in the living of it, our experience becomes a part of the collective whole.

5

The Experience of the Kingdom of God

KEVIN HART

1

Imagine that someone knocks on your door and, when you open it, the man standing there says to you, "I have experienced God." And imagine that you have walked down the hallway from the kitchen or the study with a remote in hand, a newfangled contraption with a special feature you have been dying to try out: a pause button that works with human beings. No sooner has that remarkable statement been uttered than you press the button: the man becomes a living statue, and you are left to ponder what has been said to you without having to respond. There is no question, then, of having to deal with someone who wishes to convert you, murder you, sell you a magazine, take your money, or engage you in fruitless and frustrating talk. The only thing you have to do is consider what has been said to you. If you like, you can look closely at this person, examining his face for signs of mania or substance abuse. He seems quite harmless. By now your heart has stopped thumping; and, as you take them in, those four common words must count as one of the most arresting sentences that has ever been said to you. Of course, you have heard the sentence many times before—or, at any rate, something very much like it—but never in such a direct and confronting manner.

What did this person mean by saying that to you? Thinking back a few moments, you recall those four words were pronounced without any particular emphasis; and it is that lack of stress, along with the poverty of context that you established simply by using that remote so quickly, that form the most unnerving aspect of the whole scene. Never perhaps has a sentence sounded so strange, and never perhaps has a sentence imposed itself so strongly on you. This strangeness is the spur to interpretation. First of all, as never before, the sentence strikes you as completely absurd. How can one pass from the finite to the infinite? To say that God can be experienced is to have assumed that the divine offers itself as a phenomenon, and this runs counter to everything you know about the proper usage of the word "God." No sooner is this thought coming clear, though, than a dialectic begins. You think: all that is given to us comes through experience. Perhaps experience is not the source of our sense of the divine but, if it is to encounter us, the divine must do so in the medium of human experience. There have been, as you know, men, women, and children who have claimed to have had visions: confessors are obliged to be rigorous in trying to separate delusions and demonic temptations from authentic ecstasies, while theologians are trained to draw appropriate distinctions, such as that between infused and acquired grace. Yet the most profound of the mystics play down any experiential aspect of their visions. Teresa of Avila placed more trust in intellectual rather than sensuous visions, while John of the Cross observed that ecstasies do not remain in the memory.

Perhaps God reveals himself only at the very edge of the concepts we are obliged to use, leaving the blessed soul with a sense that something wondrous has happened but with no language appropriate to speak of it. Could it be, then, that you have just paused a major mystic? Yes, indeed—or it could be only a minor mystic, like those who populate parts of William James's *Varieties of Religious Experience*.[1] You are about to rush inside and call your local bishop or psychologist of religion when you remember that the expression "I have experienced God" can be used in quite ordinary circumstances. People sometimes speak of their prayer life in words only a little less direct than those without claiming to have had visions, and, to be sure, we sometimes talk of entering a state of great calm: could this be reckoned as experience of God? The father of modern Protestant theology, Friedrich Schleiermacher, said in the second edition of his *On Religion* (first published in 1799) that if we are to understand religion we must step back to an "earlier moment" in our consciousnesses, a time when sense and object "mingle and unite"; it is this moment, he says, "which you always experience yet never experience" (*den Ihr jedesmal erlebt, aber auch nicht erlebt*).[2] If he is right, then all religious folk have felt a fleeting moment of unity with what is, and this apparently prelinguistic experience forms the basis of all piety. Similarly, in the last century the distinguished Catholic theologian Karl Rahner argued that it is normative for people to be able to say, "I have experienced God." Like Schleiermacher, he promotes a "mysticism of everyday life," but, unlike him, does so in the register of the transcendental.[3] As he says, "Transcendental experience is the experience of transcendence."[4] That is, we experience the divine mystery at the limits of our hopes and longings, our acts of love and duty, although we never receive the deity as an explicit theme. God's mystery is not to be compromised.

It is at this stage of your reflections that you are likely to become increasingly uneasy with the word "experience." Two sorts of worry come into view. The first was nicely expressed by I. A. Richards. "A word like 'experience,'" he says, "is like a pocket-knife. In good hands it will do most things — not very well."[5] So we should attend closely to the word, beginning by pointing out what is self-evident: it belongs to the English language. We should risk saying the obvious because speakers of other languages would find it odd to have only the one word to cover the conceptual range of "experience." German distinguishes *Erfahrung* and *Erlebnis*, experience in the sense of a journey and experience as lived, and in a similar fashion French has both *expérience* and *vécu*. Philosophy develops in different directions depending on which of these is taken as a starting point. One can elect *Erlebnis*, like Edmund Husserl, and ground one's account of phenomena on modifications of consciousness. Or one can choose *Erfahrung*, as Martin Heidegger came to do, and argue that a shared, public world necessarily precedes any and all private experience. The sole English word "experience" takes on varying meanings and functions in different contexts, meaning now *Erlebnis* and now *Erfahrung* and perhaps now neither, and this must always be acknowledged if confusion is to be avoided at the level of ordinary speech, let alone in philosophical debate.

This philological concern is merely the introduction to the first worry, which is at heart philosophical. It can be announced in the following way. If there is an event that is irreducible to a phenomenon, do we have the right to call it "experience"? Or, to look at the issue from the other side, if we can anticipate what is to come, specify in advance what we count as experience, and thereby notionally deny its otherness, can we strictly call it an experience? Were we to develop impeccable philological habits and decide whether the integrity of the phenomenological horizon should be respected or whether we must admit that it can be divided, we could become clearer about what the man frozen before you might be trying to say. But the other worry is the more fundamental. It, too, is best phrased in terms of a problem. Does the statement "I have experienced God" presume a passage from the finite to the infinite? Or does it bespeak a movement from the infinite to the finite? The very idea of a finite being seeking to experience the infinite makes philosophers and theologians sadly shake their heads. Yet no less an authority than Augustine gives credence to the thought. He tells us how, at Ostia, he and his mother momentarily beheld the divine: "we extended our reach [*nunc extendimus nos*] and in a flash of mental energy attained [*attingimus*] the eternal wisdom which abides beyond all things."[6] The Neoplatonism that informs Augustine's account of his experience makes it seem as though the finite can indeed reach the infinite. No later Catholic theologian would be happy with this, however, and at the least would evoke Augustine's christology to flesh out the position being evoked. To cite only one gloss: "Strictly considered, they did not ascend to God; rather, he descended to and into them."[7]

Is there a way in which one can legitimately pass from the finite to the infinite? Only if the infinite precedes the finite. The idea is found in the third of Descartes's *Meditations*, although it is not suggested there that the infinite can be experienced. For that claim we must look to Hegel. Nature is the realm of contradiction, he says: in its self-negation, the finite sublates itself and reveals itself to be a moment in the infinite. In 1821 he told his students in Berlin, "To philosophical cognition, the progression is a stream *flowing in opposite directions*, leading forward to the other, but at the same time working backward, so that what appears to be the *last*, founded on what precedes, appears rather to be the *first*—the foundation."[8] One can pass from the finite to the infinite only because the infinite has dialectically preceded the finite, and so it makes decent philosophical sense to speak of experiencing the deity. To be sure, God may not be found in "external experience" (the senses) or in "inner experience" (illumination), but is to be known in the final reaches of *Erfahrung*, understood speculatively as the return of absolute spirit to itself.[9] Perhaps the man standing before you is using a dramatic opening gambit to interest you in signing up for an evening course on Hegel's *Encyclopedia*.

The claim that the infinite precedes the finite can be taken ontologically, temporally, transcendentally, and so on. In terms of theological method, however, it amounts to the assertion that revelation is prior to revealability. "God is known only by God": I am quoting Karl Barth, and his point is that theology must begin with the premise that God unveils himself.[10] So maybe those initial fears about the finite not being capable of experiencing the infinite were unfounded. Perhaps the person frozen before you has not committed an elementary philosophical mistake; perhaps what he was about to tell you is that God has indeed revealed himself. No sooner has the thought taken hold, though, than you will remember that Barth's point is epistemological, not existential. "Actual experience begins where our alleged experiences cease, in the crisis of our experiences, in the fear of God," he wrote as a young man.[11] Then, when lecturing at Göttingen, he told his class, "*Deus dixit* is our confidence, not experience."[12] Indeed, the whole of Barth's theology, in its several maturities, is a movement away from the nineteenth-century preoccupation with *Erlebnis* and twentieth-century attempts to correlate God's Word with our sense of modern life. God is subject, not object, he repeatedly tells us; and the deity does not usually offer himself as an item of individual experience.[13]

Time is passing: you are still standing at the door, pondering what the expression "I have experienced God" might mean. In the end, the cruel invention in your hand has been of little help in explicating the sentence, although it has given you time to consider what the person standing before you might say next and what you might say to him. Perhaps, if you are reflective, it has taught you something about what modern European philosophers call "the gaze"; but at any rate the time has come to reanimate the person before you. He has something to say to you. It is this: "I have experienced God."

2

Or maybe, once the man is finally allowed to speak, he will immediately correct himself and say, "No, what I mean is I have experienced the Word of God" or "I have experienced God through music" or "I have experienced God by working for the poor" or "I have experienced God by walking in the woods during Fall" or "I have experienced God by hearing the mass in Latin" or "I have experienced God by studying non-Euclidean geometries." The possibilities are endless. Almost at once, you feel more relaxed; and if you are a theologian you will be very much at ease. Praise God, you are not being confronted by a mystic, major or minor. The man before you now appears to be someone more or less like you, and so you discretely hide the remote behind your back while you speak with him. If you want to put in the time, you can talk with this man quite reasonably. You can reach for your copy of Anselm's *On the Incarnation of the Word*; it is there, on your messy bookshelf, leaning against Eugene Ionesco's *La Cantatrice chauve*.[14] You quote from Anselm: "he who does not believe will not experience, and he who has not had experience will not know" (*Nam qui non crediderit, no experietur; et qui expertus non fuerit, non cognoscet*).[15] Far from sidelining experience as a theological concern, Anselm makes it central. He does not make it primary, however: without faith, there will be no experience. In putting this view to the man at your door, your ultimate authority is neither Barth nor Anselm. Most arguments about religion at front doors turn not on theologians but on what the Bible says. And here your authority is the New Testament.

What you would tell the man at your door is that the New Testament places faith before experience. The healings and the miracles are signs of God's strength and Jesus' intimacy with the one he calls "Abba," but they are not performed so that people may idly savor the supernatural. Unlike magic, miracles presume that faith has already been risked, not always by everyone involved but always by someone. Indeed, although the New Testament uses *peira*, from which, by way of Latin, we derive the English "experience," it is with the sense of "to attempt" or "to strive" or "to test." In the Latin church the word *experiri* does not appear with any regularity until the twelfth century; and experience is accorded a special role in understanding the Christian faith only with the advent of Romanticism.[16] Should the man at your door wish to argue only with regard to the Bible, it could be pointed out, in chapter and verse, that God is figured there as having more experience of men and women, most of it very bitter, than men and women have of him. Many people in the Hebrew Bible hold dear the promises of Yahweh, only a few are depicted as conversing with him. Moses enters a heavy cloud (Ex. 19:16) and speaks of encountering a trace of the divine (Ex. 33:22), Elijah listens to a thin voice of silence (1 Kings 19:12): when we are most tempted to venture the word "experience" we are also firmly reminded that God insists on being absolute subject. He does not also offer himself as a phenomenon, as people are obliged to do when talking with each other, but withdraws behind darkness, silence, fire.

Were the conversation on your front porch to have continued, you would probably have found yourself arguing that although Jesus met and talked with all manner of people none of them thought that they were experiencing God. That would have been blasphemy. In the narrative of the resurrected Jesus in the upper chamber we hear Thomas exclaiming, "My Lord and my God!" (John 20:28), which in terms of the narrative returns us to the proem where the Logos is claimed to be with God and God itself. Only after the christological and trinitarian controversies of the ante-Nicene age, however, do we find formulations that clarify the nature of the unity of Jesus and God. It is one thing to affirm that the full revelation of God was in Christ, quite another to suggest that this full revelation presented itself to anyone's consciousness when Jesus was alive. Had you wished to get more polemical with the man at your door, you might have even queried whether Jesus had experience of God. We cannot doubt that he had an intense prayer life and that his relationship with God was unique in its intimacy, but modern biblical criticism suggests there is little trustworthy evidence that the earthly Jesus had anything like experience of God in the modern, psychologistic sense of the expression. If he did, it was not something that impinged on his public ministry.[17] Rather, the synoptic gospels stress time and again that Jesus was convinced that God's rule, the basileia, was breaking into the world, that an urgent decision about it had to be made, and that the fellowship of an open table was an apt sign of what the kingdom would be like.[18]

But the man on the porch has long ago regretted choosing to knock on your door, and you have showed him very little by way of hospitality. He wanted to tell you something simple and powerful, and you would not let him. When he goes out tomorrow, he will bring with him that new gadget his wife bought him for Christmas, a remote that can pause people the very moment they begin to get quarrelsome or tedious.

3

I think the meditation we have just overheard begins to get interesting in its final moments. Not that the mystics are not fascinating, and not that nineteenth- and twentieth-century theology does not offer essential perspectives for our coming to terms with the theme "the experience of God." Yet the appeal to Jesus' ministry pierces the theme, perhaps even punctures it as a theme. In saying that I am not merely being pious, for I wish to draw attention to what the New Testament tells us about God and experience without linking the two words in any particular way. I think this last point needs to be underlined. The preposition "of" can spin threads of different kinds between the words it connects, and none of these can be philosophically or theologically innocent in the expression "experience of God."[19] Can one take "of" in the sense of an objective genitive, for instance, without any shadow falling from the preposition's sense of possession?

My concern, then, is how "God and experience" cuts a figure against the ground of the New Testament, and had I the time I would set both "figure" and "ground" in the plural. Rather than differentiate the Johannine, Lukan, Markan, Matthean, and Pauline experiences of God, however, I will speak more generally. In fact, I will begin by reflecting on the movement of generalizing, as it variously occurs in the passage from the New Testament documents to the patristic commentaries and debates: the movement of passing from kerygmata to a faith that can be summarized, affirmed, and presented as Catholic. I take as my point of entry a simple confession: I have sometimes felt disoriented when reciting the Nicene creed. How strange it is, I find myself thinking, that in a broad statement of our beliefs we do not say either "I believe in prayer" or "I believe in the basileia," for these are central to the Jesus who is represented in the gospels. When we say the creed we affirm a good many things that we hold to be true on the plane of being—articles of faith concerning the economy of our redemption and the nature of the Trinity—but little about what Jesus thought was important for us to practice on the plane of experience. The Jesus of the creed is born, suffers, dies, is resurrected, ascends, and will come again. He does everything except live. Certainly nothing is directly said about prayer in the creed, and the one mention of the basileia, albeit in translation (with all its difficulties) is associated not with the earthly Jesus but with his second coming.

Now I know very well why the creed came to be formulated as it is, and its dignity is to be respected. Besides, there is a freedom and a pleasure in not having to tell everyone explicitly, Sunday after Sunday, what should be quite evident anyway: that one believes in prayer and the basileia. In that spirit, I would like to make some observations about "experience and God," maybe even—if a close eye is kept on the historical and formal horizons of the expression—"the experience of God"; and I would like to do so from the vantage points of prayer and the basileia. I choose those two perspectives not because I think that one can or even should return to the Jesus movement or even the primitive church, but because Christianity is caught up in an irreducibly double gesture. On one hand, as a living force it must stretch ahead into the unknown, engaging with whatever confronts it and developing itself in every way that is consistent with its missions; on the other hand, it must return perpetually in order to confirm its bases in the witnesses of the New Testament and its roots in the Hebrew scriptures. The double gesture does not always result in an exquisite fit between the developing faith and its sources; on the contrary, the tradition can sometimes ignore the scriptural as is the case, for example, with the doctrine of creation *ex nihilo*. That said, the faith should return with gifts, and the best gifts one can bring to scripture are insights on how to read it the better. And it must go out into the world with the good news, confident that it remains news because it speaks of God's unending quest for us.

If anything, is likely to persuade us that the words "experience" and "God" can enter into a positive relation with one another, it is the simple fact that people pray. In a state of prayer, public or private, one's consciousness is directed to God. This is not to say that the deity ever offers himself as an intentional object, or that prayer is always "answered" in a straightforward way.[20] It is not even to say that there is a God: agnostics and atheists *in extremis* have been known to pray and then to return to their former views when normality reasserts itself. I think of Filip Müller's testimony when a fellow Jew in a death camp encouraged other inmates to pray. "To me it seemed sheer madness to pray in Auschwitz, and absurd to believe in God in this place. In any other situation and in any other place I should not have taken Fischl seriously. But here, on the border line between life and death, we obediently followed his example, possibly because we had nothing else left or because we felt strengthened by his faith."[21] To pray proves nothing about God's existence, yet the act presumes that one is attending to God as testified by another, perhaps because a limit has been reached and all other possibilities have vanished or corroded. No one inaugurates a relationship with God: prayer is always a response, even though it can feel like a response to silence. This is important, for no one can petition a hypothesis or a possibility. Some people posit God as absolutely real in the act of prayer. For most others, I suspect, prayer is accompanied by a hope that the very act makes sense, and that hope is itself an unspoken prayer. Faith always contains the call for more faith (Mark

9:24).[22] A moment ago I said that prayer presumes that one is attending to God. In saying that I was of course alluding to Simone Weil's well-known remark on prayer: "Attention, taken to its highest degree is the same thing as prayer," she says. "It presupposes faith [*foi*] and love."[23] I want to say something about this claim, and other observations that are related to it, but not before I reflect on the verb "attend" and its forms.

To attend to God: it is a rich notion, if one will allow it to be so. It invites us to see the soul fixed on the deity, concentrating on him, or—it might come to be the same thing—relaxing so as to draw close to him. For it certainly suggests approaching so as to be near at hand, and with the sense of offering service. Yet this service is not servitude, since to attend to God also means to accompany him, to go and stay with him as a beloved companion, perhaps even to watch with him, as people sometimes say when visiting the Blessed Sacrament. John of the Cross talks of attending to God in another way, of waiting for him, of waiting in silence for the slightest assurance that there is more than silence, even if it be the merest hint of a quality of silence that surrounds the soul, a silence that is also a calm. Sometimes the wait is immense because what presses on the soul is the sense of waiting without there being anyone or anything to wait for, and the point of this dark night is for the soul to realize, at first very painfully, that God transcends all our ideas of him. The verb "to attend" comes from the Latin *attendere*, "to stretch," and without sacrificing more to etymology than is good for thought, I would like to keep alive the image of the soul stretching itself, as one finds in Philippians 3:13 and in those theologies, from Gregory of Nyssa's to Karl Rahner's, that extend and ramify Paul's powerful metaphor.

If we meet God in prayer it is as absolute subject, not as intentional object, and this means several things. To begin with, it suggests that the encounter does not take the form of an experience; at the most, we could call it a counterexperience. It indicates a movement we cannot inaugurate or control, a rupture in the immanence of our lives. Needless to say, the recognition that God always remains absolute subject also means that we can have no mastery whatsoever of God, not even that which is given by the sheer force of the mutual attraction of lovers. When John of the Cross says, "by love they bind Him with one hair," he announces a deep truth, says it beautifully, yet causes flickers of concern among theologians.[24] For God opens the space wherein love can be ventured, and the first step is always his. As absolute subject, God never presents himself as object in any sense, and so he comes to us not as experience but in experience: not as that which we can appropriate, render proper to consciousness, but rather as a mystery that passes through our lives, a disturbance that opens our ways of being, doing, and thinking to quite other perspectives and that cannot be positively identified by introspection.

Attending to God occurs only in and through a faith that is always and already given to us, and that makes possible a symbolic transformation of our ordinary experience. Faith is freely given, not inscribed in the structure of our humanity or imposed from above, so the risk it entails is to be freely accepted or rejected. One can come without faith to the conclusion that one must accept God, if one does, in faith. To recognize that faith is always and already given to us refocuses the truth that Hegel glimpsed when he insisted that the infinite precedes the finite, while to sense that faith involves a transformation of experience can be exemplified by a contemporary theologian not especially close to Hegel but who takes him very seriously indeed. I am thinking of Eberhard Jüngel, and I am thinking in particular of his suggestive formulation that faith is "an experience with experience" (*eine Erfahrung mit der Erfahrung*).[25] In turning to God we revalue past events as well as those that are to come, and thus experience itself is reset. Reoriented though we may be, we will not have qualitatively different experiences in life. Yet our newfound allegiance to Jesus as the Christ has the potential to affect any and all events that might come our way; it sets them in italics.

This is not the whole story, however. I would say that faith is "a stream *flowing in opposite directions*," if I may borrow Hegel's fine phrase. For equally we can think of faith as the medium of counter-experience, of what breaks through the horizons of expectation that bound our lives and calls the sovereignty of the constituting "I" into question.[26] When faith is the medium, any event can contain the possibility that God will come. A woman walks past me on the street, busy talking with her son, and when she lightly touches his shoulder for no apparent reason and with no response from the child I can see just that and no more. Or I could see the event itself touched by mystery: two people cutting a figure against a vast ground of suffering and love. In that moment I can see myself there as well, connected with them not by ties of friendship or even acquaintanceship but because my being, like theirs, is constituted as "being-with" and because in faith I take that ontological sociality to be a trace of trinitarian life. What enters the event quite unexpectedly is not only *caritas* but also a renewed understanding of it, one that can have direct and indirect consequences in the world around me.

We have not stopped thinking about Simone Weil, but let us return to her writings. "Attention, taken to its highest degree," she says, "is the same thing as prayer"; and she adds, "It presupposes faith [*foi*] and love." Much turns here on the qualification "taken to its highest degree" and on the designation of faith as *foi*. If I attend with complete concentration on some thing—as Francis Ponge does with a glass of water, for example, in one of his long meditations[27]—I might uncover hidden or undisclosed horizons of my intentional relationship with that thing. I might also express a respect for its singularity and even a care for its being. But unless I already have the theological virtue of faith, I will not go any further than this, and the limit I will have reached strikes me as preliminary to prayer. If I attend with equal concentration on that same thing, this time possessing the theological virtue of faith, I will of course reflect that it belongs to the order of creation, and consequently I will attune myself to the creator. Concentration will turn to praise. The point was made by another writer deeply impressed by Plato, Augustine. In *De Trinitate* he says of someone being educated in the love of God, "Let him so accustom himself to find traces of spiritual things in material things that, when he shall begin to ascend upwards from them under the guidance of reason, he may arrive at that unchangeable truth itself through which all things have been made, and may not take with him to the highest things that which he loathes in the lowest things."[28]

In another passage, however, Weil distances herself from the point that Augustine is making. "Attention which is turned toward that which is able to be present without attention is of a mixed kind," she says, "there is a mixture of attention and impression." There is no ascent that leaves the created order entirely behind, it would seem, and yet Weil suggests that attention is able to surmount impression in a decisive manner. "Absolutely pure attention—attention which is nothing but attention—is attention directed toward God; for he is only present to the extent that such attention exists."[29] An attention that is "absolutely pure," utterly unconditioned by its disengagement with impression, is hard to imagine. It would be an awareness without an end and therefore without a desire for meaning and truth; it would come only in detachment from the world and from the self that centers a world. In a careful and provocative essay on Weil, Maurice Blanchot observes that attention in this eminent sense is "the reception of what escapes attention, an opening upon the unexpected, a waiting that is the unawaited of all waiting."[30] This formulation has the virtue of bringing the paradox at the heart of Weil's remark into sharp focus. God becomes present to us in prayer only to the extent that we open ourselves to the possibility of counterexperience.

This paradox yields to another: were counterexperience to approach us in the realm of the possible it would be a species of experience, formed by the privilege of the constituting "I." No sooner is this thought before us than one of the words that is important for Weil goes out of focus. For God cannot become present to us in an epistemological or ontic manner: that would require him to offer himself as an intentional object, which is precisely what is forbidden by attention in its eminent sense. To dig down deeper and think of God granting himself ontologically or even pre-ontologically is one way to avoid difficulties, though not if they are located on the plane of experience. True, one can adopt Rahner's solution, although in doing so one downplays the event of God, its coming from nowhere. There is no "experience" of God in prayer, then, but rather a disturbance that invites us to assent to a reordering of our experiences and our sense of what these are and can be. We come to realize that the risk of faith is not assenting to a deficient mode of knowledge but of accepting that, once it is embraced, faith can declare itself as the fundamental ground of our thought and action. We are ungrounded, made secondary with respect to God who has initiated the movement of faith. This faith is explored in prayer, and there is a sense in which the subject does not pray. Heidegger tells us that the specific being of *Dasein* is not its "I" but its "who," and without exploring the relations between *Dasein* and *Mitsein* I would say that the person in prayer is no longer simply an "I": he or she passes from the constituting "I" to the "who." Whether we wish to explain experience on the basis of internal *Erlebnisse* or by external *Erfahrung*, our very relation to experience has been reordered. One aspect of that reordering is a reorientation to the world, an opening that for us is impossible but that now beckons, a path that could never be discerned in advance and that, even now, does not offer itself fully to consciousness. It unfolds only when one begins to pass along it.

4

One thing we know about Jesus' spiritual life is that he asked his Father that the basileia might come (Matt. 6:9–15, Luke 11:2–4).

The very fact that Jesus prayed in this way, and taught his disciples to do likewise, tells us something important about the basileia: it is right and proper to pray for its coming. The explicit placing of the basileia in the prayer, directly after the hallowing of the divine name, also tells us something significant about it: it is associated with God's holiness rather than our petitions for food, forgiveness, and avoidance of being put to the test. In praying for the basileia to come, we are not so much asking for something we require for our daily well-being as asking for God himself. Of course the gift of God in the basileia has already been given, as the prayer teaches us by its very structure: we begin by saying *"Our* Father". . . . And although it is God who will bring about the basileia in all its fullness at the right time it is implied by the act of prayer that this time will come more swiftly if we bind ourselves to God in word and deed.

As soon as one passes from the fact that Jesus preached the basileia to the inevitable question of what the basileia is one gets caught up in paradoxes. The scriptural evidence points in different directions: the basileia is both here and still to come (Matt. 11:5–6; 25:1–13); it grows in and around us yet interrupts us (Mark 4:26–29; Luke 12:39–40); it is inside as well as outside us (Thomas 3); it is divine yet entirely ordinary (Matt. 13:33); it is secret yet can be seen in public (Mark 4:11–12; Luke 7:22–23). No one gospel gives us a clear account of what Jesus meant by the notion, while taking all of them together does not make things any easier. This should not come as a surprise, for Jesus tells us only what the basileia is like and never what it is. Certainly the Church Fathers do not resolve the tensions coiled in the notion: some, like Irenaeus and Justin, argue for an earthly reign of a thousand years while others, like Clement and Origen, for a heavenly kingdom.[31] Eusebius believes that the basileia is to be identified with monarchia, while Augustine holds that the church and the basileia will become one, though not yet.[32] In the Middle Ages the basileia either fuels intense eschatological hope, as with Joachim of Fiore, or—perhaps because of the ecclesial suspicions that follow this spiritual ferment—is not discussed at all. Thomas Aquinas, for example, does not consider it.

With the Renaissance the basileia goes underground as a theme until the seventeenth century when Johannes Cocceius in his *Summa doctrina de Foedere et Testimento Dei* (1660) develops a doctrine of grace that has the basileia as its historical horizon. Thereafter one finds Hermann Samuel Reimarus maintaining that Jesus proposed a political realm, not a spiritual kingdom, and Kant refiguring the basileia by way of the kingdom of ends. For the one, the basileia would have offered itself to experience had it been established; for the other, the coming of the basileia marks the extinction of all religious experience.[33] Reimarus and Kant agree to divorce Jesus' teaching from teachings about him: the one retains the former, the other stresses the latter, though solely from a moral point of view. Only with Schleiermacher do we find an attempt to argue that the basileia is precisely what disables the distinction between the Jesus of history and the Christ of faith. "Christ did what he did to found the kingdom of God," he says, "and we can represent his teaching activity only as a specific form in which he endeavored to carry out his mission. It follows that we cannot make a distinction between the teaching of Christ and the teaching about Christ. Rather, the teaching about Christ was central to all his teaching."[34]

Schleiermacher's understanding of the basileia is strongly marked by the Johannine character of his christology, and one would want to fold the synoptic parables and sayings into this understanding before developing the notion any further.[35] Once that has been done, even Barth would agree with Schleiermacher: "He spoke of the Kingdom of God, and He was the Kingdom of God."[36] Rather than dwell on this theme, though, I would like to conclude by sketching a double relation between the basileia and the Trinity. I begin by returning to Augustine. In *De Trinitate* VIII:8 he considers the objection that while one can find God in love there is no basis for discerning the Trinity there as well. "But as a matter of fact," he says to those who question his position, "you do see the Trinity if you see love" (*Imo vero vides Trinitatem, si charitatem vides*), and he goes on to offer a proof.[37] The details of that demonstration interest me less than Augustine's central insight, which I would like to explicate in my own way by linking the basileia with the Trinity. If there is love, *caritas*, then the basileia has already taken root, and it is the triune God who has brought that about: the Son has preached the Father in and through the Spirit. Our experience of being-with, entirely ordinary though it be, is in and through faith a participation in the divine life of the Trinity. There is no reason to think of this experience of the basileia by way of utopia. Of course, insofar as we can represent it to ourselves, stammering uncontrollably all the while, the immanent Trinity is the ultimate horizon of sociality: plurality in unity, perichoresis. Yet it would be a slight to our created natures to aim directly for that kind of sociality, which is impossible for us, while the very word "sociality" is theologically misleading since it implies three centers of consciousness in the deity. At the same time, though, the life of the Trinity offers itself to us as characterized by desolation: Jesus suffers and dies, and if God is absolutely one with Jesus then, as Hegel saw so sharply, there is a seriousness and a suffering within the deepest life of the Trinity. If we see the Trinity when we see love, *caritas*, then we have experience of the basileia. It is limited and mediated, needless to say, but the very adventure with the other person means that we are embraced by the deity in its endless movement of self-giving. For when the Trinity communicates with us it does so as relationality, as a being with others, not only with human beings but also with the entirety of creation.[38] It is that sense of relationality in the present, looking back on the past, and with a view to the future, which gives us our best chance of rethinking the *vestigium trinitatis*, the trace of the Trinity. Because the Trinity offers itself as eschatological reality and as social desolation we glimpse the basileia with hope and suffering. To hear the cry of justice is to hear the approach of the basileia.

When we see love we discern a trace of the Trinity. Yet it is the Trinity that reveals to us what this love truly is; and the parables of the basileia are, whatever they are, attempts to show us that this love is, from our perspective, incalculable and impossible: it overturns our expectations by its sheer excess, breaks through the horizons within which we live, and surprises us, insisting on its status as an event. This love manifests itself in the basileia, which now appears to us in all the force of not yet being here: we feel the full weight of a reversal of our legitimate expectations, and can only sense the infinite distance between how we act with one another and how we could act were we to surrender to the rule of God, a rule that is wholly consumed by *caritas* in its strongest possible sense. This is no easy familiarity with a moral commonwealth, nor is it in any clear sense "experience," even "moral experience," if Kant would allow the expression. It is eschatology or, if you like, counterexperience: that which occurs, without being lived through, when we are encountered by the absolute subject who is God. Counterexperience is awe and rupture; because it involves encountering the other, it contains the possibility of peril; and it is the realization that our homes, both familial and intellectual, have no ground on which to stand. It occurs without theater more often than not, in and around and through ordinary events, like passing a woman and her son in the street. We could testify to it, were our mouths not caked with silence because of it: how can one make sentences out of that which upsets our entire way of thinking and being? Perhaps it was something like this that the man at your door wanted to tell you.

6

Faith and the Conditions of Possibility of Experience
A Response to Kevin Hart

JAMES K. A. SMITH

I think I know the fellow who knocked at Kevin Hart's door: every Sunday, he sits just a few pews in front of me at Del Aire Assembly of God, an inner-city church in Los Angeles. And every once in a while, he comes to pester me in my adult education class. Lacking that handy remote which could stop him mid-sentence (I've put one on my Christmas list!), I don't have the luxury of turning off his testimony regarding his experience of God. And so I often hear him recount similar experiences: "Jamie, I met God in such a powerful way this week," he'll testify. Or, "Brother, I just have to share with you the kingdom experience I had on our retreat this weekend." He then proceeds to share—to testify to—his experience, what he has "gone through," continuing a long tradition of testimony that includes Augustine's *Confessions*. In fact, testimonies to the experience of God are pretty common fare in my evangelical, charismatic tradition; but reflection on just what that means—or its very possibility—is not. So I am thankful to Hart for raising these questions about the experience of God, and about the very idea of experience itself. Indeed, just as Marion suggests that it is the question of God's "phenomenality" that

---

My thanks to Barbara Wall, Director of the Office for Mission Effectiveness, and John Caputo, David R. Cook Professor of Philosophy, for both the invitation and support to engage Kevin Hart and participate in the Experience of God conference.

pushes us to the question of phenomenality per se, so an investigation of the experience of God brings us to a point of sustained reflection on experience per se.[1]

It seems that Hart, however, is immediately perplexed by the claim to an "experience of God": "that God can be experienced," he remarks, "is to have assumed that the divine offers itself as a phenomenon, and this runs counter to everything you know about the proper usage of the word 'God.'" That observation itself, however, assumes something about both the nature of "experience," what constitutes a "phenomenon,"[2] as well as the nature of God and God's "donation." In the remainder of the essay, Hart attempts to unpack just what he means by this slippery word "experience" and hence what can be characterized as a "phenomenon." There is a correlation between the two: only a phenomenon can be experienced, and experience can only be experience of a phenomenon in a strict sense. So any "encounter" with something (or someone) that cannot—or will not—be subjected to the conditions of phenomenality cannot be "experienced" in a strict sense. But this does not mean that it cannot be encountered, or that it cannot encounter us; it's just that we'll have to find a different name for that "event"—a "counterexperience." (Of course, all of the problems that Hart believes attend our claims to an "experience of God" must, Levinas reminds us, also accompany any claim to an "experience" of the other person, the Other. For Levinas, the other person is also an alterity who refuses to be submitted to the conditions of appearance imposed by phenomenality.[3] Thus Levinas must also provide an account of how I can "encounter" the other without the other being reduced to the conditions of my horizons of expectation. His "solution" is a "relation without relation."[4] In this sense, Hart carries on a Levinasian tradition that includes Marion.)

Hart locates this nonobjectifying, nonreductive encounter in prayer:[5] "If anything is likely to persuade us that the words 'experience' and 'God' can enter into a positive relation with one another it is the simple fact that people pray." This is because "if we meet God in prayer it is as absolute subject, not as intentional object, and this means several things. To begin with, it suggests that the encounter does not take the form of an experience; at the most, we could call it a counterexperience. . . . As absolute subject, God never presents himself as object in any sense, and so he comes to us not as experience but in experience."

It is at this juncture that Hart seems to oppose "experience" and "faith" (another slippery word). Faith, in fact, is understood as the medium[6] of this "counterexperience" that is not an experience. And "when faith is the medium, any event can contain the possibility that God will come." This faith then becomes the condition of possibility for the revelation of God—the encounter with God that is a counter-experience—in, for example, witnessing a mother's touch as a sacramental medium for the revelation of God.

But let us closely consider what Hart is suggesting here, particularly in the lovely example of a mother and her son. Without faith, he says, all I would "see" are just bodies touching "and no more." On the other hand, with faith, I can "see the event itself touched by mystery" and in fact see there "a trace of trinitarian life." I think the notion of "seeing" is an important matter here; it indicates that what is at stake is precisely a matter of perception. Indeed, is not Hart simply suggesting that faith is the condition of possibility for this (counter)experience of the divine? Or, to put it more precisely, is this not to say—with Anselm—that faith functions as a "horizon of expectation" which makes it possible for one to "see" God in this gentle caress? Despite the fact that Hart suggests that "what enters the event quite unexpectedly is not only *caritas* but also a renewed understanding of it," I think we must conclude that it is precisely because faith expects this, or creates a horizon of expectation for it, that one is then able and open to see the divine in this tender moment. Indeed, we might say that faith is precisely the horizon of expectation that expects the unexpected, such that nothing is unexpected (because with God "all things are possible"). This is not because everything is delineated in advance, hence eliminating any surprise (here we follow Levinas's critique of intentionality); rather, the only thing that is intended in the horizon of faith is that God is the God of the impossible. As such, the believer expects nothing but surprises. So it seems that the revelation of God, which would be a "counterexperience," nevertheless requires a certain horizon of expectation, viz., faith; otherwise, even the one without faith could encounter this "rupture" of immanence (but Hart has correctly argued that this cannot happen). Hart himself has emphasized just this point: "when faith is the medium," then I can see this (e.g., divine sociality in the love between mother and son); when faith is not operative as my horizon of expectation, this mundane event lacks this sacramental or revelatory power. Or perhaps we should say that this "power" is not operative for the perceiver without faith as a horizon of expectation. The mundane world, as creation, always carries within it this function of being *sacramentum mundi*. That this mode of reference is not "picked up" is the perceiver's "problem," so to speak. Indeed, this is precisely Paul's point in Romans 1: God is revealed in the structure of creation, but for perceivers who lack faith as a horizon of expectation, this "truth" is "suppressed"—it goes unseen (Rom. 1:18–21).[7]

I want to rethink both Hart's assumptions about the nature of experience and the constitution of "phenomena," precisely by affirming his insight that faith is the condition of possibility for experience (a bit of an attempt to deconstruct one who has written one of the best books on deconstruction and theology!).[8] It seems to me that Hart earlier rejected the notion of an "experience" of God precisely because experience involved conditions under which a phenomenon must appear, and because he assumed that the divine would not "offer itself as a phenomenon." Such conditions could also be described (pace Levinas) as horizons of expectation. But if faith is a "medium" or horizon of expectation which makes the encounter with God possible, and it is only such a horizon of expectation that makes the "encounter" with God possible (as Hart affirms), then it is not a matter of horizons of expectation per se which are the problem, but rather what kind of horizons are operative, or the way in which these horizons operate. The "encounter"—even if we want to call it a "counterexperience"—nevertheless requires a certain horizon of expectation. And if the encounter involves such mediation, why can't we call it an "experience?" God is not afraid of our horizons of expectation; indeed, he is happy to concede them (indeed, he created us in such a way that they are the conditions of finite, creaturely existence). God gives himself—reveals himself or "offers himself"—"according to the mode of the perceiver" (Aquinas). We might even offer something of a postmodern translation of Philippians 2: "Being in the very form of the Infinite, he did not consider absolute alterity something to be maintained at all costs, but rather humbled himself, making himself a phenomenon, obedient to the point of death." God shows up, on his own terms to be sure (*a partir de lui*, Marion always emphasizes), but precisely thereby choosing to show up in terms that we can understand. This is why every revelation of God is incarnational: the Infinite "shows up" in the finitude of the flesh (John 1:14)—to be heard, touched, held. "This is what we've seen," John would recount, "what we've heard, what we've touched" (1 John 1:1–3). That sounds to me like a testimony to an experience of God, made possible by God's giving himself to be experienced (not an experience that shuts down transcendence or alterity, but precisely an experience that is an experience *of* alterity, which at the same time eludes the experience).

That "experience" would only be objectifying or reductive if we consider experience in a very narrow sense of subject-object relations (here we recall Heidegger's critique of Husserl[9]). But that need not be the case. What we would have to rehearse here—if time permitted—are all of the contours of Derrida's critique of Levinas in "Violence and Metaphysics,"[10] where he emphasizes that even in Husserl (I don't think we'll ever get past Husserl) the account of experience is radically attentive to its inadequation, the way in which the other, in being experienced, nevertheless remains other—along with the correlate assertion that no "encounter" with the other could take place unless the other could be "experienced" in some sense, appearing in terms that the constituting ego can perceive. As such, the experience of God is not an objectification of God that would make God an "object" in the narrow sense; but it is an encounter in which God gives himself (in a mode of donation) to be experienced by a finite perceiver—precisely because the very conditions of encounter for finite perceivers (as created by God) demand that both experience and what Hart calls a "counterexperience" must nevertheless be an event that takes place on a register commensurate with finitude. So the fellow knocking at Hart's door, far from claiming to have objectified God (he wouldn't even know what that meant), is testifying to an encounter—and experience—with God in which the transcendence of God became more manifest. So his response—in a manner that Heidegger would appreciate—is not to invent a concept, but rather to dance and pray. Finally, I would note one other concern, regarding Hart's conception of faith. Faith, for him, "is freely given, not inscribed in the structure of our humanity or imposed from above." He goes on to describe faith in terms of a "theological virtue." Faith, then, in a good Thomistic fashion, seems to be a kind of supernatural addendum—a supplement. I don't need to explain the implications of that to Hart, who is most familiar with Derrida's analysis of supplementarity. Suffice it to note that for Derrida, supplements are original, so that the supposed "super"-character of this infused virtue must be inscribed, in a sense, in the original structure.

That is what I would argue: faith is structural, a structural mode of human existence.[11] We can see this described, in fact, in Husserl's account of "apperception" (recalling from above that the situation with respect to God is analogous to our situation with respect to other persons): from the perspective of the constituting ego, the other's subjectivity is genuinely transcendent, and thus in a sense structurally "absent"—never able to be present within the sphere of ownness, which Husserl describes as the "core of presentation" presupposed by appresentation. Thus, it is on the basis of what is present—the body of the other (*Körper*) paired with my animated body (*Leib*)—that the ego posits what is absent. What is absent is appresented on the basis of what is present. "Thus every perception of this type," Husserl remarks, "is transcending: it posits more as itself there than it makes 'actually' present at any time."[12] The other's body, as present, "signals" or "indicates" the subjectivity of the other, which can never be made present. Or to put it conversely, the subjectivity of the other is manifested or incarnated in her or his body, constituting "the 'irreal' intentional reaching of the other into my primordiality."[13] The other qua other can never be present, can never be "seen" or "show up" within the sphere of ownness, which is the very condition for knowledge in Husserl's phenomenology.

But would this not mean that phenomenology, when it comes to the Other, is operating "in the blind?" And if appresentation is characteristic of all perception,[14] would this not mean that there is a certain blindness at the heart of phenomenology? For that which is appresented, we lack intuition, lack sight. But insofar as intuition is the condition of possibility of knowledge, might we not conclude that we do not know the other but only believe the other body to be an ego (though with good reason)? Would this signal a faith at the heart of phenomenology (surprising those who thought phenomenology had no *kardia*)? Does this not mean that faith is "inscribed in the structure of our humanity"? That faith is the condition of possibility for the experience of alterity?

Je ne sais pas; il faut croire.[15]

7

Liturgy and Coaffection

JEAN-YVES LACOSTE
Translated by Jeffrey L. Kosky

When we pray, what is this "we" that prays? To answer this question, I will take on three tasks: (1) spelling out the phenomenal reality of the "we" or the "with" by evoking two accepted understandings of these notions; (2) describing the liturgy (or what people do *coram Deo*) as an experience that knows neither "subject" nor "object"; (3) and examining the extent to which the "we" of the liturgy is that of a coaffective experience, that is, the "we" of a *Mitbefindlichkeit*.

Intersubjectivity

For Husserl, who coined and popularized the word *intersubjectivity*, the other man, the other subject, the other subjectivity comes up belatedly, and his credentials demand careful examination. Regarding the other man, what first appears to me is not his subjectness, but his objectness. I appear to myself inseparably in the twofold mode of subjectivity and objectivity (for myself, I am at once an ego and a body); the other man, to the contrary, appears to me as this other body like mine, but without anything in his appearing making it apodictically necessary that I accept him as another myself. Reducing the Other[1] to his objectivity is above all not what Husserl wants to do. But this objectivity, or whatever one wants to call it, is still first for me—at least to the extent that I exist in the mode of a subject, which is that of intentional and representational consciousness. For subjectivity, intersubjectivity thus presents itself as a theoretically unavoidable task. We exist in the plural. This plural, which belongs to our "natural attitude," nevertheless cannot be considered established or indubitable if the field of the indubitable is defined as that of a self appearing to itself and if the other man is first of all the representation that I make of him. The I is the first to appear, and it is as noematic content that the other man intervenes. To make it such that the arrival of the other was not confined to this realm was what Husserl always wanted, from the first notes concerning *Einfühlung* to the fifth *Cartesian Meditation*. This arrival, however, might remain there, and it is at the end of the phenomenological process, not at its outset, that we possess the experiential and conceptual means necessary not to be stuck there. There where consciousness and the subject are master—and they are in Husserl—the I occupies such a strong position that the rights of the "we" can be established only with great difficulty.

But is it as consciousness and subject that the I appears primordially? Must the names of consciousness and the subject be the first ones uttered? Heidegger, who proposes other names, will position himself at the root of the Husserlian problematic. The first phenomenon is the world. The first name for man is Being-in-the-world. And the original or primal structure of the world includes a shared world, *Mitwelt*. When we say existence—*Dasein*—we say coexistence (*Mitsein, Mitdasein*). The Other is always already there, pretheoretically, prethematically. He is not there first as a potential intentional object, as a body I spot and wonder if it is inhabited by a consciousness. He is there from the beginning as an "other self" and as my "double." I cannot appear to myself without letting the world appear to me, and in the world we exist in the plural, each interested in the other, each concerned with or caring for the other—ever since forever. The "with" is first, and whoever asserts its primacy also asserts that the not-being-with, in all the forms of solitude, is itself only an extreme case of being-with. That the Other can be missing, that he can appear paradoxically in the mode of absence, tells us that he is ordinarily present, present first. The Husserlian problematic grants the upper hand to an ego conceived as "monad," and only afterward does it try to permit this monadic ego to encounter the Other. In Heidegger, things are completely reversed. The I is always already engaged in a We. This I is not monad, but radical openness; it is turned toward things in a way that is not that of an intentional aim but that of openness to the world. And in this world, the I dwells in the company of the Other, immemorially and indubitably.

Does that mean that Husserl, in all the nooks and crannies of all his texts on intersubjectivity, is describing nothing real? We cannot be so sure. If the with is first, it still cannot be said that it is the sole way of being or the sole structure of existence (the sole "existential"). If the with is a fact (if it enters into the play of "facticity"), a point about which Heidegger was right, we cannot infer that it alone is factic. And it is a phenomenologically indispensable task to specify on what conditions, in light of what possibilities, man can also appear to himself as monadic transcendental subject. Closing the doors and windows, existing in the mode of a subjectivity who enjoys a priori only his own company and for whom the Other is one object among all those that fall under intentionality—the Husserlian monadology is not devoted to a pseudo-possible but to a disposition or way of being that cannot be dismissed with only so much as a wave of the hand, exclaiming that it is neither originary nor fundamental. To exist as subject; to apprehend things as objects; to apperceive the Other as an other body about which I wonder if it is only a body or if it is an other ego—this set of experiences, placed beneath the authority of Descartes, is not a mistake about oneself but an exploration of a possibility given at the outset, an initial possibility. Certainly, this experience does violence: violence with regard to our everyday ways of being that take for granted the presence of the alter ego, violence with regard to the theories for which there is existence only in the plural, and so forth. But these are fruitful violations, and the experience shares in this fruitfulness. The world is for the other as much as it is for me. Each time, it appears to (an) ego. This ego is not only consciousness, but it is not less. And in each moment, therefore, that it exists as consciousness, in every extent to which it exists by opening an intentional aim, the other ego can appear to himself only as content of consciousness. In the existential reality of the "with" nothing stops the Being-with from degenerating into intersubjectivity, i.e. from structuring itself as intersubjectivity. It is possible for the me to close itself up in a monadic experience that suspends the real existence of the Other or that demands guarantees from the Other before admitting him to the status of an other ego besides my ego. This possibility is given at the beginning. We therefore cannot dispense with a theory (or a theoretical moment) capable of telling us how this possible becomes real. Husserl's investigation does indeed bear on what is, that is, on what we are always capable of being.

The conceptual clash—coexistence vs. intersubjectivity—does not have to be interpreted as an alternative, but as a dialectic. The Other is immemorially familiar to us. When we try to regain, notion by notion, experience by experience, the dawn of existence and the first evidences given, we discover that the other is in fact familiar to us in the mode of the strange, of that whose apparition is always fraught with problems. The "with" is indeed originary, but it is, we say, endangered. Being-with is also actualized as the intention of the one against the other, as objectification of the Other, as the occurrence of a subject who knows, outside himself, only the existence of objects. We do our best to say that there is peril there, and we can produce experiences that are reluctant to be integrated into the schema of intersubjectivity (experience of an Other who "gazes" at us, experience of an "I" always summoned by others or of an "I" that the other always hangs over, etc.). The critics of intentionality and objectification must, however, concede one point: the neighbor, the other who draws near to us, the other face, and so on, coexistence always runs the risk of being lived as intersubjectivity or as demand for intersubjectivity. When Husserl forces the other ego, in order to prove that it is an other subject, to have no other existence besides the noematic, he makes no theoretical error: the error or faulty perspective is to have failed to perceive that the Other appears to us by authorizing and by criticizing, both at once, the reduction of the originary "with" to a subject-object relation. To say of the other ego that he runs the risk of being reduced to noematic status is to say that the phenomenology of intersubjectivity does not rest on confusions, that it is authorized by a possibility included in the originary "with." The world is a shared world, a with-world. The Other was always already present in it, and present as other ego. The Other forever appears to us as always able to be integrated into a relation of *intentio* to *intentum*. And symmetrically I myself exist in the world as always susceptible of playing the role of subject—as in danger of being subject.

Liturgical Experience

These suggestions having been made, I can cut to the heart of the matter by interrogating a special experience, liturgical experience, to see if (and how) it runs the risk in question and if it has the means to avoid falling prey to it (and what these means are). How does the problematic of the "with" connect with that of the life lived *coram Deo*? How can it either clarify or be clarified by it? The response we need seems clear: liturgical experience is for those who know neither subject nor object, and we are only offering a caricature if we seek objects and subjects in it (and intersubjectivity along with them). This answer needs to be explained.

Absence of any object, first—what does that mean? It means, quite simply, that many things (in the pregnant sense that Heidegger gives to the word in the lecture on "The Thing"[2]) populate the space opened by the liturgy and that these things appear by refusing their objectification. If things there are, this is so in a strong, not banal, sense: on one hand, things that are not constituted for or in the intention of a consciousness; on the other hand, things that are not at our disposition, things that we let be and appear in a play that excludes all grasping, whether this be in the mode of representation or taking possession. Neither representation nor use here. Sensation and perception are present, of course. Things are visible, audible, tangible. We can apprehend them as we apprehend anything that shows itself in the horizon of the world. But whenever we apprehend them in the realm of representation, we make a mistake about the thing. Things in general, and those of the liturgy in particular, are such by virtue of a rupture or a separation. The things of the liturgy are not the sole beings to be things (even the most profane work of art, for example, also exists in the nonobjective mode of the thing). The things of the liturgy are nevertheless nonobjects in a pure state. They are signs and symbols. They often surround us in such a way that we cannot spot them (for example the places, churches or chapels, where we gather to pray). Measuring them, quantifying them, amounts to mistaking them—or at least to glimpsing only a fraction of what they are.

Let us admit that every thing runs the risk of being collapsed into objectivity; let us admit that it belongs to the thing to have its secret negative, which is to appear to us potentially as object. For there to be object, an intervention is necessary, that of a consciousness that establishes itself in a relation of *intentio* to *intentum*. Now if one characteristic of liturgical experience is clear, it is that this experience, this play, does not require any actual representational consciousness, but actors in a spectacle without spectator. The category of drama has pride of place here, and it is as dramatis persona that one participates in the liturgy—to participate in it otherwise, for the pleasure of seeing or hearing, would be the error par excellence, a pseudo-participation incapable of letting things be what they are. Of course, we do not take part in the liturgical play in order to achieve the satisfaction that the solution to a theoretical problem would bring: namely, letting-things-be-things. But if the theoretical contribution is there in addition, it is of no small interest. "A mystery is something one does, and not something one contemplates." This axiom (put forward by Maria Laach) provides us with the key to the participation of things in the liturgy. This key takes its place in a list of duties: disqualifying objectifying manipulation, disqualifying representational consciousness. And insofar as there are things, these duties (of which we cannot acquit ourselves cleanly by means of a theory) are those of a vigilance and a respect. The liturgy knows neither objects nor subjects, for it is the work of men who watch over things. (Not exclusively—but necessarily.)

In addition to not existing in the mode of subject, I can add that one dispenses ipso facto with asking if the other man exists in the same mode. Here the "we" is not to be conquered and secured. The other man does not face me. He asks nothing of me. If by chance we had a disagreement, our common participation in the liturgy supposes that we have settled this disagreement before leaving our offering on the altar—or at least that we have bracketed it. No unrest, I insist, weighs on the identity of the Other. He is obviously alter ego. His presence is self-evident. The liturgy is a brotherly work in common—it is a pure case of existence as coexistence, of *Dasein* as *Mit-dasein*.

Beyond subject and object, beyond subjectivity and intersubjectivity, the liturgical space is that of a recall and an affirmation. It is, at first glance, the field where we verify the originary "with" that governs the relations among men and where we verify the pre-objective familiarity that governs the relation of men and things. But is it only that? According to the evidence, no: for the liturgy sometimes traffics with things that bear a strange fate (as with the thing that becomes a sacrament), and because it manifests the existential primacy of the "with" only by also giving us to see modes of this "with" that are not included in the logic of the fundamental words of the experience. Let us leave it to other texts to consider things that become sacraments and focus instead on what men do liturgically who are not content to be *Mitmenschen*. Within the time of the world, the liturgy means to offer a certain image or anticipation of the ultimate, or definitive, of final realities. The ultimate, that is to say, the excess of Being-in-the-world. The ultimate, again, as life over which the shadows of death have symbolically dissipated. The ultimate, again, as the experience of a flesh made for life. These excesses and these symbols (how could they be forgotten!) are made real here and now, and we exist here and now faced with a perpetual possibility: take on the role of subject and force things to wear the garb of objects. But these excesses remain. And about men who want to associate liturgically with angelic praises, it must be conceded that they are a little bit more than just together.

To specify this "little bit more," it behooves us to see in the "with" proper to the liturgy a disqualification of the "everyday" modes of the "with." Two points are important here. On the one hand, the liturgy is the place where a word is spoken without gossip. On the other hand, it is the figure of a "dwelling," or cohabitation, within the world, that exceeds the phenomenon of Being-in-the-world. (1) The everyday world is a world where one speaks, but the liturgy is not the affair of just anyone. Ritualized, codified, cantillated, the words of the liturgy set themselves at a distance from ordinary words. That he who prays says the prayer of the church or that he speaks in the name of Christ, these words are words that "they" cannot utter. Put at the service of praise, the words say and seal the unity of a "we." To utter them is to open a discursive space where only the important belongs. The liturgy makes words un-everyday. (2) This being so, the liturgical assembly opens in advance a common dwelling. We ordinarily find ourselves together, but we are in the world as a pilgrim passing through or on reprieve. The limits of the "with" are the limits of the "there," and the limits of the "there" are those of Being-toward-death. When we pray, the "with" has the bearing of the definitive. Those who pray together undertake an act of communion. This communion is the fact of the living among them, it is also the fact of the living and the dead, the assembly of those who are and those who were, a unity that knows no barrier, neither temporal nor spatial. The liturgical play is a visible play, ranged along with every possible sort of "communicative practice." But it is above all the image of an invisible: of the "with" over which death no longer exercises any right of preemption.

I just spoke of communion. We should avoid letting ourselves be tricked by such language into believing that the liturgy institutes here and now an eschatological transparency of egos or a definitive reign of "relation," of the *esse ad*. To speak of the liturgy is also to speak of the world and to confess that the world is not experientially bracketed merely by the strength of an act of faith. The liturgy tells of a desire for communion and attempts to prove that this desire is not a figment of the imagination; it hopes that by having a part in holy things, men will rejoice together in being brothers. This is not enough, however, for describing this desire for communion. We do not participate in the liturgical play without making all that we empirically are participate in it—without making a body, a memory, an affectivity participate therein. Experience of fatigue, experience of distraction, experience of spiritual dryness, of still others . . . all that is not banished merely by a theoretical decision, by the simple fact of wanting to participate in the blessed dance from this moment and forevermore. The sway of the world remains when we want to exist beyond the world. Liturgical experience is the precarious experience of a way of being that is not factic, that is not given with Being-in-the-world, and that cannot render the world unforgettable to us.

The Affective Situation

The liturgy lives a "with" that knows as such neither subjects nor objects. "With" is not said of a collection of given beings gathered together in a perception, but of a presence made for affection as much as for perception. And just as the ego appears to itself in the life of the affects (what Michel Henry calls just "life"), so too does it "find itself" (Heidegger's *Befindlichkeit*) always in an affective situation in the world, and so too must we ask here about the affective tone in which the experience of the "we" occurs. The human community that prays, I said, is a pacified, or pacifiable, community. Men who are liturgically occupied with the Absolute are reconciled in advance . . . they must at least have it as their goal to be so. And for that reason, their "with" is not problematic; for that reason, no serious unease can arise as to the identity of the Other. The "we" is here self-evident, and in a rich way, that of a possible communion. But it is not so self-evident that the existence of this "we" is translated indubitably into the life of the affects. What we want to do liturgically clearly exceeds all that we sense. The God to whom we pray is not necessarily a God felt in the heart.[3] Similarly, the other man with whom I pray is there with me more than the sensibility can suffer him. We pray "with," and we accept with an open heart the presence of all those with whom we pray, visible and invisible, near and far, known and unknown, nameable and anonymous. To pray together is to have something to say and do together, to participate together in a drama—and it is in this common participation that the secret of the liturgy must be sought, more so than in the shared sensibility and the affective communion that we would like to make the test of our "with." On this point, I will elaborate.

Just as our relation to the Other in the element of the world is never deprived of affective tonalities, lively or depressed, foregrounded or backgrounded, never deprived of a "finding oneself together in an affective situation"—*Mitbefindlichkeit*—so too can the liturgical experience be instituted only if its participants aim at a communion felt in the heart. The liturgy mobilizes us first as bearers of a will (in it, we want to transgress the measures of Being-in-the-world and all associated phenomena) and as rich with a knowledge (we know that the Absolute has a face). But it also mobilizes us as beings with sensibility. Sensibility suffers however from an inherent ambiguity, from an inherent uncertainty about its "object" or its content. Is it the other that I sense, or is it myself? Am I affected by the other or by myself? Does affection reveal me more than it does the subtle nuances of my being-in-the-world and them alone? It is difficult to cut to the heart of the matter. The life of the emotions presents itself as a cognitive life, and in the regard of many it is—we think of the cognitive function of anxiety and boredom in Heidegger or again of Meinong's theory of "emotional presentations." To be at peace with the Other, to rejoice that he is there, and (if need be) to share his suffering with him: there is no lack of affective tonalities that would witness a "with" lived as communion.

In order to respect the fundamental ambivalence of sensibility in its worldly (historical) usage, let us resolve then to speak of presentiment to name the affections that make up and translate communion. To have a presentiment, we say, is to relate to a future on the basis of a present and to live this relation as anticipation. The rules of the game of anticipation are known to us; it is for us to use them correctly here. To speak of presentiment is first to say that one is stuck with sticking to the language of sensibility despite all the ambiguity. And this is to say, more precisely, that one is stuck with speaking this way because one acknowledges in sensibility—in man as sensible being—a destiny that goes beyond the world. We live as mortal bodies, but these bodies that go *toward* death are not *for* death without remainder. We exist in the world, but we do not belong *to* the world without remainder. And when the "with" takes, liturgically, the shape of being-at-peace or of shared joy and the like, we then have a presentiment of a use of the ego, of affection, and so forth that lives in advance of an eschatological destiny and signifies here and now an order of experience that is no longer that of the world, an order of manifestation that exceeds all being-in-the-world.

He who speaks of an other order does not speak of a break or a rupture with the facticity of the "with," but rather of a transcendence. (Perhaps one day we will have to speak of "transfacticty" or of experiences with "paraexistential" quality [O. Becker].) We find ourselves immemorially together. We do not have to await some privileged experience (for example, that of empathy in Husserl) to authorize the advent of the "we" or its acceptance in theory. But if we find ourselves together, it is also in a minimal way. Being-together is only being-together; and the "together" includes no particular experiential content, or it includes them all, including the monadic imprisonment that sets out in search of intersubjectivity. He who reaches the liturgical experience allows for an appearing of the "with" that exceeds its common appearing. The other man, he who has, ever since forever, appeared to me as and in the role of the *Mitmensch*, appears to me here as brother or sister, to be loved without delay. He would not appear to me as brother if he had not been with me ever since forever. The logic of presentiment confirms that of the sensibility. But what one senses here transgresses the everyday rules of appearing.

Presentiment is, by definition, a relation to the future, that is to say, to the unavailable. The present of the liturgy can harbor more than co-being-there. We can form the goal of perfect communion (of being as being-toward, of existence lived integrally as "relation," etc.). The last things are not anticipated in the present without their anticipation quickly vanishing. The present can therefore receive only the quality of the next-to-last. It is already too late, when men reunite to pray, for them to be content being there in the common formality of the world. But it is also too early for "proexistence" (H. Schürmann) and communion to be realized without remainder in the assembly of brothers. The liturgy compels us to want a properly parousiac presence of man to man, and such a presence can only be foreshadowed in the time of the world. To each man, each man can be present. This presence can, in fortunate experiences, take shape as parousia (for example in Levinas, in a context different from ours). But because the parousia lends itself to presentiment and only to presentiment, it is in fact in an interval—more than in the common law of interaffection, less than in the final purity of love—that men find their joy in being together.

Just as the liturgy knows neither subjects nor objects, so too is liturgical presentiment, I note quickly, not richly endowed with intentional objects. The affect has no presentiment of p or p', and it has no presentiment of x or y. Consciousness and intentionality are never far when men try to pray, but what gives itself liturgically to a presentiment is nothing other and perhaps nothing more than existence as such, or life as such, when they shatter the measure of the world (or of the earth, etc.). To ground the cognitive dignity of the affect, Scheler distinguished between sensing (*Gefühl*), which is objectless affection, and intentional sensibility (*Fühlen von etwas*) such that ethical or aesthetic values appear to it. Now liturgical presentiment gives less to know than it gives to be. Joy, peace, recollection, reconciliation, one can always connect these experiences to objects, and nothing will stop us from doing so. But to have liturgical presentiments — we are mistaken about such affects if we perceive only that they bear on all by enjoying the anticipations that give them a power of transcendence. In the provisional state that is the world and the earth, presentiments seize the definitive in advance.

Let me say in conclusion that the economy of presentiment does not govern only the presence of one man to another man, but also that of man to God. It is a truism to say so, but our sensibility never reveals to us anything except within a previous horizon (which means that there are other horizons). The God "felt in the heart" gives himself to us in the world only according to the conditions of the world. The divine presence is never parousiacal. As for the liturgy, it is inaugurated by a distancing, that is by a critique of sensibility in its "religious" use as "feeling," and what counts for the divine presence counts for the presence of the Other. The "we" that is said and constructed in common prayer is not primordially the act of a co-feeling, and all the reservations one has about feeling count as well for co-feeling. But in giving themselves common words and common gestures, men who pray clearly speak their wish — their wish for a plenary presence of the Absolute at the heart of coaffection. An affectivity that does not serve the manifestation of the world, but that of the neighbor and of God: the liturgical logic of presentiment tells us that this is not unthinkable. But for that to become reality, this world must pass . . . or at least it must be bracketed.

8

A Response to Jean-Yves Lacoste

JEFFREY BLOECHL

Liturgy and Coaffection: Jean-Yves Lacoste's title makes the reasonable suggestion that we attempt to think the relation with God together with thinking about the relation with other people, and more
precisely at the level of mood and feeling. As his text unfolds, we
are also required to heed the conditions defining the context for this
exercise. In Lacoste's work, this means, above all, recognizing the
greater emergence of what we might call the secular dimension of
our humanity,[1] but also dealing with new and sophisticated forms of
thought willing to ground themselves entirely there. His approach to
this twofold challenge is bent specifically toward what is sometimes
called philosophical anthropology, which has recently become the
provenance of thinkers no longer interested in the possibility of a religious dimension there. Formulated positively, Lacoste is concerned
to reassert an argument for the religious dimension of our humanity,
but without ignoring the depth and sophistication of analyses that do
not properly acknowledge the human relation with God. This places
a great deal of Lacoste's work, including an important strand of "Liturgy and Coaffection," close to a problem that certain theologians
and philosophers of religion have kept on the agenda, at least in
France, since the late nineteenth century. In his thesis that human
nature, for each and all of us, includes an openness toward God, we
hear an echo of Henri de Lubac's great and controversial *Surnaturel*.
But in Lacoste's willingness to hold the religious (or supernatural)

dimension apart from the secular dimension that would entail our natural existence in the world, we may also detect some reticence about the "intrinsicist" position sometimes attributed to de Lubac.[2] I can not confidently say whether Lacoste understands himself to extend de Lubac's project, or whether he considers his position intrinsicist or extrinsicist with regard to this matter of a properly religious dimension of our humanity. However, this does appear to be an important underlying concern, and at any rate, it has been in its light that I have been able to offer these few reflections on his "Liturgy and Coaffection."

One benefit of studying Christian theology through the lens of Heidegger's philosophy is a heightened awareness of the difficulty that theology has had, and perhaps always will have, freeing itself from any number of distortions owed to the simple fact that it must think from within space and time—from within the limits of a world. At an immediate level, this is hardly something that a theologian will need Heidegger to understand: experience of God, we know, must always be experience by a living person, here and now, and this is already enough to raise the possibility of forgetting that God as God is also infinitely greater than God here and now—though of course this is not necessarily a matter of choosing one over the other. But this is not the level that has concerned Heidegger. In an early discussion of theology that he saw fit to include in his 1967 collection *Wegmarken* ("pathways": this relation to theology will have been one mark along the way that became Heidegger's subsequent path), Heidegger focuses on the relation of biblical faith and its self-interpretation to the concepts employed in that work. Can Christian theology have begun to think without employing concepts already cast in a pre-Christian context? Can those concepts have made their way into Christian thought without elements unsuited to their new task also clinging to them? Heidegger, for one, is circumspect, and offers phenomenology as a possible antidote: phenomenology, he says, can provide a "corrective for the ontic and, in particular, pre-Christian content of basic theological concepts."[3]

Deciphering this statement leads us directly to the most fundamental movements of Heidegger's work. We know from *Being and Time* (§ 4) that his use of "ontic" designates that which makes a being the being that it is, as distinct from all others. Among beings (*Seienden*), the one which we are, Dasein, has the ontical character of understanding being (*Sein*). Dasein understands being as beings, or better, as a world and everything in it. Precisely this is the ontical distinctiveness of Dasein: it is ontological; it can ask about the meaning of being, and even before that has a prethematic understanding of being in and as beings. This is crucial: we, as Daseins, have always already understood being in a particular way, have always already constituted the meaning of being in terms of a particular configuration of beings into a world replete with things, tools, ideas, and so forth. And this is always already the world in which Dasein lives. Accordingly, when Heidegger says that Dasein is "being-in-the-world," he is in the first instance drawing attention to the fact that being must not be mistaken for a being, but also laying bare the existential root for any way of ordering a world, experiencing space and time, and so forth. Turning to Christian thought, Heidegger's statement may thus be heard in response to the thought that theologians may thwart their own attempt to articulate the specifically Christian way of being by employing concepts that are simply unsuited to the task. Phenomenology can help theologians maintain the necessary vigilance by providing the basis for a clear conception of Christian being-in-the-world, so that it is possible to recognize what does not belong there. In Heideggerian terms, the life of faith must be understood as that form of being-in-the-world that is toward God. The difference between being-in-the-world, as the universal condition of Dasein, and being-in-the-world-toward God, as a condition specific to the life of faith thus lays the basis for a more worked-out account of precisely what distinguishes the latter, and in turn for an informed scrutiny of concepts taken into theological reflection.

This, it seems to me, is close to how Lacoste has read Heidegger, and indeed perhaps why he continues to read Heidegger. Heidegger's philosophy will have provided us with an admirable account of living in a world, but this does not yet say anything about what might define the specifically Christian life that does exist in the world, but without supposing that that existence makes up all that a person is. Lacoste himself probes that other dimension under the heading of "liturgy," his concept for the logic of being-toward-God. The magnitude of his concession to Heidegger raises at least one preliminary question: if we accept only the arrival of a complete rationality capable of speaking within the limits of our worldly existence, and if we also suppose that theology is somehow capable of entering into discussion with it, then what would be the status of the language and concepts that do not belong exclusively to either interlocutor?

The appearance of the term (co)affection in Lacoste's title signifies a wish to debate the question of human personhood, or what he prefers to call our "humanity," against what has sometimes been argued in the name of either ego or self. This is the obvious intention of the concise paragraphs on Husserl and Heidegger, who moreover prove much closer than hasty readings might lead one to believe. What Husserl experienced as a persistent obstacle to transcendental reflection, Heidegger embraced as an inner truth of the hermeneutics of facticity: already before thinking sets out to verify an essence, an eidos, it is already directed by a particular orientation, which is to say animated by a particular mood. The locus of Heidegger's Dasein is a "mineness" (*Jemeinigkeit*) that turns up in anxiety at a death that can not be taken over by someone else. Perhaps it is moving too quickly to say that this "mineness" is lost upon the Husserl who concerned himself above all with the "ego" that comes into view when he steps back to study intuition and intention, but it does seem evident that Heidegger was much quicker to believe that there is no way to purge thinking of the most profound elements of existence (and here, too, lies the difference between Husserl and Heidegger on the "reduction" to a priori conditions: Husserl would have the ego practice it; Heidegger witnesses it befalling Dasein). It is along this line that Heidegger appears to break from Husserl by way of what can only be called an immanent critique of phenomenology such as he found it, and indeed the 1925 course on the history of the concept of time makes this claim explicitly.[4] A second question for Lacoste might ask whether his effort to go still deeper than Heidegger, beneath or before the "mineness" of Dasein, to a liturgical relation with God anterior to existence in this world, could be understood as a further instance of this same style of immanent critique. That said, it must be admitted that the question might better be posed to others (J.-L. Marion, M. Henry) who are more avowedly concerned with yet another founding of phenomenology. And in any event, it is only marginal to the central concerns of "Liturgy and Coaffection."

Heidegger's move to structures of existence anterior to the ego is filled out in his attention to the theme of affectivity. In *Being and Time*, everything is centered on the manner in which anxiety brings to the surface a pervasive, underlying sense of being not-at-home, *Unzuhause*. In contrast, later essays, beginning with the studies of Hölderlin, educe a feeling of serenity that comes in poetic dwelling, signaling a harmony with the elements, and more deeply a being-at-home on the earth. In the present context, it is already enough to underline this difference.[5] In the end, whether the early Heidegger says that we are always either fleeing from our anxiety or else resolutely facing it, or the later Heidegger says that we are always to some degree either alienated from the serenity of poetic dwelling or else somehow releasing ourselves into it, he leads us on a search for the basic mood where we may feel our primordial condition. Anxiety and serenity are Heidegger's candidates for what he sometimes calls a *Grundstimmung*, and it is this that Lacoste seeks for the specifically Christian way of life.

What does this have to do with our relations with one another? We may take our cue once again from Heidegger, this time when he says that one effect of anxiety is to uproot a person from all other structures of existence, including being-with others. It is true that the other person is always there—even during anxiety—but my anxiety is my own, just as the death it announces is my own, and upon recovering from it I now know that my togetherness with others must be understood in terms of the fact that each of us shares the condition of dying his or her own death. This sort of conclusion is no doubt also necessary with regard to the later Heidegger's notion of serenity.

If, then, it is true that Heidegger's notions of Mitsein and Mitdasein stand for the fact of a coexistence always already built into Dasein's existence, it may be asked whether Heidegger does not thus affirm the primacy of self-relation over relations with others. In anxiety or serenity, it is the singularity of Dasein's own existence that shows up, and if the world where Dasein finds itself is indeed shared, this sharing must nonetheless be among a plurality of such singular Daseins. It is this plurality that Levinas has sometimes characterized, no doubt with some excess, as "atomistic."

This element of Heidegger's thinking is also conceded in Lacoste's essay, though once only as an account of existence, of the secular dimension of our humanity. If I have understood Lacoste properly, what Heidegger has not seen or discussed, and what must be brought back into the open, proves to be a vision of plurality already familiar to the theological tradition. The stated intention is to reflect on the experience of prayer, which we should remember is always already communal, even if it often occurs in silence or solitude. To live in the presence of God is simultaneously to inhabit the world as sons and daughters of God. According to the most elementary structure of Christian kinship, filiality and fraternity imply one another. We should not mistake this statement about structure as a claim about the acts that permit us to see it.

Nothing in Lacoste's argument prevents him agreeing that the gestures and formulae of prayer can be empty, yielding experiences that are all too worldly. Yet some occasions—and *some* seems to be enough to carry the argument—do admit experiences opening beyond the world, to God, or what philosophers call the "Absolute." This means that we humans are, at least potentially, capable of welcoming the self-revelation of God from beyond the shared world. There is in us, beneath our worldly existence but without canceling it (one prays in the world, according to certain movements and gestures, etc.), a liturgical dimension that completes our humanity in being-toward-God.

"What is this 'we' that prays?" Lacoste answers the question at a level anterior to the pretheoretical intersubjectivity investigated in Husserl's *Fifth Cartesian Meditation*, but also anterior to the prethematic *mit* interpreted in *Being and Time*, §§ 25–27. As a question of affectivity, and indeed of a *Grundstimmung*, Lacoste speaks of the disclosure of being-toward-God in the Christian mood of *pressentiment*. English seems not to provide us with an especially apt translation for Lacoste's intention with this word, but the eschatological context suggested by an expression like being-toward-God puts us on the right track. Anterior to both the impossibility of being at home, which conditions the early Heidegger's notion being-in-the-world, and to the possibility of a homeland, which conditions the later Heidegger's notion of dwelling, each of us is radically open to a God whose creative act has marked us with a foretaste of his Second Coming. In a moment, it will be necessary to ask about the form of thought that would make such a proposition without returning to the narrow metaphysics of efficient causality so vulnerable to even the crudest of charges against "ontotheology." How, in other words, does this thought of "foretaste" not imply a God who simply moves us to move back toward Him?

Much of Lacoste's essay also reminds us of how terribly fragile experience of God is—how constantly subject to recuperation into a logic that is precisely not liturgical. The reflective Christian will recognize this immediately: this world makes undeniable claims on us, and we are pulled from a life patterned on the will of God into a life patterned on the configuration of the here and now. Lacoste's approach to this fact remains close to good Augustinian theology, but also Heideggerian philosophy. On one hand, "foretaste" is his placeholder for an attunement to God that Augustine tends to develop in terms of divine appeal. On the other hand, Heidegger's philosophy requires him to develop this as an appeal reaching us upstream from both the world and the earth, and indeed upstream from the difference between them. Anterior to the difference between homelessness and being at home, there is the pure passivity that alone can receive an appeal from beyond time and space. And yet, as beings who inhabit time and space—who ceaselessly temporalize and spatialize—we are bound, by nature, to always imperil that deep passivity. This cannot fail to reprise the language of authenticity, where it is always a matter of acting for or against primordial conditions. In this particular case, the alternative seems exceptionally difficult, since the very condition one must choose (passivity) would be immediately falsified by any act of choosing. Lacoste certainly knows this, and draws a lesson once more from Heidegger: in "Liturgy and Coaffection," the sort of thing Heidegger's Bremen lectures said about the "danger" of our technological configuration (*Gestell*) of knowledge is applied to the broader plane of worldly knowledge of any kind (a plane which, for all of that, Heidegger himself certainly does not fail to reach).[6]

One thing about these latter propositions does seem evident: whatever the nature and success of liturgical authenticity, attempts to achieve it will presuppose some event of awakening to God. Returning for a moment to the theme of a plurality anterior to intersubjectvity and copresence, such an encounter would not only shake one loose from every worldly attachment, but it would also mark the possibility of living in a community which is not yet made up of a group of subjects, let alone a sum of individuals or citizens. With regard to this communal relation, the aforementioned "danger" merits the word violence: truly peaceful community is rooted outside the world of rivalry and exchange, whose violences are all the more dangerous for not only injuring one's neighbor but also causing us to forget the proper depth of a call to charity. Here, the point is not to elevate liturgy over responsibility so much as to preserve their difference, as one of mutual invigoration.[7] Of course, the idea of harmony between love of God and love of neighbor is hardly new, but with the arrival of liberation, feminist, and nativist currents in Christian theology one can scarcely pretend that its meaning is either univocal or even evident.

Applied to the most fundamental level of experience and meaning, the language of peace and peril makes no sense apart from the notion of a relation transcending world and earth. In short, the root of the argument and the justification for the critique are ultimately eschatological. As a matter of our "humanity," only the notion of a soul that desires God before and beyond this world and its desires supports the claim that those worldly desires fuel a life that is violent and an understanding that is dangerous. It is here that one might ask about the way a certain conception of our humanity is affixed to a certain conception of God, such that that humanity transcends the natural order and that God is more than an ulterior efficient cause. I have understood Lacoste's argument to evade the usual difficulties simply by respecting the classical theological doctrine of analogy between the meaning of the divine "Object," as it gives itself to experience, and the human "subject" who is capable of receiving and understanding the experience. Furthermore, what seems to get that exercise started, and no doubt maintain it along the way, is a basic phenomenological commitment to stay close to acts and intentions such as they show themselves to us. At this juncture, nothing stands in the way of reprising discussion of the alleged theology-phenomenology differend, but a more interesting question might go in search of the metaphysical horizon of the traditional doctrine of theology. It is well known that Husserl already hoped to supplant the metaphysics of foundations with an epistemology of manifestation, of phenomenality. Would theology after Husserl, and all the more after Heidegger, make this same turn? The question is, of course, impossibly massive.

Leaving the foregoing to one side, I do not wish to pass over one eminently phenomenological theme that Lacoste's essay makes impossible to ignore: should we not think more about the liturgical gaze that would open itself to God before and outside our relation to world and earth?

Virtually all of phenomenology, and certainly including Heidegger, has insisted on the impossibility of a pure gaze, a gaze not encoded by some particular horizon—and yet if the eschatology set forth by Lacoste does not actually state a claim for the real existence of this very thing in human life, it certainly does entertain it as a proper and meaningful ideal. Of course, "Liturgy and Coaffection" calls us to address this question to a feeling rather than to a gaze, thus to the domain of affectivity rather than representation. It would thus be better to say that we seem attuned to God in advance of any possible interference or distraction, and if that attunement is proper to our humanity then not even interference and distraction truly extinguish it. Because we are exposed to God before we are exposed to being and beings, our relations with being and beings are never more than surface clutter that leaves intact a deeper bond. The idea that foretaste arises from a greater depth than any attachment to either world or earth agrees with the Augustinian thesis that one draws closer to intimacy with God to the degree that one empties oneself of all the things of this life. In this context, Augustine himself does not hesitate to take up the language of purity: "quid est coram Deo, nisi conscientiae puritate?" (Sermon XVI). Phenomenology, I have recalled, has long resisted such a possibility. If we nonetheless grant phenomenology the right to speak for the structures and experiences belonging to our worldly existence, theology would seem obliged to present itself, at least in the intellectual climate Lacoste evokes, first of all in the mode of denial or dissent. What would count most could be said least often and with greatest effort—and not only because these would be profound themes. Theology would have to know itself as the most untimely of practices, committed first of all to defying every presumption that an unworldly gaze or mood is one that is therefore unintelligible.

9

When God Hides His Face
The Inexperience of God

MICHAEL PURCELL

The attempt at meaning is hard, involving, as Ricoeur would say, a "long detour." How does one make sense of the seemingly meaningless? When God hides his face, and Derrida's "transcendent signified" is displaced in human experience, how then does one find meaning? What I wish to consider here is "experience of distress and perplexity," which gives rise to "lament," and how this is associated with the scriptural notion of a God who has hidden his face. When God hides his face and will not respond, what then is the human response?

We begin with a few basic presuppositions that provide a frame.

Human life is a quest for meaning, which is not always of our own creating or bestowing. We always and already find ourselves in a world that precedes us, and of which we have to make sense. From the particular "here" in which we find ourselves, to survive we embark on a process of meaning-creation and meaning-bestowing.

Yet, human life at times seems evacuated of meaning. There are days when we have no soul. There are days when "one does" (as if anonymously) what needs to be done, for no other reason than "it needs to be done." But, in so doing, the doing itself has a significance. Holding on to practice matters, for often in "doing," meaning may emerge. Thus, the truth of Levinas's words, "One must love the Torah more than God," for only in "doing" the Torah does God arise.

Where, then, might a *deus absconditus* God show his face? In the keeping of the Law. And what does the Law prescribe? Love of God and love of neighbor. Only in undertaking the obligations of the Law is God encountered and experienced, and thus is the inexperience of a God who hides his face *experienced*.

How, then, does one make sense of God's self-hiding? Clearly, God's withdrawal is allied to an evacuation of meaning. God withdraws and so a vacuum is created, an empty space. A void is opened up—a void seemingly devoid of meaning—a void, empty and threatening, that seeks some meaningful fulfillment. When the divine withdraws—when "there is" only the experience of absence, when the 'there is' (the *il y a*) is the only experience, or "inexperience" since it lacks an identifiable object, when presence is absence, yet this absence is felt as an oppressive presence, what does one do? When Levinas's "*il y a*" refuses translation into the Heideggerian donative "*es gibt*," how might one respond? Absence is a terror. There is the experience of no thing (the "there is"), but not nothing. Such is the experience when God, having hidden his face, is absent.

The Psalmody of Lament

The hiddenness of God is a frequent theme in the psalms. The psalmist laments a God who has rejected or forgotten Israel, and who remains silent and aloof, a God who has withdrawn and who "hides his face." The question is provoked, "Why has this happened?" and "How long" will the situation endure? "How much longer will you forget me, Yahweh? For ever? How much longer will you hide your face from me?" (Ps. 13:1). Again, "Why do you reject me? Why do you hide your face from me?" (Ps. 88:14)

The expectant questions are addressed to an unresponsive God. There is no answer, and the question rebounds on the one who asks the question, and in whom the answer must be sought.

Samuel Balentine's study of the theme of God's absence in the Hebrew Bible, *The Hidden God*, is helpful. The psalms of lamentation "serve to bring to expression the plight of the worshipper in his struggle to understand his own situation in relation to God." God's working cannot be seen, yet there is "an urgent need for God's intervention in an intolerable situation" which "has arisen because of God's lack of involvement."[1] The present plight is a direct consequence of God's absence: "The suppliant knows his plight to be caused by Yahweh; it was his forgetfulness, his hiddenness that had resulted in the present crisis."[2]

This lamentable situation prompts two things: an initial attempt to understand "why" God should have hidden his face, and "how long" the situation will continue; yet, such questions are self-reflective questions that do not so much seek to elicit a response as try to "negotiate encounter"; second, this attempt at "negotiating encounter" in the face of divine silence attempts to re-create presence. "What is desired is not so much dialogue with God as . . . the confirmation of God's presence."[3] The psalmody of lament "has at its core an urgent appeal for confirmation of God's presence."[4]

Take, for example, Psalm 42, the "Lament of a Levite in exile." The opening verses of the psalm give the situation. There is an experience of dereliction, so much so that even others can give the taunt, "Where is your God?" "How long" is this situation to last? "When" will the face of God show itself again? (Ps. 42:2–3).

There follows the attempt to re-create presence. There is a retreat into a past present, and the recalling of more favorable times when one entered the house of God "among cries of joy and praise and an exultant throng" (Ps. 42:4). Yet re-presentation is vain. The past is immemorial, and so the soul remains "downcast" and "sighs." The suppliant then seeks to negotiate the divine presence in the present through the intentionality of hoping (Ps. 42:5–6, 11). But this too remains unfulfilled. The intending is empty. And thus the continuing question, "Where is your God?" (Ps. 42:10).

The nature of hope is worth considering further. Paul Moyaert draws attention to the necessarily unfulfilled or empty nature of hope when he writes, "Hope will inevitably shape certain expectations and expressions, even though it cannot give them definitive content. Hope is an orientation towards a future without genuine or ultimate content: it maintains a minimal distance or discrepancy with regard to the facts and events that contradict expectations. It shatters the atemporal eternity of the present."[5] The very condition of hope is that its hoped-for object defies presence. Hope is an empty and unfulfilled intending. In terms of the psalmist's critical situation, God's presence is impossible, and there is only hope, which cannot deliver presence.

Now, Balentine notes that biblical scholarship on the hiddenness of God has tended to ignore the "merit of lament simply as lament."[6] Lament has been seen as a prelude to praise and thanksgiving.[7] In times of despair, one prays all the harder. One attempts to recall the good times of divine presence.

The critical question is whether the recovery of meaning needs to be expatriated to a God who may or may not intervene. The nature of lament is that it is solitary. It has no interlocutors, either divine or human. The one who laments is thrown back on his or her own lament, and here perhaps is the beginning of a resolution.

Balentine rightly notes that the affirmation of the praise element to the neglect of the lament element "is to misjudge the crucial function of the God question which is so frequent in the psalms of lament."[8] It is also to be deaf to "the real and present element of anxiety to which the psalms of lament give expression."[9] In the "agony of the struggle,"[10] what does one do? How does one move from despair to meaning? God provides no answer, but God in himself may not be the locus of meaning.

Lament casts the lamenter back upon himself. This is not to suggest that lament finds its resolution in a self-enclosed subjectivity, endlessly haruspicating its own entrails, and feeding on its own grief, even to the point of the subject being overwhelmed and losing its very subjectivity. It is perhaps, rather, to suggest that the singularity and solitariness of a lamentable situation in which a solitary self might find itself, finds its egress and resolution, not in a recourse to a God who purposively elects to be absent and chooses to be silent and unresponsive, but in the one who, lamenting, becomes aware of a responsibility which only she or he can bear. It is not catharsis but kenosis that will be required.

Balentine considers Psalm 80. The suppliant's prayer is that God's face will once again smile on Israel, a "languishing vine" (Ps. 80:3, 19). Yet, there is no attempt at praise. God has ravaged the walls of Israel's vineyard. Lament is the point of the whole prayer. What, then, does one do in the face of the absent and unresponsive God?

Accounting for God's Absence

Diagnosing and dealing with divine absence is a key concern for those undergoing and enduring the present time of crisis. Typically, in the prophetic literature, the questions that are raised in the psalms about God's absence and how long this might last are questions that are inverted and returned to the suppliant in the divine court. God, being accused, turns the argument on his accusers and confronts them. Yahweh, being accused, is no longer defendant but answers as accuser. "Israel's accusations against God become God's accusations against Israel."[11] Our question to God becomes God's question to us.

Generally speaking, in the prophets, "God does not hide himself from Israel capriciously but angrily; he is not hidden from the beginning of time but rather during the course of history. Hence his hiddenness is an angry reaction against a guilty people at specific points in history."[12] When God withdraws from history, "the events of history appear to be out of control"[13] and his people endure suffering, but God has withdrawn from history precisely on account of the sin and guilt of the people. It is not so much that God has abandoned Israel, but that Israel has abandoned God. God walks away from the situation with clean hands.

Leora Batnitsky makes a similar observation when she notes that the "view of suffering as punishment for sin is the most pervasive view of the Hebrew Bible."[14] One needs to note, particularly in a post-Holocaust situation (or a situation of ongoing Holocaust), that the notion of a God who hides his face because of some sin of his people is somewhat obscene and objectionable. Such a God is precisely a God who acts capriciously.

Levinas, similarly, considers the attempt to explain "deserved" or "merited" suffering, either in terms of its being endured in view of some higher good or "a kingdom of transcendent ends,"[15] or in terms of some original and ongoing falling that acts as its cause. Such an original sinning, as found in the Christian tradition, is, according to Levinas, "in a certain sense implicit in the Old Testament, where the drama of the Diaspora reflects the sins of Israel. The wicked conduct of ancestors, still non-expiated by the sufferings of exile, would explain to the exiles themselves the duration and the harshness of the exile."[16] Yet, this does not necessarily "make God innocent" nor "make suffering bearable." Indeed, being aware of situations of profound or extreme suffering—suffering in extremis—"makes waiting for the saving actions of an all powerful God impossible without degradation."[17] The scandal of suffering cannot be resolved by referring it to a "metaphysical order," whether an *arche* or a *telos*. For Levinas, suffering will only find some meaningful resolution in the "ethical perspective of the interhuman."[18]

Now, the attempt to find some reason for the absence of God in Israel's past offence against God is lacking in the psalms of lament. Here, the questions are singularly addressed to an absent and silent God, who is either hiding or forgetful. Balentine notes, "God's hiddenness is not primarily related to his punishment for disobedience. It is not basically a reflection of man's inability to understand or even perceive God's presence in the world. It is manifest in both these ways, but it is not restricted to them. It is rather an integral part of the nature of God, which is not to be explained away by theological exposition of human failures or human limitations. God is hidden just as he is present; he is far away just as he is near."[19] What reason and response, then, might one make when faced with the darkness of God's absence?

Perhaps, as I have suggested, these are not even questions since there is no respondent. The one who is the subject of the lament, and who is "subjected" as lament addresses his question to a God who does not respond. He, as it were, ends up talking to himself. Here the words of Yosl Rakover begin to surface. Zvi Kolitz's "Yosl Rakover talks to God" becomes an interlocutor.[20] How does one address oneself to God, *à Dieu*, when God—even if he had an address—has already said adieu?

Yosl Rakover Talks to God

Yosl Rakover begins his address to God with the words, "I, Yost, son of David Rakover of Tarnapol, a follower of the Rabbi of Ger and descendant of the righteous, learned and holy ones of the families Rakover and Maysels, am writing these lines as the houses of the Warsaw Ghetto are in flames, and the house I am in is one of the last that has not yet caught fire. For several hours now we have been under raging artillery fire and all around me walls are exploding and shattering in the hail of shells. It will not be long before this house I'm in, like almost all the houses in the ghetto, will become the grave of its inhabitants and defenders.[21]

The story is, of course, a fabrication, but nonetheless, as Levinas remarks of it, "true as only fiction can be." Levinas adverts to the story in his short article, "Loving the Torah More Than God," indicating that "what we must do is listen to the thought that it contains. The ultimate passion of the holocaust, like innocent suffering in general, cannot become a spectacle, for the meaning lacks transparency. It cannot be witnessed to; it can only be undergone."[22] As Elizier Berkovits notes, "the sacrificial way of the innocent through history is not to be vindicated or justified! It remains unforgivable."[23] In the face of suffering and the horror of holocaust, none can play the part of Job's companions.

To return to Yosl Rakover: Yosl refuses to see his present crisis, a present severely defined by God's absence, as the result of sin or failing on Yosl's own part. He is a faithful Jew: "I do not say, like Job, that God should lay his finger on my sins so that I may know how I have earned this. For greater and better men than I are convinced that it is no longer a question of punishment for sins and transgressions. On the contrary, something unique is happening in the world: *hastoras ponim*—God has hidden his face."[24]

In the relationship between God and Yosl, Yosl certainly does not consider himself the debtor. Rather it is God who is in debt to Yosl— "greatly in debt"[25]—and is to be admonished. So, too, Berkovits can say, "Within time and history God remains indebted to his people."[26] Yosl's situation is one of a fidelity that refuses to be extinguished, despite the absence of God. Humanity has been delivered over to its most savage instincts; yet Yosl can nonetheless continue to say, "I believe in the God of Israel, even when he has done everything to make me cease to believe in him."[27] Again, "You have done everything to make me lose my faith in you, to make me cease to believe in you. But I die exactly as I have lived—an unshakeable believer in you."[28] Yosl has faith, but it is a faith that has no foundation in anything else, nor is there any supporting evidence to sustain it.

Speaking of faith and trust in another context, Paul Moyaert notes that these "cannot be founded on anything else," nor do they "depend on rational justification or on objective grounds"; "they are in that sense invulnerable to external events that contradict them."[29] Certainly Yosl's faith is severely—and one might say deliberately— tested. The utter transcendence of God, implicated in God's self-concealing, is not a positive experience of a transcendence that could be interpreted as "an experience of an inexhaustible richness in meaning," namely God's goodness.[30] Moyaert continues: "In contrast with [such an interpretation], I consider an experience of God's transcendence to test the belief in his goodness, such that in this world and in this life—at their very limit—we no longer see, possess, or receive any sign that could support that belief, and such that even the recollection of earlier signs disappears. God's transcendence is manifest in the suspension of any sign of his goodness, which is to say, his radical absence."[31] With respect to Yosl, then, God's transcendence is something that is "suffered" or undergone.

Now, Yosl indicates that the reason why he refuses to lose faith is not simply because "I love him" but because "I love his Torah more. . . . God commands religion, but his Torah commands a way of life."[32] Implicated here is the relation between religion and ethics, and the importance of fidelity to the ongoing ethical injunctions of the Torah. Levinas draws attention to the importance of Yosl's faithfulness when, in "Useless Suffering," he refers to Emil Fackenheim: "To renounce after Auschwitz this God absent from Auschwitz—no longer to assure the continuation of Israel—would amount to finishing the criminal enterprise of National Socialism . . . and the forgetting of the ethical message of the Bible."[33]

Continuing the theme of Zvi Kolitz's story, Levinas recognizes in it "a profound and authentic experience of spiritual life."[34] The perduring question is: "What is the meaning of the suffering of the innocents? Does it not prove a world without God. . . ?"[35] Indeed, without ethics, "Did not the word of Nietzsche on the death of God take on, in the extermination camps, the significance of a quasi-empirical fact?" When God is terribly absent and silent, whence does meaning come? More, can one begin to respond theologically?

Levinas suggests a number of moves, which are helpful in confining theology, and preveniently preventing it from being too proud.

The Temptation of Atheism

First, there is the temptation of atheism. This, says Levinas, "is the simplest and most common reaction"[36] to the God who hides his face. It is the reaction of "those whose idea of God . . . was of some kind of kindergarten deity who distributed prizes, applied penalties, or forgave faults and in his goodness treated men as eternal children."[37] Now, Levinas sees a value in atheism. It is the necessary prelude to a relationship with the true God of monotheism. The way to the true God has 'a way station where there is no God. . . . Genuine monotheism owes it to itself to respond to the legitimate demands of atheism."[38]

Levinas argues the point in *Totality and Infinity*. The emergence of the self demands separation. One "comes to oneself" by affirming one's independence. As Levinas puts it "the soul [that is, the self] . . . being an accomplishment of separation is naturally atheist."[39] Again, "One lives outside of God, at home with oneself; one is an I, an egoism."[40] Yet, such an atheism is not to be understood as a negation of the divine. Rather it is "prior to both the negation and the affirmation of the divine."[41] It is that process of becoming a separate being—an existent—which is the very condition of transcendence, but which will also become the very possibility of that human responsibility that alone will fill the space of dereliction opened up by God's absence. In such an "atheism" and the abyss of responsibility that come in its wake, there can be seen also Levinas's stress on atheism, that is, a relationship with the divine which transcends theism, where theism is understood as reason's comprehensive advance on and consequent reduction of the divine to categories of understanding. Atheism becomes the very possibility of God's return. Levinas argues,

> The atheism of the metaphysician means, positively, that our relation with the metaphysical is an ethical behaviour and not theology, not a thematisation, be it a knowledge by analogy, of the attributes of God. God rises to his supreme and ultimate presence as correlative to the justice rendered unto men. The direct comprehension of God is impossible for a look directed upon him, not because our intelligence is limited, but because the relation with infinity respects the total Transcendence of the other without being bewitched by it, and because our possibility of welcoming him in man goes further than the comprehension that thematises and encompasses its object.[42]

In other words, access to the true God is more to be achieved through engagement with other people rather than through any "adventure of cognition." The sense of dereliction that the demise of the divine may cause casts back on the human the need to respond to the human: "A God invisible means not only a God unimaginable, but a God accessible in justice. Ethics is the spiritual optics. . . . The Other is the very locus of metaphysical truth, and is indispensable for my relation with God."[43] In other words, it is in the arduous undertaking of ethics that God is to be found.

What Levinas is reacting against is any tendency to make God an object of theology, and perhaps not principally because this would compromise the transcendence of God. It is true that in the theology of the Judeo-Christian tradition, positive theology finds itself countered by negative theology; the kataphatic eventually has to yield to the apophatic, though both remain counterparts in the one discourse on the divine. What Levinas is more hostile toward is the tendency of theology toward theory and its alliance with systems of thought that compromise the ethical relationship with the other person, and the irreducible responsibilities that well up from this ethical relationship. Theology can only ever be pursued in an ethical move, and from an ethical point of departure. In a way, the Holocaust—and all those crimes committed in the name of religion—is the practical outcome of the onto-theological tradition, which is not so much a Heideggerian *Seinsvergessenheit*, but fundamentally a forgetfulness of the other person. "Who can say that he loves the God whom he cannot see if he does not love the other person whom he can see?" (John 1). Thus Levinas rightly stresses, "The Other is not the incarnation of God, but precisely by his face, in which he is disincarnate, is the manifestation of the height in which God is revealed."[44]

These words—that "the Other is not the incarnation of God"— may be apparently difficult for Christian theology. Yet, they offer a critical question to theology: is the other person to be understood and valued in terms of an initial divine revelation that culminates in an incarnation of God; or does the significance of the incarnation of God and divine revelation flow from the relationship with the other person? Is the other person to be loved and respected because we somehow or other see in his or her face the incarnation of the divine, or is the other to be valued as being of inestimable worth in his or her own right, and in such a valuing of the other person, God thereby enters into his world anew? Is access to the divine by way of the human, or does one gain access to the human by way of the divine? For Levinas, there is no possible approach to God other than by way of the other person. Ethics gives access. Thus can Levinas write, "Metaphysics is enacted in ethical relations. . . . Everything that cannot be reduced to an interhuman relation represents not the superior form but the forever primitive form of religion."[45] This is not to compromise the initiative and freedom of God with respect to his creation. Indeed, one can argue that it is precisely to maintain the utter freedom and transcendence of God with respect to creation that Levinas stresses the value and importance of atheism. The affirmation of God's utter freedom and transcendence with respect to creation makes that creation in its human form the focal point of any theological reflection on the divine. A theology that seeks to be phenomenologically adequate is a theology whose point of departure must be shamelessly anthropological (and ultimately incarnational). The way to God can only start from here, even though further phenomenological and theological reflection may open up those further and unknown horizons, which in Husserl's terminology are unfulfilled, yet to be fulfilled, but may never be fulfilled.

Methodologically, Levinas articulates this in terms of the "anteriority of posteriority" (and its corollary, the posteriority of the anterior). In terms of theology, it can only ever have an anthropological point of departure, but this point of departure opens onto an origin that predates the epistemic subject. Writing of the effecting of the separated self that "is produced in the form of an inner life," Levinas notes that "even its cause, older than itself, is still to come. The cause of being is thought or known by its effect as though it were posterior to its effect."[46]

Heidegger's Dasein's construction of its dwelling remains the perennial point for critical comment. Husserl's notion that "thought" is here—a point of departure—finds its existential translation in Heideggerian Dasein, which becomes the focal point of meaning. In terms of Husserl, there is discovered after the event of "thought" as "representation" something that precedes that event, and that can only be welcomed, and that representation cannot measure. Consciousness, or thought, which is a point of departure, knows itself in its very conceiving to have been conceived. As Levinas notes, the event of separation is already a transcendence.[47] Similarly with Heidegger: the dwelling that the separated self achieves as a first concretization opens on to "an overflowing of concretization," but this is encountered "only after the event, a posteriori."[48] It is as if the house that I have built as shelter in view of my self as the ultimate "for-the-sake-of-which" (Heidegger) is discovered after the event actually to have been built not as a place of security and shelter, but as a place of welcome and hospitality. The doors and windows, integral to my dwelling, do not so much close off a world beyond, but open on to a world, already there, and the advent of the other, an advent that is the "paralysis of possession."[49] Thus Levinas can write, "The fact of having limited a part of this world and having closed it off, having access to the elements I enjoy by way of the door and the window, realizes extraterritoriality and the sovereignty of thought, anterior to the world to which it is posterior."[50]

This phenomenological detour, which is perhaps a "way station" in which there is no God, is a necessary prelude to theology. But it also points to an ethics, which is anterior to both, but whose apriority is only uncovered in its aposteriority.

In respect of a theology that is more fundamental than dogmatic, "the God who veils his face is neither . . . a theological abstraction nor a poetic image."[51] The God who hides his face is a God who is always anterior to the posteriority of the human, but who hides his face in order, starting from the human, to be recovered in the human, and by way of the human. God indeed arises as the counterpart of the justice I render to my neighbor, and who in the very rendering of that justice, makes a discrete return as the true God. Theology can only ever have its adequate origin in an adequate consideration and treatment of the human person.

The Burden and the Abyss of Responsibility

A second theological reflection is demanded by the "atheism of the metaphysician." Atheism is not so much the refusal of the divine but an affirmation of the ethical, in which the true God makes his return. The refusal of theology as *theoria*, which is also the "temptation of temptations,"[52] is an initial positive aspect of atheism. But, as indicated, this is not a "negation of the divine." When Yosl experiences the absence of God, the response is not atheism, for he believes and refuses not to believe. This refusal not to yield to the temptation to reduce the divine to knowledge opens on to a further positive dimension of agnostic atheism, or "life without God." Positively, God's withdrawal gives the possibility of encountering him in our opening on to the other person. Levinas comments, "Yosl experienced the certainty of God's existence with new force in an empty world. Because Yosl exists in his utter solitude, it is so that he can feel all God's responsibility resting on his shoulders."[53]

In other words, God withdraws in order to create a space wherein the individual can achieve full humanity, which is, for Levinas, to be understood as "responsibility-for-the-other." Just as, in the creative act, God, as it were, removes himself or stands back in order to create a space, in order that there be a "world," so now God withdraws in order that that world might become ethical. A like sentiment is expressed in *Totality and Infinity*: "It is certainly a great glory for the creator to have set up a being capable of atheism, a being which without having been causa sui, has an independent view and word and is at home with itself."[54]

The self-absenting move on the part of God enables the place of an ethical humanity by its very otherness from God, and the heavy demands that this otherness brings. There is no "external reprieve"; there is no institution to which one might take recourse and surrender this responsibility; there is no "consolation of divine presence." God "renounces any manifestation of himself that would give succor, and calls on man in his maturity to recognize his full responsibility."[55] Again, "His divine grandeur is shown when he veils his face in order to ask everything, to ask the superhuman of man; it is shown in his creation of a man capable of responding, capable of approaching God as a creditor, and not always as a debtor."[56] And this inevitably will entail suffering, for, in the absence of the divine—an interventionist God—man is thrown back on his own resources. He "can triumph only in his own conscience, which necessarily means through suffering."[57] The mature stature of the person arises in the movement from self-consciousness to conscience, which is response to the plight and the demands of the other person. "This God, this distant God, who veils his face and abandons the just man to a justice in which there is no victory, springs immediately from within."[58]

But conscience finds its aid and its direction in the God-given Torah, the ultimate doing of which is the sole access to the true God. The law prescribes ethical activity. One must fulfill the Law. One must keep the commandments. "The Torah embodies the highest law and the most beautiful morality."[59] This fidelity to the demands of the Law opens the way to God's return. "The connection between God and man is not a sentimental communion with the love of a God made flesh, but a relation of minds mediated by instruction, through the Torah."[60] Again, "God manifests himself not by incarnation but by absence. God manifests himself not by incarnation but in the Law."[61] It is by doing the law that the experience of God is made possible, but only as justice. But, if "God arises as the counterpart of the justice we render to one another," then this is an impossible justice, a justice "in which there is no victory," a justice that may never come, a justice whose very impossibility is, paradoxically, its very possibility—and so the perpetual presence of God in the continual enactments of justice.

The Question of Innocent Suffering

If Yosl's plight opens onto a plea to a God who has hidden his face and does not answer, then how is he to make sense of his own innocent suffering and the innocent of all those others in the camps and ghettos of yesterday and today? "What," asks Levinas, "is the meaning of the suffering of the innocents?"[62] I think one has to say with Levinas that innocent suffering—however one may try to specify that, as if suffering could ever be specific—has no intrinsic meaning. The attempt to specify sufferings is a specious endeavor. One may try to interpret it, but it can only be undergone. So, too, the attempt to value and evaluate suffering is a proud endeavor that needs humiliation in the face of the human. There is suffering incapable of being distilled by understanding. This has been especially brought to the fore in the post-Holocaust situation. Batnitzky notes, "The tension between recognizing the ethical and theological value of suffering without assigning it an intrinsic value is important for post-Holocaust Jewish thinkers."[63] The Holocaust cannot be theologically justified. Thus, the question: "How can Jews believe in an omnipotent, beneficent God after Auschwitz? Traditional Jewish theology maintains that God is the ultimate, omnipotent actor in historical drama. . . . To see any purpose in the death camps, the traditional believer is forced to regard the most demonic, antihuman explosion of all history as a meaningful expression of God's purposes."[64] To justify my neighbor's suffering is a scandal. "My neighbor's suffering is beyond justification; it is, in a word, meaningless."[65] Referring to Levinas, Batnitzky writes, "The Jewish tradition often maintains a difficult balancing act when it affirms both the theological and ethical value of suffering for others, while denying the necessity of suffering itself."[66] One cannot justify suffering. Thus an end to all theodicy, and "to all attempts, theological or otherwise, to justify suffering."[67]

Perhaps Christian theology has been guilty of the attempt to explain suffering, whether in those theodicies that would see suffering as a punishment for sin, or even in the notion of God being present in the sufferings of the innocents. Consider attempts to answer the question of where God was in the sufferings of the holocaust with the response that God was in the sufferings of the innocent. Even the theology of the cross needs to be approached with a certain care and sensitivity lest we say too much too soon. Does the theology of the cross offer an answer to the question of innocent suffering? Well, yes and no. One needs to recall that the experience of the cross was, for Jesus, also an experience of dereliction and emptiness. One should not move from Good Friday to Easter Sunday with unseemly haste. There is the "long detour" of Holy Saturday. Despite the positive note with which Psalm 22 ends, it is also an expression of dereliction: "My God, my God, why have you forsaken me?" is a cry that resulted from the absence and silence of God. One has to recognize that the suffering and death of Jesus, considered in itself, was meaningless. In itself, it is an innocent suffering. Theology seeks in various ways to invest it with meaning and interpret it, whether adequate or otherwise. But, perhaps what makes the suffering and death of Jesus—and the cross—theologically significant is that it was a death "for-others," a death that exhibited the "for-structure" of ethical humanity; in other words, humanity betrays the structure of responsibility, a structure made visible on the cross. Insofar as I respond to the suffering of the other person by suffering the suffering of the other, then suffering opens on to redemption. Suffering is only meaningful insofar as it becomes a "suffering-for." In suffering the suffering of the other person—in "suffering-for"—I am redeemed.[68]

Redeeming Suffering, and the Return of God

What then of the suffering of the innocent, whether my own or that of others? Suffering, argues Levinas, is meaningful only when it can become a suffering for and with others. The suffering of the other person (and its very uselessness) issues in an ethical imperative. When confronted with the other's suffering (and one wonders whether there can be too hard a distinction between innocent suffering and "merited" suffering), one is challenged and obligated to respond. One does not only suffer the transcendence of God who has withdrawn and hidden his face; one also suffers the suffering of the other person who faces us—a suffering which the psalmists see as a direct consequence of God's self-concealment. Yet, it is precisely in the response we make to the suffering of others (even from a situation of my own intolerable suffering) that the God who has withdrawn and hidden his face makes his return in the faces of others, and the responses I make to them.

Levinas is keen to situate the redemption of suffering in ethical terms. I may be able to do little in respect of my own suffering, but perhaps I can do something in respect of the suffering of others. The meaning of suffering can only be situated in the interhuman perspective. It is meaningful in me inasmuch as my suffering can become a suffering for and of the suffering of the other person—the intolerable burden of responsibility. Levinas writes, "[A] radical difference develops between suffering in the Other, which for me is unpardonable and solicits and calls me, and suffering in me, my own adventure of suffering whose . . . congenital uselessness can take on a meaning . . . in becoming a suffering for the suffering—be it inexorable—of someone else."[69] Yet one should not see this "adventure of suffering" as some kind of martyrdom in which I can give witness to the suffering of others. Witnessing to those who suffer, as Agamben points out, is not possible, for we would be attempting to witness to the unwitnessable. The sufferings of others are sui generis. Useless and meaningless in themselves, and outwith the scope of my meaning-bestowing intentionality, I cannot make the suffering of others meaningful. Suffering, like death, is an isolated experience. My singular inability to make the suffering and death of the other my own is well expressed by the Welsh poet R. S. Thomas, where the isolation of the death-watcher becomes the focus. In his poem "Evans," he relates his ministerial experience of tending to Evans, who is dying:

It was not the dark filling my eyes
and mouth appalled me; not even
the drip
Of rain like blood from the one tree
Weather tortured. It was the dark
Silting the veins of that sick man
I left stranded upon the vast
And lonely shore of his bleak bed.

Paradoxically, it is not only Evans who is isolated in his suffering and dying, but also Thomas, the poet, who cannot enter into that singular experience of suffering in extremis that belongs to Evans alone. All Thomas can do is suffer the suffering of Evans, and that by way of an attentive and singular response, and in the responding is the space wherein God's return is opened up.

Suffering for Others, and Working for the Coming Kingdom

Responsibility-for-the-other is the mark of an ethically mature human subjectivity, but this responsibility, since there are many, also impels that ethical subject to work for the establishment of justice, for, there being always at least three, one finds oneself in the situation of trying to compare the incomparable. Liturgical, or eucharistic, humanity is not only "for-you" but also "for-many." Comparing the incomparable is a matter of justice, a justice borne of responsibility, yet a justice that is always called into question by the demand that it also be responsible. The justice that responsibility demands, as Jean-Yves Lacoste might have suggested, is always "in danger." Things can be objects, and others can become subjects. Justice, having fleetingly been done, is constantly having to be undone by the demand to be responsible, and thus constantly having to be done again and again. While we pray that the kingdom may come—which is a kingdom of justice and peace—that it has not yet come, and indeed may never come, impels the working toward justice. Or, we might say, our prayer for the coming of the kingdom that does not come, opens up a space in our world in which it may come, but might not. It is the absence of the Just One and the kingdom he promises that makes possible the work of justice, which, like the responsibility which Yosl realized was his own, is given back to us as our own work.

Paradoxically, it may well be that the kingdom, or the rule, of God is necessarily utopic, and must remain so. Utopia is both a-topic (that is, it has no place), and eu-topic (that is, it is a good place). It may well be that justice is, in this sense, a utopian dream for which we pray, and for which we hope. But, we can only hope for it—and that hope can only be true hope when that kingdom of justice for which we hope is impossible. Paradoxically, what this means is that the very possibility of justice has as its condition of possibility the impossibility of justice. Justice is only possible because it is always impossible. The possibility of justice is injustice. Certainly, the lack of justice—the injustices that provoke us into action—enables the working for justice, but what sustains justice is the radical impossibility of its achievement. For having fleetingly been established, it needs constantly to be undone by the counterdemand of responsibility, that same responsibility incumbent upon us because God has hidden his face.

10

Schools for Scandal
A Response to Michael Purcell

KEVIN L. HUGHES

Perhaps I can only begin where Michael Purcell does, with his pre-suppositions. He begins with the assertion that "Human life is mean-ingful . . . we are entered into a 'world' in which there is already meaning." His second assertion is that this same life, the meaning of which we find ourselves already "in the middest," can seem evacu-ated of meaning. What stands between the "world" of the first and the "appearance" of the second, I wonder? In other words, if to us the world from time to time "seems evacuated," then is the problem one of perception (what it seems) or what it is? Is the "world in which we find ourselves" evacuated of meaning?

Levinas seems to say (I find it difficult to escape the unseemliness of the "seem" in this case) yes—at least, for a time. Levinas invokes the kabbalistic notion of *tsimtsum*, of the divine contraction, which makes space outside of divine presence for creation to inhabit—a space still scattered with divine fragments, but without divine pres-ence per se. For the great kabbalist Isaac Luria, and for the kabbalist and Hasidic thought that is rooted in him, the work of redemption, *tikkun*, is in human beings, especially in Jews, in the observance of the Law, which reunites these fragments with the divine presence. As Gershom Scholem notes, this makes the figure of the Messiah symbolic only, for it is "not the act of the Messiah as executor of tikkun, as a person entrusted with the specific function of redemp-tion, that brings Redemption, but your action and mine."[1] Here, in a mystical nutshell, is the shape of Levinas's thought: God withdraws, hides, veils his face, and space is made for human responsibility, the keeping of the Law, to close the gap. Michael Purcell suggests in his paper that "this fidelity to the demands of the Law opens the way to God's return," and he quotes Levinas to this effect: "The connection between God and man is not a sentimental communion with the love of a God made flesh, but a relation of minds mediated by instruction, through the Torah." But if the basic lines of Levinas's thought are correct, then what we see here is not the way open for God's return to us, but rather the way open for our return to God. We close the gap between God and humanity through our ethical action, through our keeping of the Law. Ethical responsibility is possible only in the midst of the withdrawal of God.

But the doctrine of Incarnation in the Christian faith seems to suggest precisely the opposite: As we stand on the edge of the Christian season of Advent, we recall that Jesus, Yeshua, is Emmanuel, "God saves" is "God with us." Incarnation is the sign of a God who comes to meet us, not the other way around. "Though he was in the form of God he did not count equality with God as a thing to be grasped, but emptied himself, taking the form of a servant, being born in the likeness of men. . . . And being found in human form he humbled himself and became obedient to death, even death on a cross" (Phil. 2:6–8). Kenosis suggests that the motion of redemption is not fundamentally the ethical action of the human reuniting the divine, but rather the self-emptying love of God meeting humanity in its brokenness.

So I wonder if the notion of "God's purposeful withdrawal" is in the end compatible with or helpful in expressing Christian faith, in which not only is the figure of the Messiah central, but the stakes are raised—the Messiah is the "image of the invisible God" (Col. 1:15), God Incarnate.[2] From this Christian theological perspective, Michael's announced presuppositions are dead on—the problem is in fact one of perception: God does not withdraw; God pours God's self out, God gives himself as gift. Eucharist, *ecclesia*, these two "bodies of Christ" are pledges of "real presence," re-presentations of the sacramentality of a creation deemed good and never failing in that. But this fundamental difference by no means solves the problem of suffering; in fact, it may make it more difficult. For what it may force one to say is that the coincidence of opposites—God's presence and innocent suffering—is in fact coincidence and not contradiction after all. And this is, as Michael Purcell's essay suggests, a scandal.

But, in the end, part of the problem is in conceiving of suffering as a problem to be solved. We all agree, it seems, to cry "Ecrasez l'infame," where "l'infame" is this strange modern creation called "theodicy." One cannot think of the account either of divine presence or of divine absence as an "explanation" of suffering. So what, then? What we are left with is, I suppose, the need to narrate suffering, to tell the tale, to remember.[3] And we must then decide which story of suffering is more scandalous, and which more true. Or maybe, which more true and more scandalous. Is it the story of God's presence to or absence from suffering? Which story tells the tale of a world in which we cannot live?

Levinas's account has a certain poignancy, and, while it may cut against the grain of what Rubenstein calls "traditional Jewish theology" of a certain stripe, it is certainly in keeping with Kabbalah, a wisdom tradition deep and wide. Purcell's essay sinks the roots of this kabbalistic argument deeper, in the soil of psalmody, the psalmody of lament. He notes, and quite rightly, I think, that biblical scholarship has tended to subsume lament as a subcategory of psalms of thanksgiving. To the contrary, "Perhaps lament has its own meaning," he wonders with Balentine, "and contains within itself its own resolution. . . . Lament is its own meaning, which may cry out for a resolution which is not to be found in a divine response. . . . Lament finds its egress and resolution, not in a recourse to a God who purposively elects to be absent and chooses to be silent and unresponsive, but in the one who, lamenting, becomes aware of the responsibility which only s/he can bear."

On such a foundation, the Lurian-kabbalist-Levinasian narrative follows as a development and explication of this experience of lament on its own terms, when God is silent. And I suppose the response is, "when God is silent, I must speak, and I must act."

But there is, I would suggest, another meditation on and development of this theme of lament, the "other son" of Israelite biblical religion, Christianity. That is, the synoptic gospel narrative offers us a lament, and it is offered, as Purcell's essay notes, precisely on its own terms, as lament and not as thanksgiving. Upon the cross, just before his death, Jesus cries out a verse of Psalm 22, "My God, my God, why have you abandoned me?" From this, Purcell concludes that "the suffering and death of Jesus, considered in itself, was meaningless" and takes on its meaning (or is "invested with meaning" by theology) as a "death for." But I wonder what this could mean? What is this pretheological, and thus, it seems, extrahermeneutical "suffering and death in itself"? Suffering and death is always of someone, and thus it necessarily includes their history, their memory, themselves in it. The suffering and death of Jesus already includes the question, "Who and what is Jesus?" And, in fact, according to Mark, the suffering and death of Jesus is the key to who Jesus is. The centurion, "when he saw how he died, said 'surely this man was the son of God'" (Mark 15:39). What we see on the Cross is precisely the Lament, and the Lament without answer. But, precisely as such, the Cross points to a God who is found in the lament, is no stranger to it, and thus is no stranger to those who lament in turn. The paradox of the cross is that the one who laments and is not answered is himself the revelation of God, the coincidence of full humanity and full divinity in suffering is the coincidence of lament and God's presence.[4] Or, if you prefer pre-Chalcedonian language, if in suffering it seems that God has withdrawn behind the veil, it is the suffering of Christ that rends the veil of the sanctuary in two and "reveals" (*revelatio*, unveiling) the Holy of Holies, the Mercy Seat of God.

Based upon these reflections on the Cross, I am led to ask, does the notion of purposeful withdrawal suppose that God's presence is of necessity a heroic presence, deus ex machina, or else there is no presence at all? The scandal of the cross is the manifestation of God as weakness, as lament.

This is a scandal, to be sure. But this should not surprise one, since St. Paul has already asserted that the Cross of Christ is a *skandalon*, a scandal, a stumbling block. But before leave it at that, let me try to suggest the ways in which it is and is not a *skandalon*. I do not think that this implies or necessitates an atonement theology of "vicarious suffering." I have to confess that I have always found this notion of "suffering in place of" troublesome and difficult to believe in after Auschwitz, or even in the midst of the sufferings we face in every life, simply as part of the human condition. If the Cross is vicarious suffering, one finds it difficult to imagine that we could still suffer as we do—that we still inflict such suffering as we do. Such an account of the cross as vicarious suffering is, it seems to me, another "explanatory" theodicy, and not a very good one at that.

The *skandalon* I am trying to sketch is of the Cross as the completion of the Incarnation—that God takes up simply everything in the brokenness of the human condition, even death, even innocent death. That part and parcel of the "self-emptying" of God in Philippians 2:5–11 is the being obedient to death, even death on a cross.

Does this make suffering divine? Does it apotheosize suffering? Julian of Norwich, the fourteenth-century recluse, visionary, and theologian, pondered the same questions. As a young woman raised in the tradition of the imitation of Christ, Julian prays early on for the grace of experiencing the sufferings of Christ. When she gets her wish, she is distressed by the brutality of the crucifixion and is overwhelmed. "I thought to myself, 'I little knew what pain it was that I asked for' and repented like a wretch, thinking if I had known what it would be like, I would have been loath to pray for it. . . ." But then, as she watches the Passion unfold before her eyes, just at the point of death, Christ smiles, and she understands the suffering of the Cross differently. "I understood," she says, "that we are now, as our Lord intends it, dying with him on his cross in our pain and our suffering." Rather than seek out suffering, Julian now perceives through this paradoxical suffering while smiling that we are already suffering. The brokenness of sin is experienced as a wound, and it is as if Christ comes to meet us, imitates us, embraces us in our suffering. Precisely at the point at which we experience ourselves to be most vulnerable, most un-godlike, God is present and shares that condition. It is there, where divinity comes to meet us in our brokenness, as brokenness, that we can understand the experience of God in suffering. Suffering is not something to be sought, as some spiritual traditions may have encouraged us, but neither is it to be pushed away, as we who live "in a civilization that is death-dodging, death-ducking and death-denying" work so diligently to do.[7] Instead, suffering must be recognized and acknowledged. It is only in the recognition of our own suffering, our own brokenness that we come to see that even it is not beyond the reach of the love of God. For Julian, the power of this realization is so great that she chooses the Crucified Jesus "as her heaven." As she contemplates her vision of the Crucified, she is tempted to look beyond the sufferings of the Cross to the heavenly bliss beyond it:

> And then I saw clearly with the faith that I felt, that there was nothing between the Cross and heaven which could have distressed me. Either I must look up, or I must answer. I answered inwardly with all the strength of my soul and said, "No, I cannot, for you are my heaven." I said this because I did not wish to look up, for I would rather have suffered until Judgment Day than come to heaven otherwise than by him; for I well knew that he who bound me so painfully would unbind me

when he wished. Thus was I taught to choose Jesus for my heaven, though at that time I saw him only in pain.[8]

Julian sees and understands that in the midst of suffering, one need look no further than the Cross for "heaven," that is, the presence of God. What seems at first the utmost suffering to be escaped is disclosed as divine presence to be embraced. And it is an embrace that anticipates the end of suffering, when one will be "unbound."

What of the search for justice, then? Insofar as justice seeks to end suffering, it is doomed to fail, I think, and perhaps to perpetrate worse crimes in its pursuit. In the world as we know and experience it, love is forever touched by suffering, and we long for what Kevin Hart calls the "heartrending possibility of the separation of love from suffering." So then what is justice? Or what is just action? Well, following Julian, and drawing on another saintly representation, I might suggest *imitatio Christi*, in the Franciscan mode: solidarity with the poor, care for them, fearless proclamation of God's justice and mercy, rigorous self-examination in the light of the Crucified. *Nudus nudum christum sequens*, in Francis's shorthand expression—to be naked following the naked Christ. It is, therefore, responsibility, but it is "responsibility with." It is action, but it is "action with." Ethical responsibility in this account is not predicated upon the purposeful withdrawal of God, but rather upon God's paradoxical presence as brokenness, as weakness. Not a complete answer, but, in the end, I hope, not a bad place to start.

11

Faith Seeking Understanding
The Impossible Intentions of Edith Stein

MICHAEL F. ANDREWS

Similar to many contemporary postmodern philosophers, the phenomenologist Edith Stein rejected certain "modernist assumptions" concerning the human self and the self's experience of God. Although she did not live to participate in contemporary discussions on modernism,[1] I submit that Stein would, in fact, be quite sympathetic to several postmodern philosophical trends. In this essay, I shall describe how Edith Stein rejects an Enlightenment view of the self in a manner similar to that of Jean-Luc Marion. I will also show how Stein, like Marion, remains genuinely committed to the apophatic tradition, drawing effortlessly on the negative theological imagery of Dionysius the Areopagite and John of the Cross.

My reflections in this essay explore three poignant images drawn from a late and theologically rich essay written by Edith Stein while she was living in Echt, Holland, during the turbulent years 1940–1942.[2] On May 9, 1940, Marvin Farber wrote to Stein from North America, notifying her of the newly formed International Phenomenological Society. The "Council of the Phenomenological Society has voted to make you a charter member of the organization," he wrote, and formally invited her to submit an article to its nascent journal. This decision was due in part to Fritz Kaufmann's testimony that Stein's "first works belong to the most valuable and authentic contribution to phenomenology in the line of the *Ideen*. We honor Husserl's memory by asking her to be with us."[3] Although "Ways to Know

God"[4] was not accepted in that first volume of *Philosophy and Phenomenological Research*, Stein's article was subsequently published by the American journal *The Thomist* in July 1946.

In her article, Stein describes the experience of God by drawing upon three significant images: (1) The order of knowing in the writings of Pseudo-Dionysius; (2) the meaning of symbolic theology and the supernatural experience of God; and (3) the "veiling and unconcealing" of the visible and the invisible. Now, let me be perfectly clear: I do not think Edith Stein offered a definitive solution to all the complex issues raised by philosophers and theologians with reference to the experience of God. But what I think Edith Stein does offer is an understanding of the experience of God that contends that the human self is not isolated and disengaged from the social world, but is in some sense constituted by it.

The Constitution of the Human Person

Edith Stein was keenly aware of Husserl's transcendental position regarding constitution, especially after having worked through the problem of empathy with him in her own dissertation.[5] But shortly thereafter, she began to voice serious misgivings concerning Husserl's transcendental project.[6] My argument is that Edith Stein's modification of Husserl's strict cognitive description of transcendental constitution echoes a deep methodological rift that ensued between Husserl and other members of the Göttingen circle (including Scheler, Reinach, and Ingarden) shortly after the publication of Husserl's *Ideas* in 1913. In the first volume of *Ideas*, Husserl described constitution in terms of structural cognition founded upon the transcendental ego, including the constitution of other egos. But what if the alter ego is first experienced or given emotively? Such a distinction between emotive and cognitive experience would not merely reflect a disparity between two equal a priori starting points. On the contrary, such a modification of Husserl's strict epistemological orientation could also put into radical question the very notion of transcendental egology. Max Scheler, for example, held a position, contra Husserl, that foreign experience in fact precedes individual ego. Consequently, any modification of Husserl's strict epistemological orientation would eventually lead to even more significant modifications concerning Husserl's theory of transcendental constitution.

What distinguishes Stein's position from Husserl's entails a difference of orientation, a modification (though not a reversal) of the genesis and motivation of constitution.[7] By stressing a strict cognitive description of empathy in terms of the constitution of the alter ego, Husserl remained largely unaware of the primordial role that emotions and feelings play in every encounter between persons. Consequently, for Husserl the predominant experience of the constitution of alterity is characterized by cognition and tends toward greater autonomy. But what about the preservation of social bonds and emotional integration?[8] Could Husserl's notion that the individual monad precedes the community in the order of knowledge be offset by Scheler's and Stein's argument that the community precedes the ego in the order of experience?

Of course, a model of constitution that does not privilege cognition would be more radical than Husserl's transcendental model only if it can account for a genuine, primordial experience of alterity—something that Husserl's cognitive approach simply fails to do. By genuine alterity I take to mean any experience of otherness that comes from outside the self, rather than what is constituted cognitively within the sphere of ownness.[9] Either the Other qua other comes from outside the economy of sameness or the Other must somehow help constitute it.[10] It is my contention that Edith Stein addresses this tension in her description of ways to know God. For Stein, the experience of God describes the phenomenon of foreign experience in terms of a precognitive, prethematic nonexperience that is felt prior to my cognitive constitution of it as foreign and alien (*fremde*). The felt experience of the Other would thus be as equiprimordial as my own conscious stream of inner-lived experience (*Erlebnis*).[11]

The Human Person and the Experience of God

Stein's phenomenological description of the human person is in a certain sense closer to Scheler's analysis than Husserl's, since, as with Scheler, Stein insists that person is not equivocal to "individual."[12] A human person is innately intersubjective, an embodied network of act-being, an intrinsic, value-oriented conscious embodiment that includes the "world of values she lives in, which values she is responsive to, and what achievements she may be creating."[13] Every individual person is always and already part of the "we" that makes "I" and "Thou" possible in the first place: "We empathically enrich our feeling so that 'we' now feel a different joy from 'I,' 'you,' and 'he' in isolation. But 'I,' 'you,' and 'he' are retained in 'we.' A 'we,' not an 'I,' is the subject of the empathizing. Not through the feeling of oneness, but through empathizing, do we experience others. The feeling of oneness and the enrichment of our own experience become possible through empathy."[14]

In contrast to Husserl and in debt to Scheler, Edith Stein asserts that it is in principle impossible for a person to ever exist as an isolated "I." Person points always toward a "Thou," an external world, a genuine experience of alterity. Foreign experience therefore essentially constitutes the human person as a being-in-the-world. In each act there exists the entire person, which varies from act to act without ever being exhausted in its infinite possible variations.

Evidently, what Edith Stein means by person is not the same as what Husserl calls the isolated ego. Following Scheler, Stein defines person as dynamic, act-oriented, and originarily constituted in a social, cultural, emotive, and reciprocal environment.[15] Person thus signifies an embodied soul, a porous and multiply stratified way of being-with-and-among-others that includes the physical, sensate, and psychic realms of existence. This is why, for Scheler and Stein, the human person as act-being is essentially empathic, sensuous, value-oriented, and constituted by and toward foreign experience. Whereas for Husserl the transcendental ego is a pure condition of possibility, for Stein and Scheler the ego is always and already an embodied person-in-the-world.[16]

We may thus tentatively conclude that for Edith Stein, the Other—that is, foreign experience in its eidetic structure—is not merely constituted but constitutive of the self. What is the significance of foreign experience in terms of the order of knowing? This question shall guide our subsequent reflections.

The Order of Knowing in the Writings of Pseudo-Dionysius

The experience (*Erfahrung*) of God does not denote a problem that needs to be solved. Rather, the experience of God manifests a tension with which we must learn to live. In terms of lived human experience, this means that we do not most fundamentally experience God through a cognitive relationship, that is, through the understanding (*Verstehen*) alone. The experience of God is not merely speculative. In an attempt to describe what is meant by the experience of God, Edith Stein notes the following: "Seeing with the eyes or in the imagination does not necessarily have anything to do with [the experience of God]. When both are absent there may still be an inner certainty that it is God who is speaking. This certainty can rest on the 'feeling' that God is present; one feels touched in his innermost being by him, by the One present. We call this the experience [*Erfahrung*] of God in the most proper sense. It is the core of all mystical living experience [*Erlebnis*]: the person-to-person encounter with God."[17]

Stein likens genuine experience of God to the mystical journey of the soul through a dark night. It must be undertaken singularly and interiorly. Johannes de Silentio — Kierkegaard's disciple of postmodern Christian reflection par excellence — endured the same deafening withdrawal of presence in his (failed) attempt to understand Abraham's journey to Mount Moriah as Stein did in her ascent to Mount Carmel. The experience of God, even for the most faithful seeker, is wrought with divine absence, fear and trembling, the loss of hearth and home. In a manner reminiscent of John of the Cross, one might even argue that Edith Stein actually denies the experience of God except as a nonexperience, as a withdrawal, an experience of absence, an experience beyond experience. (Or, as Jean-Luc Marion describes it, the experience of God constitutes a [non]experience beyond Being.) Such an experience of God, that is, an experience beyond experience, may best be described as "symbolic" but not intuitive, as a matter of faith and revelation, not experience.

God, the Holy Other

In her doctoral dissertation written under the direction of Edmund Husserl, Stein defines empathy (*Einfühlung*) as a nonprimordial experience that announces a primordial one. In what sense can I ever claim to truly "know" foreign consciousness as such? Conversely, if the experience of other persons is given, in what sense can it be said that the other's experience remains essentially "foreign" to my own experience (*Erlebnis*)? Can the experience of empathy include what both announces and hides itself? Helmut Kaiser, the noted existential psychoanalyst, argued that authentic empathic experience must remain distinct from pseudo-empathic experiences in which, for example, a Freudian model of analysis is maintained at the expense of a client's health. Arguing that empathy is essential for psychological well-being, Kaiser notes that the true healing element in a patient-client relationship is founded on an egalitarian model. In I-Thou relationship, each person being addressed comes to experience himself or herself in an originary, nonjudgmental way.[18] I think this is what

Edith Stein has in mind in her notion of empathy. She says, for example, that in empathy a nonprimordial experience announces a primordial one. Hence, I do not empathically merely "feel-into" the inner life of an Other; rather, the Other always appears as an essential and constitutive realm of unknown claims and responsibilities that are always addressed to me.[19]

In "Ways to Know God," Edith Stein hints at just such a possibility—or, perhaps more accurately stated, she hints at such an impossibility—concerning the essential structure of every authentic experience of God. Reflecting on her life in Carmel, Stein describes the experience of God much as she had previously described the constitution of the alter ego in her earlier work on empathy. In both cases, my own primordial experience is led, or constituted, by an encounter with alterity, that is, with what is radically Other, foreign, beyond my (cognitive) grasp. As an encounter with foreign experience as such, the experience of God can in principle be apprehended neither by the understanding (*Verstehen*) nor by cognition alone. This "empty" experience is what Stein calls experience (*Erfahrung*) of God in the most proper sense. It is, Stein tells us, "the core of all mystical living experience [*Erlebnis*]: the person to person encounter with God."[20] Authentic experience of God is thus constituted through empathy, that is, a person-to-person encounter. Such a confrontation with radical alterity paradoxically constitutes a withdrawal of presence, what John of the Cross called a "dark night of the soul" and Pseudo-Dionysius described as negation, emptiness, withdrawal.[21]

What this means in phenomenological terms is that the experience of God is constituted outside the sphere of ownness. The experience of God is something visited upon me; it is something similar to what Meister Eckhart described when he spoke of the impossibility of being able to adequately define the cloud of unknowing. In its most radical appropriation, what we are talking about is the Christian doctrine of sanctifying grace. As a gift, grace is wholly outside my capacity either to give or to receive.

Pseudo-Dionysius and the Ways of Knowing

Stein acknowledges that the hand behind the pen of Pseudo-Dionysius enjoyed a good game of irony. For almost one thousand years, the author of *The Divine Names* was assumed to be Dionysius the Areopagite, recorded in chapter seventeen of the Acts of the Apostles as the disciple converted by St. Paul on the steps of the famed Areopagus in the mid-first century. Today, most scholars would probably acknowledge that the author was most likely a monk from Paris who wrote in Greek around the year 500, and whose work was later translated into medieval Latin before his pseudonym raised suspicion in the early fifteenth century. Whatever their origin, the writings of the Areopagite present two very different ways of speaking about God, one positive and the other negative. On one hand, Pseudo-Dionysius contends that human discourse affirms God's self-revelation to creation. This cataphatic *via affirmativa* describes, albeit metaphorically and symbolically, both the proximity to and the remoteness from creatures to God in terms of an incarnational abundance of divine presence. Knowledge in this positive sense is always mediated, connected and formed like beads along a continuous chain of orders or degrees of more and less perfectability. Many scholars today in fact attribute the coinage of the word "hierarchy" to Pseudo-Dionysius.

In his work *The Celestial Hierarchy*, the Areopagite writes: "Hierarchy, for me, is sacred order, knowledge and activity assimilating itself, as far as it can, to the likeness of God [*deiformity*] and raising itself to its utmost, by means of the illuminations granted by God, to the imitation of God."[22] In terms of positive theology, hierarchy is a "science of order," and it entails what Thomas Aquinas calls the *exitus* and the *reditus* of all creatures to and from God. As well, Pseudo-Dionysius's inner hierarchy mirrors St. Augustine's maxim from the *Confessions*, namely, that "God is more interior to me than my inmost self." *Noli foras ire, in to redi, in interiore homine habitat veritas*: Do not go outside, return within yourself; truth dwells in the interior of man.

On the other hand, the experience of God derives not from what we can say about God, but precisely from what we cannot say. Pseudo-Dionysius calls this way of speaking about God "negative" theology. The *via negativa* points to a hermeneutics of suspicion, a tension in the attempt to think always in terms of presence. In his quest to liberate the experience of God from the imposition of human limitations, Pseudo-Dionysius employs the biblical imagery of Jacob's ladder. Jacob, of course, was the Hebrew patriarch whose dream dared connect heaven and earth, flesh and divinity, ego and alter ego, and whose name in Hebrew means, "He who overreaches." Jacob's ladder thus creates for the Areopagite a sort of "hermeneutical space" within which experiences of God are constituted in terms of a dialectical relationship between the apophatic and the cataphatic. Karl Rahner, the Jesuit philosopher and theologian who writes of the experience of God in terms of an encounter with silence, calls the experience of God constituted outside the range of human intelligibility "an ineffable and incomprehensible presupposition, a ground and abyss, an ineffable mystery."[23]

It is important to note, then, that for Pseudo-Dionysius (as well as that other ladder-climber, Johannes Climacus), negative theology does not annihilate affirmative theology. Rather, "negation" purges all conceptual frameworks and circumscribes all perceptual attributes that theology naively assigns to God. Theological discourse does not define the experience of God. It merely points to the ambiguity that underlies every human experience and, at the same time, attempts to expose its limits. What Dionysius argues is that human language is constituted in some sense by apophatic experience. The experience of God begins and ends in silence; its aim is to mark the limitless incapacity of human language to preserve the sense of transcendence — experienced now in human terms as an absence — of divine presence.

Edith Stein is quick to point out that the meaning of theological discourse does not imply a systematic doctrine about God, even in a strictly negative sense. Citing the Areopagite, Stein insists that theology always implies Holy Scripture, God's Word. By the word "theologians," Pseudo-Dionysius refers to the authors and sacred writers whose experience of God has become normative within the biblical tradition. Given this normativity, in what sense can we say that Pseudo Dionysius is significant for Edith Stein's understanding of the experience of God? First, Stein agrees with the Areopagite that speaking about God must remain necessarily distinct from every experience of God. Second, she intimates that the experience of God does not constitute a discipline or field of study apart from how such experience can be expressed. Third, she holds the position that different experiences of God imply different ways of speaking about God. This, in turn, implies that there are different ways or manners of knowing God. Edith Stein comments:

> When Dionysius calls Daniel, Ezechiel, or even the Apostle Peter "theologians," he does not mean only nor even primarily that they are the authors of the books or letters bearing their names, but that they are (as we would say) inspired: they speak of God because God has taken hold of them or God speaks through them. In this sense the angels, too, are theologians, and Christ, the living Word of God, is the highest of all theologians.

Indeed, we shall in the end be led to call God the "Primal Theologian."[24]

Stein notes that even negative theologians use the cataphatic imagery of hierarchy and ascent in order to distinguish operations of consciousness: experience, understanding experience, affirming or negating our understanding of experience, taking decisive action based on our affirmations or negations of our understanding of experience, and so forth. In Stein's analysis, operations of consciousness are transcendental, that is, they are conditions of possibility without which the experience of God cannot be raised as such. By "hierarchy" Stein does not mean an ontological hierarchy composed of different grades in the order of being. Rather, she refers to an ontic ordering of experience that begins with the lowest, what is furthest from God, an experience of confusion and chaos. "When we are plunged into darkness beyond all understanding," Pseudo-Dionysius reminds us, "we will find ourselves not only short of words but utterly at a loss for words and understanding."[25]

This sense of a loss for words and understanding is not constituted by a merely negative (albeit cognitive) experience. It is also a positive experience. For Stein, such tension does not constitute a difference between hierarchy and no hierarchy, but between different kinds of hierarchy. Knowing and not knowing are part of a single, unitive experience. Hence, the experience of God is a negative ascent insofar as one's prior experience of God is cataphatically obscured by rendering ethereal the divine human mystery. That is why John of the Cross, like Edith Stein, speaks in terms of an "ascent" of Mount Carmel by the soul in its dark night. The loss of the world of sense and sensibility becomes, paradoxically, the very condition of possibility of the experience of God. The religious name that Edith Stein took for herself, "Teresa of the Cross," signifies her assent of this apparent contradiction: "Negation is an ascent, too, in the sense that it begins with the lowest."[26]

Experience of God and the Alter Ego

We are now in a better position to consider how Edith Stein's notion of the experience of God is bound to her phenomenological model of empathy in terms of the nonprimordial givenness of foreign experience. Similar to empathy, the experience of God violates the law of cognition because it modifies the origin (not the direction) of intentionality. What is radically and wholly foreign (*fremde*) cannot be constituted within the sphere of ownness; otherwise, it would belong to me, that is, it would no longer be foreign, alien, *fremde*. My contention here is that, for Stein, the order of experience precedes the order of knowledge.[27] If it were otherwise, then the experience of God qua God would be constituted cognitively in the sphere of ownness. This, consequently, would make "God" one experience I can have alongside every other mundane experience constituted by me as a for-itself. Such proximity to the philosophical threat of solipsism is unacceptable for Stein's comfort. Consequently, she contends that the experience of God—like the experience of empathy—is an impossible experience, an experience of impossibility, a "dark encounter" that "lacks the evidence of insight [*Uneinsichtig*]."[28] Experience of God is therefore constituted the same way that I am motivated to constitute any foreign experience. Through empathy, I feel into (*Einfühlen*) what is structurally absent. To experience God means to lose God, to forgo God as a concept, as a foundation, as a point of reference and return, as a ground of sufficient reason. Every genuine foreign experience thus entails its own undoing. Alterity both reveals and withdraws itself from the world at one and the same time.

In terms of the nonprimordial givenness of foreign experience, apophatic theology may thus be described as being wholly derivative: what is positively given in experience must always be given with a sufficient reason "why." But for Edith Stein, authentic mystical experience of God is without why. Analogous to the constitution of the alter ego, experience of God first and foremost signifies a response, a reply to a call that originates from outside the self, from a source that is foreign, strange, alter, alien, unknown.[29] Of course, such a radical experience of alterity remains, in principle at least, utterly impossible for Husserl, in that it clearly violates the strict, cognitive laws of constitution. Nevertheless, we should note that Edith Stein's modification of Husserl's position contains no such homage to suprarationalism. On the contrary, Stein points to a noncognitive, coprimordial experience of alterity that neither implies violence nor leads to the self's annihilation. This nonexperience is not an experience of the self's annihilation, but is rather a constitutive experience. In it, the subject fully comes to rest in a kind of silent, meditative repose. In and for itself, the subject rests fully outside the boundary of sufficient reason." (Or, as Kierkegaard would say, the self rests transparently in the Power that established it.)[30] Paradoxically, such a moment of silence, of rest, of repose, is not without language. Yet, what is said is precisely what cannot be said or, better still, what is left unsaid: "God's speaking in its most proper sense is that before which human speech must grow dumb; it finds no place in the words of man, nor in the language of images. God's speaking seizes the person whom it addresses, and demands personal surrender as a condition for hearing him."[31]

Edith Stein characterizes "genuine, full, supernatural faith" as a "dark light."[32] She asks, "How is it possible for us, starting with the things of experience, to reach something lying beyond all experience?"[33] In other words, how is it possible to speak meaningfully of the experience of God as something so utterly transcendent, so unreachably Other, so foreign to experience, that it resists even the capacity to name it?[34] For Husserl, such an experience of the wholly other (*tout autre*) is impossible to constitute. Edith Stein, on the other hand, believes that the experience of God is such an experience of impossibility.

The experience of God signifies a nonexperience, an experience of absence, a nonprimordial experience that announces the unimaginable, the unthinkable. As such, it turns the word upside down and heralds the unexpected. For Stein, foreign experience cannot be constituted merely cognitively in the sphere of radical privacy, or else it would contain a trace of "mineness" and thereby cease to be authentically "foreign."[35] No matter what language is used to describe the experience of God, it can never accurately describe the experience of something so radically foreign or strange (*fremde*) that it can only be described as a nonexperience, as an experience that rises above all meaning and beyond Being. "In the end," Stein tells us, "[language] must abolish itself, since denial no more applies to [God] than does affirmation."[36] What Stein wants to find is a moment, a place prior to the experience of God, so as to escape its range of influence. Now, how would we constitute that?

The Meaning of Symbolic Theology and Supernatural Experience of God

An important element of the Christian tradition is the insistence that God is primarily known through analogy and symbol. Edith Stein writes that we must always start with the things of natural understanding and so "reason from effects to a first cause and from the purposeful and lawful order of the universe to a being that orders it by bestowing purpose and law."[37] In discussing the role of symbol and allegory, Stein emphasizes that the general meaning of a sensible thing serves as a "meaning picture" of something nonsensible. She says, for example, that everyone understands a poet's intention when one reads that the "face" of a flower "speaks" to us, even though it is clearly understood that flowers possess neither face nor speech.

In phenomenological terms, a symbol is what gets brought into "immediate contact" with "something quite different and yet . . . something that makes the expression relation possible and enables the expression to be understood."[38] Classically formulated, a symbol functions for Stein as a sort of icon: It allows what is visible and tangible to point to the invisible, to what is not there.[39]

Yet the visible does not make present what is not there. Rather, what is made present through the symbol is the absence of presence, that is, what essentially cannot be made present:

> The symbolic relation, however, does not necessarily presuppose that the two things bearing the relation are known. Actually, the meaning of symbol is perhaps most properly fulfilled when what we know leads us to something we do not now. In a way, the symbolism of the human body is like this. Its whole external appearance points beyond itself to something disclosed thereby. All knowledge of ontic being and living is essentially built upon it."[40]

Edith Stein's definition of symbol in terms of the experience of God functions mainly as a critique of hierarchy, by which I mean that the experience of God both presupposes and at the same time undoes the very conditions that make knowledge of God possible. The higher the order of knowledge of God is, the darker and more mysterious it becomes, and the less it can be put into words. Consequently, for Stein the ascent to God is an assent into darkness and incomprehensibility. Conversely, this ascent in the order of experience constitutes a descent in the order of knowledge. Stein's image of inversion is striking. She argues that, when a person stands at the base of a mountain, that individual can express himself or herself in great detail. One's experience is lucid, descriptive, sensual, based on the sciences of natural knowledge. But as an individual ascends the mountain of faith, experience of God becomes more obscure the closer that individual approaches the summit. Symbolic theology climbs the ladder of creatureliness in order to state at each higher stage that the Creator is not to be found there. Stein likens the experience of God to the way children learn to interpret the world around them: "Certainly for most children human ideas are a bridge to thoughts about God. But they go beyond to the 'totally other,' other than anything their experience encounters or can encounter in the world."[41]

For St. Thomas, of course, any parallelism between creature and Creator is merely the result of the *analogia entis*. In order to say that the creature enters into union with the Creator, one must first acknowledge the presence of the Ineffable. In Thomas's view, negative theology rests on the fact that alongside *similitudo* lies a *maior dissimilitudo*. In this respect, at least, Stein and St. Thomas share a great deal in common: Climbing the summit of the mountain of faith, Thomas admonishes the seeker that genuine experience of God does not in any way entail an experience of knowing God. Just as the finite cannot know the infinite, so the constituting ego cannot know what is nonprimordial outside its own lived stream of inner conscious life: *adequatio rei et intellectus*. God unveils the mystery; but, at the same time, the mystery that is unveiled is the impenetrability of the mystery itself. For neither St. Thomas Aquinas nor St. Edith Stein, the experience of God does not entail a merely cognitive relationship between the knower and an object known.

The Insufficiency of Reason

Insofar as all images and words used to describe God are inadequate, symbolic knowledge does more than merely "re-present" or "make present" something that is no longer present. Following Husserl, Stein argues that a symbol does not merely help us recognize an absence that was once a presence. On the contrary, symbolic knowledge leads to the knowledge of what is and what must remain unknown. Words and images do not give us meaning; instead, they bring to presence the absence and inaccessibility of what remains hidden as such. Language used to describe the experience of God is therefore essentially symbolic. It does not give us the meaning of the divine so much as it makes present divine absence and impenetrability. Symbolic language leads to a kind of Socratic wisdom in the sense that the word or image gives me what it cannot give.

This is what Edith Stein means by supernatural experience of God. "God" is neither the name nor the experience of an otherworldly entity who "pops" in and out of the world of nature in order to violate the laws of cognitive reasoning. The image of God is an ideal one, but one that nevertheless presupposes a higher level, spiritual penetration into what is originally given in sensible experience. The experience of God is therefore an experience constituted initially by *feeling*, in this case, the feeling of uncanniness. Such experience can never be constituted merely cognitively. In a phenomenological sense, this means that the experience of God would have to include something of what Jean-Luc Marion calls the "insufficiency of reason." Of course, such redress to insufficiency is not entirely alien to the Western philosophical tradition. Pascal warns us that, "the heart has reasons that Reason knows not of." So, too, Angelus Silesius says eloquently, "the rose is without why." In a fashion similar to Jean-Luc Marion's postmodern notion of the God beyond being, Edith Stein urges us to contest the *principum reddendae rationis* as a condition of possibility of talking about the experience of God.

In effect, Stein argues that the experience of God cannot aim at giving reasons for constituting God as the highest degree of reason. Otherwise, the experience of God becomes simply reducible to what is merely knowable, objectifiable, synthesizable, constructible, comprehensible, in short, recognizable. Hence, the experience of God must either violate the formal meaning of the Infinite on the one hand, or it must somehow lead to a kind of knowledge of what is unknowable on the other hand. To coin an image from the Areopagite, symbolic theology includes all of creation, but a "whole of creation" that is itself necessarily and unequivocally permeated throughout by absence.

Intuition

The world that forms the intuitive basis for arguments of natural theology also serves as a possible intuitive basis for image-language as well as for understanding the symbols that both veil and unveil the reality of inward experience. Stein understands "natural theology" as doctrine about God gained from natural experience through natural reason. Its core is the argument for the existence of God, and thus includes metaphysical doctrines of God's essence as well as scientific properties gathered from our physical knowledge of the created order. It proceeds by conceptual thinking, but—as with all conceptual thinking and scientific procedure—it has an intuitive basis. Stein insists that intuition (*Anschauung*) needs to be taken in a very broad sense, in contrast to "conceptual thinking," which presupposes something given. In this broader sense, intuition includes both sensitive and intellectual intuitiveness, that is, it includes what is given as present along with what is represented.

Of course, whenever we think in the attitude of the natural sciences we are motivated to presuppose sense perception. Intuition supplies what is given, it places before our eyes the sensible world and everything that actually falls under the senses. But intuition always reaches beyond what is here and now given to the senses. Stein argues that this is done in two ways. First, intuition apperceives what is given along with what is actually sensed in terms of empty intuition. When I see the front facade of a building, for instance, I intuitively constitute the sides and back of the building. Through apperception and imaginative variation I "build up" a far richer and mediated context of meaning than is emptily given to me by immediate sense perception alone. Second, intuition always grasps what is not given along with what is sensed in terms of the "inner structure" of consciousness. Stein's point is that consciousness must always conform to laws of spatial-corporeal nature, that is, to the laws of cognition. Let us take a moment to explore Stein's analysis more closely.

The Veiling and Unconcealing of the Visible and the Invisible

In her essay "Ways to Know God," Edith Stein argues that, regardless of our "common sense" perception of causality or our intuitive grasp of the laws of physics, such experience never falls directly under the senses. For example, whenever I perceive an animate body moving in the world in the same way that my body moves in the world, I am intuitively motivated to constitute that foreign animate body with a soul or with psychic life. "Life and soul," Stein comments, "are seen along with what we actually see in our outward perception, but they can never be seen in the proper sense from the outside. They are nevertheless truly experienced form the 'inside,' and what we conceive along with the outer world can in a certain way come to dovetail with what we experience inwardly."[42]

What is foreign experience in its givenness? How does the perception of foreign experience look? In response to these questions, Edith Stein attempts to describe the phenomenon of alterity in its pure essence, that is, she wants to free the Other from all accidents of appearance.[43] Experience of God, then, places into radical inquiry the way in which the radical alterity of the *tout autre* is constituted for me as a for-itself within my inner stream of conscious life (*Erlebnis*) without reducing the Other to the givenness of my own horizon. Such a proposition clearly stands outside the limit and sufficiency of reason, since it calls for believing in the impossible without any shred of evidence why. My argument here is that the experience of God, like the experience of empathy, is a condition of possibility that shatters every horizon, which makes possible what I can know with sufficient reason.

Stein's point is that the phenomenological structure of the Dark Night constitutes a similar rupture in representational thinking in the same way that the alter ego remains outside my grasp as a for-itself. Through empathy (*Einfühlung*), I perceive the other's body but must apperceive the other's stream of inner lived experience (*Erlebnis*). As we noted earlier, Edith Stein designates the experience of something foreign by the name, "empathy." By empathy she means that I am given the other's body but must analogically apperceive what remains hidden "inside" the other's stream of inner lived experience (*Erlebnis*), or spiritual life. "Conceiving a body in its physical aspect [*Körper*] as human [*Leib*] means regarding everything about its shape and movement as "expression," taking everything "outside" as a symbol of something "inside.""[44] Stein notes that the body functions as a kind of icon, or expression, in that what is perceived on the outside surface (facial features, expressions and the like), points beyond itself to something quite different (psychic life), and yet has "something in common with it that makes the expression relation possible and enables the expression to be understood."[45] Intersubjectively speaking, empathy not only describes how a multiplicity of egos constitutes a cultural world of shared, higher order values. Empathy describes the essential role that alterity plays in the constitution of every experience of the Other qua other.

Edith Stein is clear on this point: I cannot experience the "inside" of an Other's originary sphere of lived experience (*Erlebnis*), just as I cannot "experience" God except as a constituted phenomenon. Therefore, I must approach the human other essentially the same way that I approach the Divine Other: as a ground of transcendent mystery, an experience of what cannot be experienced, that is, a matter of revelation. By virtue of alterity, the human other is paradoxically no different from the Holy Other in terms of the givenness of foreign experience. The experience of the human other qua other remains always and everywhere *mysterium tremendum*, veiled, hidden, precisely in its flesh. If it were otherwise—that is, if I could have primordial access to the interiority of what lies hidden within the Other's flesh—then the Other would merely be consumed within an economy of sameness. For Stein, the invisible becomes accessible only through the visible, yet what is essentially concealed never becomes merely visible. In terms of apophatic theology, this experience of a nonexperience is structurally identical to the constituting ego's encounter with the *tout autre*. It is my contention, then, that for Stein, empathy and the experience of God are structurally similar. As a nonprimordial experience that announces a primordial one, the experience of God as *tout autre* is constitutive of a nonphenomenon, a nonexperience:

> Human ideas are a bridge to thoughts about God. But they go beyond to the "totally other," other than anything their experience encounters or can encounter in the world. And this they allow to move them to accept the teaching of supernatural revelation as the fulfillment of what they at first grasped in but empty fashion as the "totally other," and as the answer to the riddles that experience itself poses without ever being able to solve them. In this case passing from the world of natural experience into the world of supernatural faith comes about as a matter of course and almost imperceptibly."[46]

The Shattering of Horizons

As early as 1916, Edith Stein began to describe herself as a phenomenological "heretic" in terms of her desire to free the alter ego from Husserl's transcendental bonds and, thereby, liberate the order of experience from what is given cognitively in the order of knowledge. Yet, it is only in her later, more mature theological reflections that we glimpse a sense of the radical implications that her emotive modification of Husserl's strict, cognitive theory of empathy might actually entail. For Edith Stein, the experience of God is not founded merely as a cognitive phenomenon. In fact, the experience of God is no phenomenon at all. Anticipating Levinas's critique of Husserl by a quarter of a century, Stein holds that the experience of God is a nonexperience; hence, the experience of God emanates from outside the "I" as subject. It is a response to a call that comes from outside myself.

The experience of God arises from a primordial experience of alterity that is itself not grounded by the order of sufficient reason. For

Stein, the structure of the experience of God is similar to the structure of empathy in that it feels-into a nonprimordial experience that announces a primordial one.

The experience of God is, therefore, primarily a calling, an invitation, a command to respond, a "being laid claim to" without intention, without limit, without cause or sense, without reservation, without sufficient reason why. In Husserlian terms, this amounts to nothing less than a substantial change in the direction of Husserl's arrow of intentionality. It requires that the Other first lay claim to me before I can ever hope to begin to imagine how I could possibly respond. Transcendentally speaking, God's self-communication is grasped at one and the same time as both a revealing of supernatural experience as well as an address and invitation to respond. We are, after all, hearers of words long before we ever learn to speak. Knowledge of the experience of God is a kind of dark knowledge insofar as faith is never apodictic: "However, the kinds of mediate knowledge we mentioned should also be counted as supernatural experience and thereby distinct from faith. All forms of supernatural experience — but especially personal acquaintance — stand to faith as in the natural order our very own experience stands to knowledge based only upon what we are told: as the fulfillment of what we now grasp only in thought without ourselves becoming originally aware of it."[47]

Hence, although I may be motivated to constitute a deeper spiritual significance to a word or an encounter or an experience, nevertheless that experience or word or encounter is itself not God. In sacred scripture for example, long revered as "God's Word," God draws near to us in a sense of radical and definitive self-disclosure. Nevertheless, God is not sensibly present, nor does God speak in first person narrative. What makes God present in a person's encounter with scripture, or the eucharist, or even one's neighbor, is the changed reality in which I become inwardly moved and transformed by an encounter with the Holy Other. In the interiority of my transformative experience, God is speaking, and God is speaking to me. But the moment I attempt to constitute this experience cognitively, the radical immediacy of alterity vanishes. All that remains is an echo of the primordial experience. This means that even the most personal and intimate experience of God is never immediately given, but must be constituted through language as an event in and for consciousness. The experience of God qua Holy Other is always and everywhere a mediated phenomenon; it is therefore not merely constituted but constitutive.

Concluding Reflections

What remains essential in every experience of God is that we are always addressed, we are inwardly and immediately moved to respond to an address. *Shema Israel, adonai elohanu, adonai ehad*: "Hear, O Israel. . . ." Consequently, the experience of God is not constituted by a strictly cognitive relationship with the Divine. It emanates from my responding to a call that comes from outside myself, a primordial experience of alterity that is not itself reducible to the order of sufficient reason. Stein's argument is similar to Pseudo-Dionysius's in that both mystics are saying that the essence of the experience of God is not knowledge about God, but rather my being "transformed in that new way of knowledge."[48] But whereas Descartes believed that God must somehow be thought within the horizon of creatureliness (*ens creator*), Edith Stein argues that the condition of the possibility of the experience of God is that God must get out of the way precisely in order for me to experience the experience of God as a nonexperience. To "experience God" means that I who am finite must transcend the infinitely Other without having any clear or sufficient reason why. This means that an emotive, nonthematic experience of God is at least as equiprimordial as any cognitive constitution of such an experience. Otherwise, every foreign experience must necessarily remain within a closed system, trapped within the sphere of ownness.

I submit that the paradox to which Edith Stein points is a "third term" of ecstatic wonderment, to what Bernini called the "spiritual ecstasy" of that other Jewish convert to Carmel, Teresa of Avila. It is the paradox of excess, of supplement, of joy; it is the surplus of desire without concern for self. Such nonexperience is the necessary condition that makes possible an excess of experience; it gives expression to a dialogical and reciprocal exchange between the visible and the invisible, the cataphatic and the apophatic, ego and alter ego, totality and infinity. Similar in this respect to both Levinas's and Jean-Luc Marion's postmodern projects, Edith Stein's understanding of the experience of God places into radical question the whole world opened up by language in which reality is present for us. How can I encounter the Holy Other without the Other being reduced to my horizon?

Edith Stein seeks an impossible intention. In one sense, the experience of God opens up and makes possible the paradox of transcendence. From below, this paradox reverses all hierarchies, even as it upholds them; whereas from above it upholds all hierarchies, even as it reverses them. The experience of God is thus the experience of a nonexperience, the experience of God's presence even in its withdrawal. To remain faithful to a God who hides in the negation of experience means to remain faithful to a future that never quite arrives — or that arrives in the unexpected terror or Auschwitz. Such a future, I submit, is structurally messianic. Like the messiah, the impossibility of the experience of God arrives by virtue of its never arriving.

It is, then, precisely the impossibility of the experience of God that makes the experience of God possible. For Stein, the journey of the Dark Night is a rupture in representational thinking. Like the constitution of the alter ego, God is structurally absent from this experience. Alterity in effect gives presence to what both "is" and "is not" at one and the same time, it manifests what in principle is an impossible intention. Phenomenologically speaking, the constitution of neither God nor neighbor can be justified by sufficient reason. What Edith Stein discovers in her encounter with Pseudo-Dionysius is that the Other qua other both shatters and constitutes at one and the same time every horizon of expectation and foreseeability. The experience of the Other is therefore analogous to the experience of God. The Other is constituted by an act of faith; hence every encounter with every Other constitutes an act of saturation, a gift given without expenditure, without justification.

For Edith Stein, faith means to make a radical commitment of one's life to being, to the stranger who is other than one's neighbor, to God . . . but without sufficient reason why. Faith means to see through a glass darkly, to cry out without any proof of being heard: thy will be done, *nei secoli secolorum*; in a word, *Amen*. Faith, Stein tells us, is a gift that bids us always to ask for more.[49]

12

The Twilight of the Idols and the Night of the Senses

JEFFREY BLOECHL

The question of experience of God may be taken to respond to the thought that experience of God has become questionable. Heard in this way, the question summons the idea that what we call "God" is in fact not God, whether this is taken to mean simply that there is no God or that God is somehow other or more than what we say. The fact that the experience of God can be the theme of questioning and inquiry thus informs us that reflection on the experience of God is always accompanied by doubt, whether this doubt is only the leading edge of violent suspicion or the first gesture of desire for intimacy with the true God. Following this line, one may observe these two possibilities to meet and challenge one another in the wake of the death of God. For some, the death of God signifies the realization that "God" is an idea that has somehow outlived its usefulness and plausibility. For others it signifies only that God is beyond usefulness and plausibility—which is not to say that God is either useless or implausible.

This debate over the meaning of the death of God permits us to see that the difference between a claim that God is no longer plausible and a claim that God is beyond all criteria of plausibility— between a refusal of God and an elevated faith in God—is concentrated in conflicting notions of what constitutes an idol, and of what would be required to transcend it. Does idolatry appear in the faith in God that falls short of God, or already in faith itself?

Above all, when it is a question of experience of the one true God, this matter of the idol is unavoidable. And it bears specifically on the nature of experience—its structure, its status, and its proper limits. After all, God does not need experience in order to remain God, as Anselm teaches the *incipiens*. What would it mean for this *Deus semper maior* to have entered our experience? Or rather, what does it mean for us to feel and think that this is so? How could we experience God without somehow making God our own, giving God a place within a wider context of things already familiar to us, and in the process mistaking as God something that is essentially less than God?

Experience, Egology, Idolatry

These questions have always been close to philosophy and theology, and they have always been understood to be a matter of experience in general before they are a matter specifically of faith and God. Let us first distinguish the immediacy of an experience from the understanding that commits the experience to an idea or at least an interpretation. When we read Aristotle's classic definition of understanding as the identification of causes for what enters experience,[1] we must not fail to notice how this supposes that what we seek to understand has already arrived in experience. Something enters experience, and if there is any reason to doubt its status or meaning, we turn to ground it in some ulterior cause or causes. This is to say that when something enters experience, we tend naturally to accept it; even if we do not see it clearly or recognize it well, we believe that it exists. Husserl considered this spontaneous belief to be the root of meaning-giving, and he sought to trace its fate through the many steps required to make a well-founded statement of understanding. It is a defining feature of our natural attitude, he says, that we accept the being of things as such; we accept things into experience as "really there," and this spontaneous belief in them is the condition for any possible doubt we may subsequently have about them, as well as any understanding of them that we may eventually achieve. In the first book of his *Ideas*, Husserl focuses on an elemental "correlation" to be found already here: any experience must be composed of, on the side of the subject, "belief-characteristics" and, on the side of the objective reality that shows itself to experience, "being-characteristics."[2]

The question of experience of God, if it is attuned to theme of idolatry, directs attention to this notion of basic belief, or doxa, in a way

that seems left aside by Husserl himself, with his concern for a philosophy that would be rigorous science. Rather than following him
directly into a study of the constitution of meaning and expression
of truth, one might first ask about the status of the belief that they
presuppose. How is it that we immediately accept the real existence
of what enters experience, before any question of doubt or eventual
correction? According to what conditions, or from what existential
situation? One must grant that it would be extremely difficult to produce an example in which experience does not proceed on this basic
belief, but is it certain that no exceptions are possible? In order to
even begin with this hypothesis, it would be necessary to think that
existence has a root that reaches beneath consciousness itself, which
is to say beneath our openness to being, and it would be necessary to
also think that there may be moments and events in which we are
touched from beyond consciousness, which is to say from beyond
being and the play of presence and absence in which being shows
itself. Without these two propositions, there is no avoiding the conclusion that what presents itself as meaningful will have first been
accepted by the basic belief of a living subject. We should not forget
that Husserl himself has contributed profound analyses of the strata
of existence and experience anterior to the consciousness of the subject, but we may also see that it is not for nothing that many of his
readers have expressed reservations about a perceived reduction of
phenomenology to egology—that is, a reduction of the study of the
manifold forms of appearing to a study of the life of the meaning-
giving ego.

If the word "egology" designates the premise or assertion that the
ego is the inevitable locus of meaning, then egology is the existential
condition for idolatry. Egology and idolatry are paired in this way
from earliest reflection on experience of God, and in God. Among
theologians, it is present as early as Paul's letter to the Romans,
which begins with an excoriation of idolaters, who "became fools,
and changed the glory of the incorruptible God for the likeness of
corruptible humanity, birds, beasts, and reptiles" (Rom. 1:22–23).
There is no mistaking Paul's deep concern, as it reaches beyond criticizing worship of false images of the divine, to highlighting the stunted mode of existence that goes with it. The idolater does not merely
worship the wrong gods, but limits himself to an outlook restricted
to the terms of this world, without any greater dimension. Already in
Paul, idolatry is the expression of a gaze that never sees beyond the
limits of the world, so that what counts as meaningful never goes

beyond what can be oriented to our situation in the world. A Christian sees things differently, or perhaps otherwise; a Christian knows that "an idol is nothing . . . and that there is no God except one." (1 Cor. 8:14). A Pauline critique of egology and idolatry therefore proceeds directly from the most radical commitment of monotheism, which the epistles express with frequent reminders that "God is one" (Rom. 3:30, Gal. 3:20), "there is one God" (1 Tim. 2:5), "the blessed and only Sovereign, the King of kings, Lord of lords" (1 Tim. 6:15–16), and so forth.[3] Paul's sense of wisdom and the way it fulfills humanity in openness to the Invisible God could not be farther from the modern notion of a humanity that would instead be fulfilled when it emancipates itself from this faith in God, now considered immature, at best. Feuerbach manages to take this path even while nonetheless asserting the paramount importance of Christian faith for human progress: in Judaism, we will have advanced from a pagan worship of nature to a worship of national or ethnic identity, but it is only in Christianity that we will have reached worship of the human spirit, as projected on the God of Jesus Christ.[4] Perhaps more recent, typically cognitive uses of this word "projection" (*Vergegenstandlichung*) have made us forgot the sense Feuerbach gives to it. In *The Essence of Christianity*, "projection" is intended only to designate a spontaneous externalization or objectification, according to a tendency that is innate and more or less constant. The important claim behind this word says that each human being is simply attached to himself or herself in a way that drives us to invent and then believe in the perfect embodiment of what we value most in ourselves: justice, strength, mercy, and so forth. This notion of attachment to oneself both identifies his work as one version of a claim for egology, and locates it at a deeper level than the more strictly cognitive theories of religion proposed by a sociologist like Peter Berger, who defines religion by a sacred view of the cosmos that serves to conquer chaos,[5] or a psychologist like Erich Fromm, who perceives it as a shared system that gives each individual member a basic orientation and object of devotion.[6] Whereas Feuerbach leads us to think of the relation with God first of all as a relation with the one who already has everything worth having and already is everything worth being, those more contemporary theories reduce that relation to interest in the one who might provide, specifically, order. The relative poverty of the sociological and psychological definitions of "projection" show up as soon as it is pointed out that experience of God can hardly be reduced to its cognitive dimension, though few would deny that it is present there. This effectively dispenses with Berger or Fromm, but it has not yet reached the level of discussion with Feuerbach. In that sense, Feuerbach's theory of religious experience still deserves attention — and indeed it defines the stake of subsequent debate — because it remains able to assert that there is idolatry in all such experiences because the fundamental horizon for experience of any kind is always self-idolatry. According to Feuerbach, we love "God" because in the first instance we love ourselves, and it is in fact this self-love that lies behind claims for the experience of God.

When we return to Paul after Feuerbach, it seems that a Christian critique of the foolish attachment to the world expressed in idolatry is more deeply a critique of the foolish attachment to oneself that comprises self-idolatry. This tells us something about what would be required today to think a genuine experience of God. In order to think the experience of God as God and not as some idol, it will be necessary to describe a mode of existence in which the ego does not identify first or finally with itself. It must be conceivable that the ego is sometimes dislodged from any natural tendency to install itself as center or locus. It must be possible for the ego to lose or surrender any tendency to grasp things on its own initiative — any tendency, in other words, to comprehend them. For in the end, idolatry is an event of comprehension, of holding something up in a light that can be crossed effortlessly by an imperial gaze. It is an affair of vision and illumination, as recent phenomenology has reminded us. With this, attention to the themes of "darkness" and "night" become inevitable.

What ensues when the light fades and the lines that profile subjects and objects become blurred, until vanishing entirely? What are we to expect from the darkness beyond the horizon of intelligibility? If we are unsure about these metaphors of darkness and night, we can feel endangered by the desire to enter their domain. What will be the destiny of those who move past idols into darkness? It seems unlikely that it could be under their control, for night approaches only when, or to the degree, that those who would enter it surrender the freedom and confidence that only daylight offers us. What this will require can be said in sharp terms: the price of getting beyond idolatry must be a suspension of the faculties by which the comprehending subject constitutes the meaning of its experiences — thus the faculties that enable a subject to maintain itself and all the privileges it assumes at the center of its world.

The gravity of the question of experience of God requires us to open the field of reflection on this matter of darkness as wide as possible, before moving toward any sort of conclusion about its nature and its meaning: after all, mystical theology is not the only source of a call to suspend the faculties of comprehension. Most of us will know that Book Three of John of the Cross's *Ascent of Mount Carmel* describes the stilling of intellect, memory, and personal will as the condition for a movement toward greater intimacy with God. How many of us like to remember that virtually the same faculties are targeted in Nietzsche's *Twilight of the Idols*, this time as the essential features of a subjectivity that is the source of every illusion and inhibition imposed on life?[7] What are we to think of this unexpected encounter at the end of the day? What, if anything, might either of these two lines of thought enable us to see in the other? More important, what might that new insight say to us about the human encounter with God? Let us content ourselves, for now, with a start from only one side of the encounter: what might the possibility of nihilism teach us about the nocturnal approach of God? What distinguishes the dark night of the soul from the profound chaos embraced by Nietzsche's solitary wanderer? And what might that difference permit us to say about the experience of God beyond idolatry?

Night of Chaos

Night lies waiting beyond the penumbra of daylight; it approaches only as light fails or withdraws. If we associate that light with intelligibility, then "darkness" must signify a condition in which we are no longer in the presence of intelligible things. As one moves from experience by light to experience in darkness, the world and everything in it cease to appear intelligible, and indeed cease to appear at all, so that all the powers by which one had previously lived would now be diminished, if not brought entirely to a halt. What distinguishes darkness from anything given in the light is the fact that it gives itself without possibility of being ordered, and we know this: the deeper we enter true darkness, the more inclined we are to surrender any attempt to search for order. This surrender of all comprehension leaves us exposed in a way that can never be the case during the daytime, when experience always navigates ordered relations and any gaps that might interrupt them.

What comprises this darkness, and what defines the experience that undergoes it? It seems possible, in preliminary fashion, to distinguish two possible answers simply by attending to their respective metaphors. If the surrender of comprehension means reducing the life of the subject to complete receptivity, then the darkness that succeeds dusk would pour over a newly immobile ego, which has become its helpless interlocutor. The night would murmur and rustle, as Levinas has written, and I would be nothing more and nothing less than this one who must hear it. But if surrendering comprehension means breaking down the structures that set me, as myself, apart from my world and everything in it, then darkness would swarm from the cracks between old boundaries, consuming everything in its path. The night would rush and roar, and I would be swept along with it, disintegrating. Freudians describe a decomposition of the subject that releases an impulse that has never known the light of day.

The second path into night has been positively advocated (and not only described, as in Freudian thought) by Nietzsche. His argument develops from pursuit of the basic question of motivation: Why do we attempt to comprehend things? And why do we believe that comprehension is reliable? Under Nietzsche's pen, the first question draws attention to a willing that is older than understanding and that even generates understanding. The second question suggests that that willing conceals its achievement by withdrawing quietly from sight, so that understanding governs our relation to the world and everything in it with unquestioned rights. Nietzsche reacts to this self-suppression of will by calling us all to abandon our trust in understanding so that will may surge forth without inhibition. This could not stop at the "death" of any single God, but must continue all the way through to a dismantling of the subjectivity that believes in any god whatsoever. According to Nietzsche, the ego—or, in his favored locution, the subject—as the site from which every god is projected and then embraced, is the primary idol that we must endeavor to see as it truly is, and then jettison. What we call "God" would be nothing more than a term in the grammar that supports a subject by linking it to an indubitable object.[8] It is therefore necessary to get beneath that grammar, beneath language, to the will to power that urges us to speak, and beneath the life of the spirit to a source that is both deeper and, at least to eyes accustomed to the light of understanding, immeasurably darker. For Nietzsche, it is necessary to overthrow spirituality altogether. The spiritual, he tells us, is only "the semiotics of the body."[9]

This is not a thought that can be easily accommodated by religious thought, and for that reason it is also a thought that religious thought must take as seriously as possible. When religious thinking has permitted itself to be moved by Nietzsche, it has often begun by observing that his affirmation of will to power defines itself in and through a rejection specifically of the Christian God. On a certain level, there is certainly something to be said for this argument, which then hears the *a* in atheism as a confession of the point. Yet on another level, this is obviously too easy, since that sort of rejection would have to be exercised by the very sort of subject that we have already seen Nietzsche himself identify as an idol. It is true, therefore, that atheism can be as idolatrous as the Christianity it would nullify, but Nietzsche does not contest this. However, will to power is constantly defined as an active force, rather than one that is reactive, and attempts to affirm it are properly understood in the spirit of Merleau-Ponty's insistence that the true meaning of his own nonbelief lies in a positive affirmation of our true humanity rather than in some negative gesture toward religion.[10] Is it possible to concede this point and still characterize will to power as "idolatrous"? One would have to follow Heidegger's claim that will to power, despite Nietzsche's intention to the contrary, takes its turn as the metaphysical ground for all else, thus insuring a new form of closure from any "other is only "the semiotics of dimension," which is to say, again, idolatry. Jean-Luc Marion has taken this approach, citing Nietzsche's own acknowledgment that will to power ceaselessly produces new, pagan gods.[11] For Marion, these new gods would indicate idolatry not because they proceed from the situation and intentions of subjectivity, but simply because they must be understood as moments of coalescence, and in this sense closure. And according to the remarkable phenomenology of light and vision undertaken in the early passages of his *God Without Being*, an idol is found wherever the gaze comes to a stop or accepts a limit for itself, and thus closes the field of vision within a specific perimeter. The gaze that rests on an idol does not see into the infinite distance that only its counterpart, the icon, holds open.

Is it certain that this argument has taken the full measure of Nietzsche's position? One reservation seems unavoidable: if there is a gaze in the uninhibited thrust of will, it is precisely one that must circulate without possibility of stopping. And for that matter, the only way to assimilate the notion of chaos to the notion of will would be to think that the latter is indeed in such an endless circulation. In view of this, it seems that Nietzsche's reference to the gods of will to power must be understood with particular emphasis on the fact that they are ceaselessly produced, countless of them at a time and with each one immediately succeeded by others, in a blind rush of uninhibited force that would not merely reject the notion of divine transcendence, but—at least this would be the claim—positively absorb it into natural immanence.[12] Each of Nietzsche's gods would be an efflorescence of this uninhibited will, leaping forth for a moment, even as it is already burst from within by the next eruption, which leaps higher, or still more intensely.

The most one can therefore say about this will to power—and it comes close to an essential definition of Nietzsche's idea—is that it always thrusts forth without possibility of stopping or even slowing. There are passages where Nietzsche seems to deny that will to power is ever any more than its activity in a present moment. Will to power is movement that does not know, and cannot know, any end. It does not merely deny itself rest and fulfillment, but is positively indifferent to the very possibility. Each moment is hunger without even the image of satisfaction ever in view, and life itself is desire without any dream of fulfillment.

These are punishing thoughts, but they may at last betray an unmistakable weakness in Nietzsche's thinking. Does it not belong to the essential nature of any hunger or desire, any willing deserving of the name—with or without a "preeminent" subject—that it lives from at least the possibility of some satisfaction? This would not be the same thing as actually projecting a well-defined object or source of satisfaction, let alone finding one. At his most extreme, Nietzsche seems to deny that will power operates on any sort of premise that some satisfaction, regardless of its form or degree, may eventually come. What he wants most is to define a willing that neither has anything, since possession supposes minimal identity, nor even wants anything, since wanting supposes a projected aim and thus, again, minimal identity. In this image of a pure willing, a willing that neither responds to anything else nor refers to anything else, one must therefore see a denial that will to power responds to any sense of lack that it moves toward filling. Undoubtedly, Nietzsche's resistance to this sort of analysis is of a single piece with his resistance to any form of subjectivity, which always imposes meaning on chaos, thus inhibiting our most natural forces. It is for this reason that will to power is always considered (positively) mute and blind: it moves without surveying the field or projecting an end for itself. But this is still not enough to deny that will to power does thrust toward some fulfillment, before any question of identifying a way to get it. Against Nietzsche, it seems necessary to insist that willing—or, if one prefers, wanting, desiring—is always already on its way toward fulfillment. If life moves at all, life must already contain within itself, as a necessary condition for movement, the dream that the movement may eventually receive everything it wants. The restless movement of life, its ceaseless thrust forward, is stirred by a longing for complete and final satisfaction. As finite beings in a finite world, we are unable to give this satisfaction to ourselves. But we are also unable to make the longing for it disappear.

Does anything prevent us from thinking of this as a natural desire, or at least a desire natural to our humanity? Of course, it is also an excessive desire, a desire that aims past any limited satisfaction and even works against the service of basic needs that bind us to the world. One always wants more, always desires beyond what satisfies basic needs. In this sense, life itself is a tension that never eases, since there are always both those basic needs and that excessive desire. Our being in the world consists, in one or another form, of living in this tension, and if we can catch sight of it we can also begin to live with it in a positive sense—negotiating the relations between what it asks and what reality may dictate. We know that too much interest in need (or even lower things) causes us to neglect the desire that points us beyond this world. We should also bear in mind that abandonment to that desire may cause us to disregard the conditions necessary for human life in this world. Pursued far enough, the desire for perfect fulfillment eventually turns back to contest the rule of a subject that sometimes sets limits on it. This does not always yield self-destruction. In remarkable instances, desire for perfect fulfillment, for what an older tradition has called beatitude, turns back on the subject only to still it, or empty it of selfish attachment. If contemporary thinking has been slow to account for this phenomenon of self-emptying, this may be because it has first had trouble with the more basic experience of hope. For it is plainly through hope, and perhaps hope alone, that one might enter a darkness beyond every idol, emptying oneself of every attachment to the world, and yet stop short of abandoning one's very life to the chaos roaring, at that moment, so close at hand. Hope is the name of a desire for intimacy with God that is experienced in full view of the fact that that intimacy cannot be made to arrive by human means. But hope, in turn, therefore seems to suppose faith in some antecedent promise or, if we dare to force the issue, sacrament. Hope, faith, and the promise are the basic lineaments of the Christian experience of God. These are lain bare in the mystical experience of night.[13]

Night of Annihilation

If we note, when reading Nietzsche, that the Christian God he identifies and then rejects is always, at bottom, a God who demands rather than promises, this is not only to conclude that his argument is built on negating only the moral God, the God of Justice, but also to suggest that he has failed to understand the experience of hope. How could hope implicate the experience of God in any of the things Nietzsche attacks so relentlessly? Hope is not expectation, which looks into the future through the lens of experience, so that it has already committed itself to seeing the new object or event in terms of the past one. Expectation continues to receive new experiences from the perspective and situation of the one who expects. To expect God would be to worship an idol. Hope is also not anticipation, which goes out ahead toward new objects or events, drawing them into the time of the one who anticipates. To anticipate God would also be to worship an idol. Hope desires, and it moves as if that desire is not futile, but it also knows that if indeed anything or anyone may come to that desire, it will come in its own time, and not in the time of those who hope. Hope is therefore neither expectation nor anticipation, but an opening to what precisely comes from beyond expectation and anticipation. Pure hope is both beautiful and terrifying, because it endures after every reason for it has disappeared and even while the reasons to abandon it multiply. But this does not mean that hope is desperate flight or denial. The God of hope is first of all, and still, the God of the promise on which hope is nourished.

When it is a matter of Christian hope, the unique promise nourishing it must be that of intimacy with God. Hope has already heard the promise that God will come, and responds by opening itself to that coming. A mystic like John of the Cross has tasted something of the fulfillment of that promise. How are we to understand his experience? Among scholars of John of the Cross, Huot de Longchamp stays closest to the spiritual language of his author, and brings us closest to the heart of the matter: the mystic comes to the point where spirit enters matter, which is the "reality of the Incarnation."[14] This interpretation can be immediately clarified by joining it to both the Carmelite emphasis on identifying with Christ, and the dogma that says that in Christ the human and the divine are one. Concisely, the experience of the reality of the Incarnation is an experience of intimacy with God in which God is still God and the mystic is still human. It is Christ, as gift, entering humanity from beyond, and opening us to the God who transcends it. This would be a first approach to John of the Cross's statement that what is received in mystical experience is "sublime," for it surpasses what is "naturally attainable."[15] A second approach, and one that we may feel more readily, rejoins the theme of hope: mystical intimacy with God is not an experience that we could ever make happen on our own, not even by the most strenuous spiritual efforts. How could I, as I, ever climb all the way to perfect communion with God? Per definition, the experience and the knowledge it imparts arrive suddenly, from beyond expectation and anticipation, beyond idolatry, apart from any exercise of a free will. If this is so—if mystical experience occurs beyond what is naturally attainable, and out of reach of human accomplishment—then the only way to act on our desire for intimacy with God can be to open ourselves to God. This is why the dark night in which intellection, memory, and personal will are stilled must be understood as an emptying of self of everything that tends to affirm the self as center of meaning. The name for this self-emptying way of being, the fundamental attitude in which it occurs, is humility, which John of the Cross understands as a quiet receptivity to God, who "will do His work at the time and in *the manner that he* wishes" (emphasis added). How is this made known to us? By the example of Jesus, who "accomplished the most marvelous work of His whole life" when He was "most annihilated in all things." When we are brought to nothing according to the example of Jesus, "the highest degree of humility, the spiritual union of the soul and God will be effected."[16] As the expression of faith in the promise of Jesus—the faith that takes Jesus as the preeminent example, the "exemplar"—humility, life in hope, defines the Christian being-in-the-world as being open to God. It is the life of this humility, as self emptying, as annihilation," as stilling of the faculties—which leads this movement toward God through the dark night of the soul.[17]

There is no need, in this context, to study the distinction between the active night, or "night of the senses," in which a person strives to commit exclusively to the glory of God, and the passive night, or "night of the spirit," in which God enters into communication with the soul, completing the work of the active night. In describing the latter, the *Dark Night of the Soul* simply confirms what the *Ascent of*

Mount Carmel assumes from the beginning: "night" is not the result of some confusion or loss of faith in the "one God who unites," but to the contrary expresses growing focus and intensity in that faith. This is why it is necessary to resist the notion that a crisis of faith within certain currents of contemporary culture may be understood according to the model of the mystical dark nights. Whereas the nineteenth and twentieth centuries saw the emergence of an apparently viable and even comfortable way of life that is no longer nourished by faith of any kind, the mystical night is constantly permeated by faith and love of God. Moreover, only this faith and love can explain its considerable pain. During the passive night, the night of the spirit, God's communication with the soul teaches one that the human condition is always defined by some separation from what it loves most, and the soul cries out with a longing that is all the greater for having seen that intimacy with God is also distance from God.

This endurance of faith and hope is of course a primary index of what truly distinguishes the mystical night from the Nietzschean chaos. In the mystical night, the soul still leaps toward some invisible dimension, as a flame will do when the air becomes rarefied. Nietzsche's darkness would be more unqualified because it would belong to a night that does not merely appear endless, but is without any inclination to end—a night in which, as Fitzgerald once put it, "it is three o'clock all the time." But if one wishes finally to understand this Nietzschean darkness, it is not enough to suppose, though no doubt correctly, that this would be an experience in which neither hope nor humility is to be found. What explains those features of the experience, as their deeper condition, is a detachment from any positive relation to an original promise, a promise that comes from elsewhere and beyond. It may be true that Nietzsche's human being can make promises and keep them, but it is also true that Nietzsche incites us to mistrust the promises of others, and above all God's, as sources of diminishment. If we accept Nietzsche's claim that none of this vision deserves to be called negative or reactionary, then it becomes necessary to ask for a positive source for it. Is it possible for the night itself, in Nietzsche's sense, to announce itself to us? Can darkness call to us? Does it voice an appeal? Such an appeal, if it is to be found, would evidently be the contrary of that other appeal in which we experience God. What would be the relation between these two? We may find such a nocturnal call, a call of darkness and to darkness, in Nietzsche's remarkable confessions that he hears the voice of instinct in attunement to certain music (and apparently most often while in Italy[18]). How could this "instinct" be anything other than the vital willing he has called us to liberate from that last idol of existence, our subjectivity? And how could the word "music," which Nietzsche constantly associates with instinct, signal anything other than the call of everything he has tried to express with concepts like "will to power" and "chaos"? When Nietzsche hears the "music of instinct" he finds himself in a mood, or indeed—accepting Heidegger's equation—a voice[19] that has spilled into his thinking from beneath it or beyond it, and determines its course. What Nietzsche eventually leads us to understand as "chaos" is first something that calls to him, or awakens in him, at an affective level, which is to say a level anterior to the concept. It enters his thinking not as an idea, but in a feeling that orients him from the moment he says "Yes" to it. This, and not some negative reaction or deliberate act of revolt, would explain Nietzsche's hostility to, among other things, the Christian faith in God. Nietzsche had no "feel" for Christianity, no sensibility for the divine promise, the hope it makes possible, and the humility that embraces it.

Experience of God and Being

Should we also accept the converse thesis that the Christian has no feel for a truly godless existence? How would the Christian mode of existence, animated by hope and humility, permit us to understand and relate to the mode of existence that seems to be without them? How does the Christian mode of being relate to this other mode of being? After Nietzsche, the question of the experience of God finally reduces to this difficulty: if being may genuinely be experienced as chaotic night, then the divine approach that communicates with the believing soul either comes only to those who are already disposed to experience being as a night infused with hope, or the divine approach would have to come from wholly beyond any experience of being, with or without hope.

I will return to the former alternative in a moment. The latter alternative is more immediately appealing, since it seems to agree with a theological emphasis on divine transcendence. However, it also comes at the price of investing being with a dangerous ambivalence: insofar as we exist, we are capable of hope and its ascent toward God but also of a rejection of hope or a loss of hope, and a descent into increasing darkness. It is difficult not to see an ultimately negative evaluation of being, in this vision. Being becomes the horizon from which it is necessary to free the experience of God, and yet that horizon will always threaten to contaminate any such experience so long as who have the experience are beings—so long as we are, and the experience is. This ambivalence turns up not infrequently in prominent contemporary—that is, post-Nietzschean—philosophies of God and religion. In Levinas's later work, for instance, the same self-emptying of the subject that is necessary for one to escape the snares of egocentrism and idolatry may also bring confusion and exhaustion, risking a fall all the way into chaos that he calls *il y a*.[20] The horror of an encounter with *il y a* is the expression of a religious desire woven into being, or even animating it, as being transcends itself—but therefore never without the possibility of also collapsing back into itself. For Marion, this is more straightforwardly a matter of a spiritual hunger that can be struck with vanity and then derail into melancholia. In melancholia, we always want infinitely more, but never see farther than the "absent vanishing point" of what transcends being and the world—never see more than the point at which God withdraws from reach. Just this is the pain of melancholia: one is not satisfied by what is offered in being, but one does not, or cannot, receive more. Melancholia comes to a spiritual hunger struggling to loosen itself from the grip of being.[21]

This sort of thinking tries to concede the darkness of being made thinkable by Nietzsche, but then always sees it alongside the superior light that comes only from God. It is not certain what this implies, beyond the depiction of a humanity with access to God but also a real susceptibility to other lures. Perhaps it is true that even within the life of faith darkness can appeal to us in alternation with the appeal of God. This approaches the model of antiphony suggested by Jean-Louis Chrétien, in his exploration of the theme of night in modern poetry (Novalis, Claudel, Peguy. . .).[22] The night touches us with an excess that defies language, and we hand that excess immediately over to a word that can only be the poetry of abjection and petition, since these poetic words never pretend to grasp. God also touches us with an excess that defies language, and we hand God's different excess immediately over to the poetry of praise and adoration. Night exposes us in a way that calls for words, and God exposes us in a way that calls for other words. The alternation of words for night and words for God, of words for darkness and words for light, comprises the song of our complete humanity.

Have these arguments, as beautiful as they may be, truly clarified the relation between the experience of godless being and the experience of God? From within the horizon opened up by experience of God, the experience of being as godless expresses a religious desire (Levinas) or spiritual hunger (Marion) that has not yet surpassed the sphere of immanence. This much seems incontestable, but it does not yet address Nietzsche's claim that such immanence is not only all there is, but is also inexhaustible. What is the relation between this experience and the experience of God? The two are evidently different in reality, and it is not inconceivable that they strike one and the same person, from time to time. As calls, they may even challenge and interfere with one another, so that a person sometimes feels hopeful and uplifted but at other times torrid with brute vitality. But would this mean that those feelings mark the same register in us differently, or does each strike a different register? Is there something like an Ur-affectibility in us, a sort of basic receptivity where different appeals stimulate correspondingly different feelings, or is the compass of our feelings irreducibly complex, so that we are at one and the same time susceptible to different appeals, each stimulating its own response? These questions do not disappear if we insist that the alternative between an openness to God and a closed ignorance of God does not describe the encounter between two distinct two modes of life, but the living oscillation of our full humanity (Chrétien). One still wants to know whether this indicates a dualism at the heart of human nature—as if we are composed of distinctly, and perhaps even opposed, spiritual and material elements—or rather a deeper template for both the call of matter and the call of spirit.

This is a question—or, rather, the concept of affection is a theme—that requires separate, lengthy attention. However, the fact that accounts of human existence and experience as far apart as Nietzsche and Christian mysticism seem to invoke it is highly suggestive. Who could deny it: we are beings whose experiences stimulate feelings that orient understanding and reflection, and this includes both our aspiration to beatitude and our fascination with the infernal.

Still, it may be fairly said that Christian hope and humility appear closer to expressing this conception of humanity than is the Nietzschean celebration of aggression. Humility is a feeling or attitude intent on confessing its own dependence, and hope is a desire aiming to make itself receptive. Aggression, in contrast, strikes toward mastery—and if the effort itself does betray a hidden insecurity, this is still something that aggression is far from recognizing and accepting. Perhaps only faith makes it possible to say that humility simply is more authentically human than aggression, but is it not necessary for everyone to admit that humility at least exhibits our humanity better? From time to time, philosophers of religion and human nature have supposed that the mystical experience of God represents a privileged opportunity to understand our basic humanity. The attempt to preserve that experience from the challenge of Nietzsche reminds us that there is something to that claim.

Finally, then, it deserves notice that the humility of the mystic eventually rejects even the distinction between finite and infinite, or immanent and transcendent, insofar as they might otherwise permit us the minimal degree of vanity that would say God is, precisely, not here.[23] Going beyond this, in the name of a greater openness to God, can only mean, eventually, accepting the constant and unqualified presence of God in every moment of life. This is why it would be wrong to say that humility and hope are preconditions for God to enter experience. The extreme expression of humility that occurs in the mystical "annihilation" of self, reaching toward an experience of non-opposition between finite self and infinite God, teaches finally that God never holds back from us. There can be no precondition for God to draw near because God is already there, though our human condition does not admit easily knowing this. The fact that desire for God is thus answered in an experience of divine abundance does not indicate idolatry, as if God were an object finally projected to provide some final reward. Recognizing the threat of this mistake, should we then renounce all desire for God, precisely out of humility? To the contrary, this may lead to the subtlest idolatry of all. When someone professes belief in God, or a conviction that God exists, but then rejects the legitimacy of any desire to experience God, to transcend our limited understanding to the perfect illumination that can only come from beyond us, they risk committing themselves to the idea that experience of God can never exceed the limits of our human condition. If this is so, then what starts out as a willingness to confess the limitations of the human condition has soon enough approached the claim that human understanding is the inevitable and therefore rightful measure of what counts as meaningful. It is difficult to imagine a more impoverished relation to God, and for that matter to anything else. In contrast, what is most striking about the path that embraces desire for experience of God beyond idolatry is its promise of endless riches. For the life committed to a God who is already alive in all things would also be a life in which what one wants most, and what makes one truly happy, can be discovered endlessly anew, without possibility of any recurrence of the same.

13

The Black Women's Spiritual Narrative as Sermon

CRYSTAL J. LUCKY

In 1836, itinerant preacher Jarena Lee offered her Philadelphia readership a brief spiritual autobiography to teach them of salvation and to give an account of her call to preach the gospel. She employed the prophetic words from the biblical book of Joel—"and it shall come to pass . . . that I will pour out my Spirit upon all flesh; and your sons, and your daughters shall prophecy [*sic*]"¹—as the epigraph to the first autobiography written by a black woman in the United States, *The Life and Religious Experience of Jarena Lee, A Coloured Lady, Giving An Account of Her Call to Preach the Gospel.*² In 1846, as a parting gift to her friends and colleagues and in preparation for her return to the United States after a five-year stay in London, Mrs. Zilpha Elaw referred on the title page of her autobiography to the Apostle Paul's words to the Corinthians—"Not that we are sufficient of ourselves to think any thing as of ourselves; but our sufficiency is of God"³—indicating her unwillingness to make authorial claims without divine sanction. In 1879, Mrs. Julia A. J. Foote, to "testify more extensively to the sufficiency of the blood of Jesus Christ to save from all sin," followed suit by asking of herself the same question as the prophet Zechariah, "is not this a brand plucked out of the fire?"⁴ And finally, at the close of the nineteenth century, Amanda Berry Smith, known also as "the Colored Evangelist," borrowed the prophet Samuel's declaration after Israel's military victory over the Philistines—"Hitherto the Lord hath helped me."⁵ She offered her "little" book (of 506 pages) "that many of my own people will be led to a more full consecration, and that the Spirit of the Lord may come upon some of the younger women who have talent, and who have had better opportunities than I have ever had, and so must do better work for the Master." By using the Bible as the foundation for their self-authorization to tell their life's stories, to claim their own spiritual birthrights, and to expand their participation in evangelical ministry, these black women used autobiography to enter the public sphere in an effort to add their powerful voices to those of the men already crying in a religious, social, and political wilderness.

Taken together, these works, along with others, comprise a genre I have termed the black preaching women's spiritual narrative of the nineteenth century. Like the Protestant spiritual narrative, it demonstrates the narrator's quest for spiritual perfection in an imperfect world, witnesses her conversion in an effort to influence an unredeemed readership, and records her trials, temptations, and final triumph.[6] Initiated by an itinerant woman preacher in 1836, the black preaching women's spiritual narrative accomplishes these narrative tasks and includes the spiritual experiences of black women who believed themselves called to preach the gospel and endeavored to enter formal ministry. The narrator calls both a black and white readership to moral reform and urges male church leadership to recognize the validity of women's evangelical ministry. Specifically, they are authored by black women officially or loosely associated with the African Methodist Episcopal Church (A.M.E.) and engaged in itinerant preaching careers. Their act of life writing enabled them to chronicle significant details of their lives and to reflect on the presence of God in their lived experiences, the existence of which many male church leaders simply denied.

This essay offers a reading of Julia Foote's *A Brand Plucked From the Fire* to illustrate one of the distinct characteristics of this narrative form, the way that orality functions on the printed page. Orality is a key component in the study of African American literature and culture, as evidenced by the emphasis placed on the role of religious and secular song, political and public speech, and the preached word in contemporary literature and culture. For nineteenth-century black women preachers turned autobiographical narrators, the characteristics associated with oral preaching were part and parcel of their written work. As I argue, they created written sermons in the form of autobiography in order to claim the right to preach the gospel in a Western society that privileged both print and men.

1

> But, all de same Ah said thank God, Ah got another
> chance. Ah wanted to preach a great sermon about col-
> ored women sittin' on high, but they wasn't no pulpit for
> me. . . . So whilst Ah was tendin' you of nights Ah said
> Ah'd save de text for you.
>
> — Zora Neale Hurston, *Their Eyes Were Watching God*

> Her authority in the pulpit, her dance in the Clearing, her
> powerful Call (she didn't deliver sermons or preach —
> insisting she was too ignorant for that — she called and the
> hearing heard) — all that had been mocked and rebuked by
> the bloodspill in her back yard.
>
> — Toni Morrison, *Beloved*

This section's epigraphs, taken from novels written in the twentieth
century, reflect the spiritual black woman's marginalized and unrecognized place in a racially and sexually bifurcated society that consistently sought to exclude them from participating in the activities to
which they felt divinely called. Both fictional characters, created as
products of American slavery in the nineteenth century, desire a vehicle through which they can express their spiritual selves. In the
first epigraph, Nanny, the protagonist's grandmother of Zora Neale
Hurston's *Their Eyes Were Watching God*, looks to her granddaughter,
Janie, to deliver the text of the sermon for which Nanny has had
neither the time nor the pulpit to preach. In Toni Morrison's *Beloved*,
Baby Suggs, holy, is the virtual anti-preacher — unchurched, unli-
censed, uncalled, unrobed, unanointed — who is, nevertheless, willing
to preach to whomever will listen. She goes to the A.M.E.s, Baptists,
Holinesses, and Sanctifieds in the winter and preaches in the Clearing to whomever will come in the summer. Morrison's Baby Suggs
is a relevantly telling character, for through her preaching of self-
love and imagined grace, she enables disenfranchised, dislocated, formally enslaved black people to embrace themselves, as it were, their
own flesh:

> "Here," she said, "in this here place, we flesh; flesh that weeps,
> laughs; flesh that dances on bare feet in grass. Love it. Love it
> hard. Yonder they do not love your flesh. They despise it. They
> don't love your eyes; they'd just as soon pick em out. No more
> do they love the skin on your back. Yonder they flay it. And O

my people they do not love your hands. Those they only use, tie, bind, chop off and leave empty. Love your hands! Love them. Raise them up and kiss them. Touch others with them, pat them together, stroke them on your face cause they don't love that either. You got to love it, you! And no, they ain't in love with your mouth. Yonder, out there, they will see it broken and break it again. What you say out of it they will not heed. What you scream from it they do not hear. What you put into it to nourish your body they will snatch away and give you leavins instead. No, they don't love your mouth. You got to love it. This is flesh I'm talking about here. Flesh that needs to be loved. Feet that need to rest and to dance; backs that need support; shoulders that need arms, strong arms I'm telling you. And O my people, out yonder, hear me, they do not love your neck unnoosed and straight. So love your neck; put a hand on it, grace it, stroke it and hold it up. And all your inside parts that they'd just as soon slop for hogs, you got to love them. The dark, dark liver—love it, love it, and the beat and beating heart, love that too. More than eyes or feet. More than lungs that have yet to draw free air. More than your lifeholding womb and your life-giving private parts, hear me now, love your heart. For this is the prize."[7]

Baby Suggs's sermon brings to light the complex and multilayered relationship between the spoken word, the printed word, and the embodied word. As readers, we never physically see or hear Baby Suggs deliver her sermon. Morrison describes the Clearing as a "wide-open place cut deep in the woods" outlined by trees. In the center is the "huge flat-sided rock" Baby Suggs uses as a pulpit. The members of the congregation, at first, stand behind the trees, but as they look on and begin to laugh, cry, and dance as Baby Suggs commands, they come out into view. Baby Suggs's sermon celebrates black flesh in that she exhorts her interlocutors (relevant to a call-and-response oral tradition) to celebrate themselves despite what others think of or do to them. Taken a step further, her words enable the listeners to embody the Logos or, in terms of incarnational theology, the Word made flesh.

In "Moving On Down the Line," literary and cultural critic Hortense Spillers examines the literacy skills required for the churchgoer to "read" the African American sermon and constructs the following parallel after processing her experience of gazing up into the ceiling of II Duomo de San Carlo: "What the feast of the gaze is to the great churches of Europe, built in early Christian centuries with the money of the Prince, the feast of hearing is to the church of the insurgent and the dispossessed, whose 'Prince' is surrounded by clouds and darkness . . . his pavilion . . . dark waters and thick clouds." She goes on to say that "in this church of democratic forms, attested by a far humbler architectural display, the listening ear becomes the privileged sensual organ, as the sermon attempts to embody the Word."[8] In the absence of vaulted ceilings, stained glass windows, and other pleasures of the eyes, the black preacher's spoken word becomes the vehicle through which insurgent and dispossessed listeners encounter the sublime. Whether in a church building or in a clearing, preaching and the preacher are of paramount importance in black church worship. Although fictional representations, Nanny and Baby Suggs symbolize black women's historic alienation from the clerical ranks of the black church and from the act of preaching. Baby Suggs is even uncomfortable characterizing her words as homiletic or her actions in terms of preaching; she simply puts forth the Call and considers herself too ignorant to define her work as anything else.

Definitions of what constitutes preaching and the sermonic form are varied and widespread. Spillers defines the sermon in its customary social context as "the driving words of inspiration and devotion" and in its modified secular state as an urgent political address. In either case, she perceives it "fundamentally as a symbolic form that not only lends shape to the contours and outcome of African Americans' verbal fortunes under American skies, but also plays a key role in the psychic configurings of their community."[9] Literary historian Carla Peterson freely exchanges the words "sermon," "speech," "address," and "message" in her analysis of the works of nineteenth-century writers and speakers Maria Stewart and Jarena Lee.[10]

In his book *The Sermon and the African American Literary Imagination*, critic Dolan Hubbard views the black sermon as "the cultural signature of the children of the African Diaspora" and acknowledges the sermon's inextricableness from the oral context out of which it sprang. "The preacher and the people," Hubbard argues, "engaged in a dynamic exchange, transform language as they empty language and fill it anew; that is, they impose through language their moral vision of the world. Replete with drama, the classic black sermon arises out of a richly symbolic context."[11]

James Forbes defines the sermon as an organic and dynamic form relative to the Holy Spirit's involvement in the preaching moment: "The person who preaches the gospel makes a statement about the Holy Spirit just by entering the pulpit," he argues in *The Holy Spirit and Preaching*. "Even before the first word is uttered, presuppositions and definitions from across the centuries speak volumes about the Spirit-led event to be experienced by the preacher and the community of worshipers. The preaching event itself—without reference to specific texts and themes—is a living, breathing, flesh-and-blood expression of the theology of the Holy Spirit."[12]

One of the most outstanding characteristics about the preaching styles of black women preachers of the early holiness movement of the early nineteenth century was spontaneity. Jarena Lee writes in her autobiographical narrative *The Life and Religious Experience of Jarena Lee*, "I had the power to exhort sinners" and "I was aided from above to give an exhortation." At other times she says that her "stammering tongue" was "cut loose" and that the scriptures were opened to her mind right at the time of her preaching. These qualities stand in stark contrast to seminary-style preaching, which is shaped by the written expository form. Hermeneutical debates across racial lines have focused a great deal on the place of women in such sacred work. Almost as intense is the question of homiletics or the science of sermon preparation in the Greek *kerygma*, the act of preaching. For some, the Holy Spirit functions to direct the minister in the homiletical process. For others, the act of putting a sermon in written form inhibits divine inspiration. For nineteenth-century black preaching women, extemporaneous exhortation epitomized successful kerygma.

Whether a conservative or liberal concept of the sermonic form is adopted, it is hermeneutics, the science of interpreting the Holy Scriptures, and who should engage in this practice that have been most intensely debated. And although it is best to hear sermons in their original context and space, since orality is valued within African and African American cultural practices, the privileging of print is evident in a Western literary tradition. Thus early African American church officials gave credence to the written word as they sought to institutionalize religious practices. It was that process of working through their impetus to preach and to situate themselves within the preaching sphere—or the tension between impulse and institution—that yielded the black preaching women's spiritual text. The two most important components of the text are the recounting of the author's individual conversion experience and her receipt of the Call. According to critic William Andrews, as the narrators of the spiritual narrative related their conversion experiences, they recorded both the process by which they were saved from sin and the subsequent empowering effect that the appropriation of the Logos had on them when they became preachers. Such spiritual autobiographies are, therefore, much more than conversion narratives. They serve as preacherly texts, as models of the act and impact of biblical appropriation on the consciousness of the black narrators as bearer of the Word.[13]

Thus by appropriating biblical text in written form, they wrested for themselves the privilege, even the right, to interpret scripture. Their resulting preacherly texts functioned on one level as sermon, which in this instance I define as the combination of autobiographical form and black preaching rhetorical strategies that enabled black women to participate in the vocation to which they felt called. Except for places where spiritual narrators directly addressed their readers, contemporary readers are unable to experience their messages in print. In *Doers of the Word*, Carla Peterson explains the nonexistence of manuscripts as the speakers' refusal to record ecstatic language in writing. She sees the narrators as negotiating a space between "the private language of mysticism and the public language of the institutional church."[14] I read the spiritual narrator's failure to record her sermons in writing, not in terms of refusal, but in terms of her implicit understanding of the unchartable, unpredictable, and dynamic quality of classical Pentecostalism and the power of oral expression versus what is lost in a print translation. If these preaching women, as I believe they were apt to do, received their messages at the moment of delivery and refined them as dynamic works in process depending upon the audience present, they would have been unable to predict the contours of their sermons. And given the absence of electronic recording devices, retroactive transcription would have been virtually impossible.

Yet, since black preaching women spiritual narrators deemed their experiences worthy of telling and the trend among black male church officials moved toward print, the resulting autobiographical document was a narrative that combined the tenets of self-writing and spirit-writing or homiletics.[15]

2

Henry Mitchell identifies three parts of the black sermon: the introduction, in which the preachers introduce themselves and launch the biblical text; the exposition, which includes various levels of personal, social, and biblical storytelling; and the climax, which concludes the sermon enthusiastically.[16]

During a typical preaching moment in a black church worship service, the preacher approaches the pulpit, addresses the congregation and other clergy present, acknowledges God's presence, and offers any other prefatory remarks. The preacher then takes a biblical text and sometimes contextualizes the sermon with a title. In most cases, in either extemporaneous or manuscript-prepared preaching, the minister takes a deductive approach to the subject and begins with general comments that historicize the biblical reference, defines biblical terms, culture, and customs, and identifies characters. The preacher then illuminates the relevance of the text by pointing to similar contemporary events or parallel character types.[17]

The amplification of the text through storytelling and the preacher's use of the first person make black preaching particularly intimate and conducive to a call-and-response pattern with the listening congregation. When, for example, the preacher relates the story of Daniel in the lion's den or Shadrach, Meschah, and Abednego in the fiery furnace, a dialogue ensues between the speaker and the hearers, especially if the preacher effectively connects the ancient stories to contemporary scenarios. Because of the value placed on a tradition of oral expression derived from African social systems, the congregation feels comfortable giving verbal response. The lyrical and chanting style of the preacher combined with the chorus-like responses of the hearers enacts a "homiletical musicality" that theologian Evan E. Crawford argues characterizes the black preaching style.[18]

In *Interpreting God's Word in Black Preaching*, Warren H. Stewart argues further that there are five basic hermeneutical principles in good black preaching. Except for the fifth point, the methodology is applicable to oral or written sermons. Whoever interprets and preaches the Word must accomplish the following:

1. know God to be actively involved in the continuous process of humankind's holistic liberation;
2. identify with the Word in such a way that the Word will both support and challenge those to whom the message is directed;

3. allow the Holy Spirit working through his or her gifts and talents to create a living experience with the Word in himself or herself first, and then in the lives of those to whom the message is directed;
4. proclaim the Word in the common tongue of the majority of those who will hear his or her message on any given occasion;
5. proclaim the Word as dialogue with the audience and utilize the voice and body to communicate interpretively one's message and its meaning.[19]

The sermonic form of the black preaching women's spiritual narrative is two-layered. The overall structure, if we accept Mitchell's definition, is like a sermon. The narrator introduces her life-writing by taking a biblical text, uses her life as a means of expounding on the biblical theme, and climaxes with detailed descriptions of her travels—souls won, miracles performed, and prayers answered. Additionally, embedded in Julia Foote's narrative are subhomilies that carry social and political messages. The words are directed at specific audiences whom Foote admonishes to take heed to her prophetic words concerning moral behavior, child rearing, spiritual regeneration, eternal damnation, and sexism. At these critical junctures, mostly at the end of the chapters, Foote establishes a dialectic, a call-and-response dialogue between herself as preacher and her readers as congregants.

3

Julia Foote's narrative, published in 1879, was introduced by Thomas K. Doty, founder of the *Christian Harvester*, an evangelical publication that subscribed to the tenets of the Holiness movement. Although Foote's narrative does not reference her race or sex in the title, Doty explicitly does so by attesting to her worth as a person of color, a woman, and a pastor with a heart for ministerial labor. Referencing it as a postbellum narrative, Doty points out that although black people were no longer slaves, they continued to exist "under the bondage of society." Yet "Holiness," he declares, "takes the prejudice of color out of both the white and the black, and declares 'The [heart's] the standard of the man'."[20] This distinction between the worth of the soul and heart despite the condition of the body, I would argue, addresses the potential dismissal by racist and sexist critics of the worth of the work. Despite the dissolution of the slave system, the fact of this interior / exterior contrast remains a reality for black women.

For Foote, the sermonic narrative served primarily as an evangelical tool and was directed toward black people, as the preface to *A Brand Plucked From the Fire* indicates: "My object has been to testify more extensively to the sufficiency of the blood of Jesus Christ to save from all sin. Many have not the means of purchasing large and expensive works on this important Bible theme. . . . My earnest desire is that many—especially of my own race—may be led to believe and enter into rest; 'For we which have believed do enter into rest' [Heb. 4:3]—sweet soul rest."[21]

Her narrative follows the pattern established by earlier black preaching women spiritual narrators. Although some points of her natural existence are revealed—her family background, education, and marriage—they are related only in connection to her salvation and visionary experiences. In addition, each of the thirty chapters is punctuated by dogmatic commentary on the evils of worldly pleasures, admonitions to both parents on child rearing and children on obeying their parents, and various discourses on prevalent societal concerns such as racial discrimination, temperance, and capital punishment. Yet the evangelist had another motive in writing, for as the first woman to be ordained deacon in 1894 and the second woman to be ordained an elder in the African Methodist Episcopal Zion Church,[22] she was an outspoken proponent of a woman's right to preach.

Julia Foote's decision to leave the A.M.E. Church and to join and work within the A.M.E. Zion Church was complex. Initially, she did so as a result of marrying her husband, George, a sailor from Boston, and then joining the local congregation in that city, which was pastored by the Reverend Jehiel C. Beman. Foote likely would have anticipated being allowed to work freely within that local church as the A.M.E. Zion connection, long known as "the Freedom Church," boasted abolitionists and preachers like Sojourner Truth, Harriet Tubman, and Frederick Douglass. The denomination's members and pastors had been deeply involved in the work of the Underground Railroad and other aspects of achieving social justice.[23] Yet, Foote's dealings with Beman proved antagonistic from the start because of her desire to operate as a woman within the preaching ministry and to adhere strictly to the tenets of holiness. One of the most vehemently articulated portions of her narrative is titled "Women in the

Gospel" and follows her description of an emotional encounter with Beman, in which he attempted to terminate her membership from the local church and to excommunicate her from the denomination completely because of her insistence on preaching. Despite the turmoil of her early years and although nothing is known of Foote's work in the 1880s, her ministry, nevertheless, was formally recognized in 1894 within the A.M.E. Zion Church.

Julia Foote was born to free parents in 1823 in Schenectady, New York. Her father, who purchased his freedom, along with that of his wife and first child, was converted to Christianity under the Methodist Episcopal Church after his wife's harrowing experience crossing a river one night as they returned from a local dance. The "nearly fatal accident made such an impression upon their minds that they said, 'We'll go to no more dances,' and they kept their word."[24] Although Foote had her first religious impression at eight years old after a white woman came to her house and taught her the Lord's Prayer, she says that she was converted at a Sunday evening worship service. By this time, Foote and her parents had moved to Albany, New York, and joined the A.M.E. Church there.

At this place in the narrative, Foote focuses again on "worldly" dancing as key to her own conversion during her teenage years:

> The last time I made a public effort at dancing I seemed to feel a heavy hand upon my arm pulling me from the floor. I was so frightened that I fell; the people all crowded around me, asking what was the matter, thinking I was ill. I told them I was not sick, but that it was wrong for me to dance. Such loud, mocking laughter as greeted my answer, methinks is not often heard this side the gates of torment, and only then when they are opened to admit a false-hearted professor of Christianity. They called me a "little Methodist fool," and urged me to try it again. Being shamed into it, I did try it again, but I had taken only a few steps, when I was seized with a smothering sensation, and felt the same heavy grasp upon my arm, and in my ears a voice kept saying, "Repent! repent!" I immediately left the floor and sank into a seat. The company gathered around me, but not with mocking laughter as before; an invisible presence seemed to fill the place. The dance broke up—all leaving very quietly. Thus was I again "plucked as a brand from the burning."[25]

Foote's negative emphasis on dancing serves as a metaphor for the sanctified individual's alienation from the natural and material world.

For those who espoused the tenets of holiness, the problem loomed large of how to negotiate between being "in the world" but not being "of the world." Strict biblical prohibitions against "worldly" behavior warned against having a love for this world and a disregard for God's principles and his world to come. It was not just dancing that was prohibited but "worldly" dancing, practicing secular dance steps to music unsanctioned by the church and its Christian doctrine. The same was true of drinking alcohol and smoking. William Andrews phrases the problem eloquently: "The 'world' was the spiritual wilderness through which the pilgrim soul had to travel and be tested before attaining ultimate blessedness. The fewer entanglements in the world, the less likely a Christian was to veer from his or her moral and spiritual course. The question was, how radically to break with the world?"[26] Foote's friends laughing her to scorn, calling her a "little Methodist fool," and leaving her alone and alienated on the dance floor point to her future state of isolation as she attempts to fulfill her calling. As the "brand plucked from the burning," she is at the same time chosen and separated. The incident points again, as well, to the dual nature of existence faced by black women spiritual narrators, except in this case the problem is on two planes (the seen and the unseen worlds) as opposed to the interior/exterior being.

After the dance, Foote spent several days in prayer begging for mercy, but the initial conviction wore off as she returned to her usual activities. She recounts, however, that at fifteen, during the sermon at an evening worship service, an inner voice repeatedly told her, "Such a sinner as you are can never sing that new song," about which the minister was preaching. The result was Foote falling unconscious to the floor. During her stupor, she appears to have answered the voice with "Lord, have mercy on me, a poor sinner!" She writes that the inner, condemning voice ceased and a "ray of light flashed across my eyes, accompanied by a sound of far distant singing." She jumped from the bed in which she had been lying for twenty hours shouting, "Redeemed! Redeemed! glory! glory!"[27]

As is the case for black preaching women's spiritual narratives generally, Foote's narrative follows the pattern of employing images of light and white garments and troubling mental attacks that cause her to doubt the truth of her experience until she is assured through sanctification. The text reads, on one level, like the polemical works published throughout the nineteenth century by the American Sunday School Union that warned young people against disobedient and immoral behavior and instructed Sunday school teachers in the ways of effective instruction.[28] One such publication, *The Sunday-School Journal*, was directed toward teachers with a variety of articles ranging from teacher health to instruction on how to start a Sunday School to advice on parenting. For instance, on January 20, 1858, the *Journal* offered an article on "Parental Duties":

> Scripture teaches us that it is a parental duty to answer the inquiries of a child. . . . Converse, then, much with your children, wise and good parents. Read and pray much that you may be wise and good. Be not satisfied with gazing fondly upon their angel forms as they play around you, or by pressing them to your bosom when they climb upon your knees; but talk with them as you rise up and as you lie down, as you sit in the house and as you walk by the way; — and let the subject be not elegance, nor affluence, nor genius, nor honor; — but the words of God; the wonders He has done; the precepts He has taught. Shut not your eyes to their sinful nature, nor believe them incapable of injustice or unkindness; of deceit or covetousness. Withhold not due correction for grave transgression, but let solemn admonition and affectionate explanation of your motives precede the punishment; and, finally, — desire NOTHING so much as to see your beloved children renewed in heart, and devoted to the Lord.

Compare this passage with Foote's message below on child rearing:

> Children were trained very differently in those days from what they are now. We were taught to treat those older than ourselves with great respect. Boys were required to make a bow, and girls to drop a courtesy, to any person who they might chance to meet in the street. Now, many of us dread to meet children almost as much as we do the half-drunken men coming out of the saloons. Who is to blame for this? Parents, are you training your children in the way they should go? Are you teaching them obedience and respect? Are you bringing your little ones to Jesus? Are they found at your side in the house of God, on Sunday, or are they roving the streets or fields? Or, what is worse, are they at home reading books or newspapers that corrupt the heart, bewilder the mind, and lead down to the bottomless pit?[29]

In both passages, the didactic admonitions to parents call them to greater responsibility in child rearing through direct instruction. Parents are instructed to be aware of their children's behavior, to administer discipline, and to offer themselves as good examples primarily by attending church with their children. It is likely that in her work with the local church, Foote spent time with children in the Sunday School and became familiar with its publications.

Although Foote is overtly instructive, if we expand the notion of what constitutes autobiography, we find a woman fervently and ardently committed to her calling despite familial or institutional discouragement. While Jarena Lee initiates a dialogue with black men about black women in the ministry by setting up her life and body as a public example, Foote takes the message further and sermonizes on both the social ills of the day and a woman's right to preach. To do so, she risked marital stress and the threat of excommunication from the A.M.E. Zion Church.

My reading of Foote's narrative as sermon highlights the tensions between the oral and the literary and the virtual impossibilities of transposing (in a musical sense) the one to the other. As a case in point, literary scholar Dolan Hubbard quotes the late Rev. Martin Luther King Jr. as saying that "a sermon is not an essay to be read but a discourse to be heard. It should be a convincing appeal to a listening congregation. Therefore, a sermon is directed toward the listening ear rather than the reading eye."[30] Although King allowed his sermons to be recorded in print, he was "mindful that the published sermon loses much of its spontaneity, that it is apt to be read as a frozen text."[31] The same is true of attempting to describe for modern readers unfamiliar with the black church experience the building up in a service to the preached word and the preacher's subsequent rebuilding in the sermon to its climactic ending. But in the ensuing discussion, I have attempted to guide the reader carefully through the sermonic portions of the narrative as I read them.

4

Respecting Mitchell's sermonic components of introduction, exposition, and climax, Foote's narrative follows form and in some ways mirrors a live preaching moment in a church setting. In many cases, particularly if the preacher is unknown to a congregation, the pastor or another member of the church will introduce the speaker, reassuring the potentially skeptical hearers that the minister is acceptable. Doty's introduction serves this function for the narrative's readers and is directed undoubtedly to those readers unsupportive of women preachers.

Upon mounting the pulpit, as the term is used, the preacher offers prefatory remarks by acknowledging the introduction and providing the scriptural text for the sermon. In this instance, Foote abbreviates the chosen scripture, "Is not this a brand plucked out of the fire?" from a telling passage in Zechariah 3:1–4:

1 And he shewed me Joshua the high priest standing before the angel of the Lord, and Satan standing at his right hand to resist him.

2 And the Lord said unto Satan, The Lord rebuke thee, O Satan; even the Lord that hath chosen Jerusalem rebuke thee: *is not this a brand plucked out of the fire?*

3 Now Joshua was *clothed with filthy garments,* and stood before the angel.

4 And he answered and spake unto those that stood before him, saying, Take away *the filthy garments* from him. And unto him he said, Behold I have caused thine iniquity to pass from thee, and I will *clothe thee with change of raiment* (emphasis added).

Foote, who titled her sermonic autobiographical narrative *A Brand Plucked From the Fire,* assumes the persona of Joshua, who is depicted as a live coal torn from the fires of hell. In the passage, the Old Testament prophet Zechariah sees a vision in which the Lord rebukes Satan on Joshua's behalf and removes the reproach of iniquity from him as evidenced by clean clothes. The seventh verse of the passage is also relevant, for the Lord tells Joshua, "If thou wilt walk in my ways, and if thou wilt keep my charge, then thou shalt also judge my house, and shalt also keep my courts, and I will give thee places to walk among these that stand by."

Foote's narrative is then contextualized by the scriptural text as she tells the story of her birth and parentage, childhood, conversion, marriage, ministry, and trials within the scope of Zechariah's vision. The narrative climaxes with the final three sermons of chapters 28, 29, and 30 that contain topics that would be appropriate for live experiences: an outright encouragement to women to preach; an admonition to readers not to love the world and its pleasures; and a poem/hymn on how to obtain sanctification. Foote is a woman determined "to walk in the ways of God" so that her ministry will be assured prominence as a result. Thus she appropriates prophetic language and images as she reads herself into the biblical text.

The preacher achieves a lively and effective call-and-response in the midst of homiletic delivery by creating a rhythm that builds to an ultimate climax. By using her life as the basis for explicating the biblical text, Foote, as narrator and preacher, becomes the "brand" of the scripture and poses rhetorical questions at the end of specific chapters to illicit a collective reader response similar to the responses of the hearers in a live experience: "Yes! Well? That's all right! Amen! to the point of loudest praise and highest joy, Glory Hallelujah!"[32] Through the accumulation of subhomilies, Foote employs persuasive rhetoric in order to win her readership.

At the end of chapter 1, for example, Foote recounts that at the age of five, she found a bottle of alcohol and drank all of the contents. Her playmates became frightened by her drunken behavior and summoned adults who helped her become sober. She says, "I was like a 'brand plucked from the burning,'" and uses her experience as the foundation for a temperance message. "Dear reader, have you innocent children, given you from the hand of God? Children, whose purity rouses all that is holy and good in your nature?" Her questions end with an ominous warning: "No drunkard shall inherit the kingdom of heaven."[33] The same is true at the end of chapter 2, where she addresses child readers and warns them to remember God while they are young, to pray, and not to be afraid to come to Christ. Again, she poses two questions as a segue to her brief homily: "Why was Adam afraid of the voice of God in the garden? Why did he flee away, and hide himself among the trees?"[34] In chapter 6, her admonition to readers regarding dancing is made up mainly of staccato interrogations:

> Had I persisted in dancing, I believe God would have smitten me dead on the spot. *Dear reader, do you engage in the ensnaring folly of dancing? Reflect a moment; ask yourself, What good is all this dissipation of body and mind?* You are ruining your health, squandering your money, and losing all relish for spiritual things. *What good does it do you? Does dancing help to make you a better Christian? Does it brighten your hopes of happiness beyond the grave?* The Holy Spirit whispers to your inmost soul, to come out from among the wicked and be separate.[35]

For the intended audience of Foote's narrative, who were Camp Meeting attendants and probably regular churchgoers, the questions were easily answered. At stake were issues concerning societal good and moral uplift in which the collective answers were designed to gather momentum to carry the reader to her final expositions.

Chapters 17 and 18 describe Foote's call to the ministry and her subsequent divine visions, but they also detail her life of alienation. The Reverend Beman never supported her ministry and was equally antagonistic toward Foote's espousal of the doctrine of holiness. Despite Beman's jeers and snide remarks—telling Foote, "You don't know anything"—the lady preacher became popular among church members, who urged Foote to preach in private homes. Beman not only threatened those who opened their homes with excommunication, but on several occasions, he also sent a committee to confront Foote about her activities. Eventually, as Foote describes in chapter 19, he informed her that she was no longer a member of the church. Although Foote appealed to the General Conference, her inquiries were largely ignored, for she says, "it was only the grievance of a woman, and there was no justice meted out to women in those days. Even ministers of Christ did not feel that women had any rights which they were bound to respect."[36]

As was the case for several black women spiritual narrators of the nineteenth century, Foote's husband threatened to send her home or to put her in an institution because of her ardent beliefs. Shortly thereafter, he accepted an offer to go out to sea for six months. Foote describes the days of his departure as "one of close trial and great inward temptation. It was difficult for me to mark the exact line between disapprobation and Christian forbearance and patient love."[37] In her despair over her marital troubles, Foote consults her Bible and is reassured of God's divine guidance, protection, even sanction when her eyes fall on Isaiah 54:5, "For thy Maker is thine husband."

In effect, the narrative reveals a woman who endures institutional ridicule and social isolation but unfailingly pursues her right to work in ministry. The resultant text is bipolar; her adherence to both radical and feminist ideals concerning any woman's right to preach the gospel and to the controversial doctrine of sanctification and holiness positions her narrative as both a vehicle of church activism and as an evangelical tool.

By the end of the text, the momentum escalates to the sermonic apex. In chapter 28, titled "A Word to My Christian Sisters," she addresses those who lack the potential courage to follow their spiritual convictions: "Sisters, shall not you and I unite with the heavenly host in the grand chorus? If so, you will not let what man may say or do, keep you from doing the will of the Lord or using the gifts you have for the good of others. How much easier to bear the reproach of men than to live at a distance from God. Be not kept in bondage by those who say, 'We suffer not a woman to teach,' thus quoting Paul's words [1 Cor. 14:34], but not rightly applying them."[38]

She indicts the church community, accusing those in clerical ranks of loving the world at the expense of their spiritual flocks in chapter 29. As well, she calls for courage in Christian sisterhood to those women who believe they are called to preach and invites them to join with heavenly beings against church leaders who, she feels, misinterpret the Apostle Paul's words to the Corinthians:

> Dear Christians, is not the low state of pure religion among all the churches the result of this worldly-mindedness? There is much outward show; and doth not this outward show portend the sore judgments of God to be executed upon the ministers and members? Malachi ii. 7, says: "The priest's lips should keep knowledge," etc. But it is a lamentable fact that too many priests' lips speak vanity. Many profess to teach, but few are able to feed the lambs, while the sheep are dying for lack of nourishment and the true knowledge of salvation.[39]

She warns her readers against misinterpreting her position as well, asserting, "I am not teaching absolute perfection . . . but Christian perfection—an extinction of every temper contrary to love,"[40] and concludes her narrative in chapter 30 with a distinct call to her readers to become sanctified.

Many traditional black preachers incorporate familiar hymn lyrics to bring the message to a close. The frenetic timbre of the preacher's voice heightens, the excitement builds, and if the hymn is familiar, the congregation recites along with the preacher. In keeping with this style, Foote begins the final chapter with the hymn, "How to Obtain Sanctification":

> Mixture of joy and sorrow I daily do pass through;
> Sometimes I'm in the valley,
> Then sinking down with woe.
>
> Chorus: Holy, holy, holy is the Lamb
> Holy is the Lamb of God,
> Whose blood doth make me clean.
>
> Oh, come to Jesus now, and drink
> Of that holy, living stream;

Your thirst he'll quench, your soul revive,
And cleanse you from all sin.

(Chorus)

Each of the seven verses of the hymn is followed by the refrain, "Holy, holy, holy is the lamb, Holy is the Lamb of God, whose blood doth make me clean." She ends the entire narrative with the familiar chorus, "Hallelujah! Tis done! I believe on the Son; I am saved by the blood of the crucified one," a song sung often during the altar call at revivals and camp meetings and one that was well known to her audience.

Julia Foote's work is complete, both narratively and sermonically, for like the ending of a live worship service, Foote ends with a benediction, the words of the Apostle Paul to the Ephesians: "Now, unto Him who is able to do exceeding abundantly, above all that we ask or think, according to the power that worketh in us; unto Him be glory in the church by Christ Jesus throughout all ages, world without end. Amen" (Ephesians 3:20–21). The move is deliberate and the narrative self-contained. In her reliance on biblical form, Julia Foote positions her life and ministry within the possibilities envisioned by the Apostle Paul, making her potential triumphantly limitless.

14

Wisdom of the Heart
The Human Encounter with God in Pensées
and Moby-Dick

KIM PAFFENROTH

At first glance, the comparison proposed by this essay might appear counterintuitive at best, idiosyncratic and misleading at worst: there would seem to be an insurmountable number of differences and contrasts between the seventeenth-century French scientist, mathematician, and theologian, devoutly Catholic (though not necessarily orthodox), who set as his goal to write the ultimate defense of Christianity, and who lived the last years of his life as a sickly hermit; and the nineteenth-century American novelist, raised Calvinist, married to a Unitarian, who came up with his own brand of skeptical, confrontational theism, who penned perhaps the greatest and most strangely satisfying story of human beings challenging the Deity in the proudest, most outrageous, and most virile way imaginable, and

The ideas in this essay come directly from my experience teaching in the Program of Liberal Studies at the University of Notre Dame (where the students graciously tolerated my first time teaching *Moby-Dick*, and all my simplistic and repetitive interpretations), and in the Core Humanities Program at Villanova University. It never would have occurred to me to compare these two thinkers if I had not assigned them in my class on Modern Thought, and if I had not been blessed by such insightful and perceptive students, from whom I have learned much more than they from me. Special thanks also go to Dan Morehead, Tom Bertonneau, Dave Schindler Jr., and Rick Bolles, for their comments on the essay, parts of which appear in my book *In Praise of Wisdom: Literary and Theological Reflections on Faith and Reason* (New York: Continuum, 2004).

who lived his life sailing all over the world, while fathering four children. But obviously, I must now say what general similarities led me to begin to compare the works of these two men, before I get to the specifics that constitute the purpose of this essay. It would be hard to find two men more characterized by melancholy, a quality of which Melville himself says, "All noble things are touched with that."[1] And in one of the many breathtaking paragraphs scattered throughout his ponderous novel, as he is building to his comparison with the soaring mountain eagle, which, "even in his lowest swoop . . . is still higher than other birds," Melville mentions Pascal as one of those "sick men," whom one must read and understand if one is to "break the green damp mould with unfathomably wondrous Solomon,"[2] that is, if one is to conquer human mortality and limitation by confronting and defying them. But most important, what struck me as most similar between the two is that both men's ruminations on God are profoundly anthropocentric and experiential. Pascal pointedly disparages the possibility or the utility of proving the existence of God, and instead focuses on proving what kind of human nature we possess that makes a certain kind of God necessary,[3] if we are to be saved: "That is why I will not try to prove here by reasons from nature either the existence of God, or the Trinity, or the immortality of the soul, or anything of that sort . . . because such knowledge, without Jesus Christ, is useless and sterile."[4] Likewise, although *Moby-Dick* constantly tantalizes us with divine images applied to both the sea and to Moby Dick the White Whale, "the grand god,"[5] it always anchors those images in a sea of human subjectivity and brings them back to the characters' reactions and interpretations of them, as shown most vividly by the juxtaposition of the characters' reactions to "The Doubloon": "And some certain significance lurks in all things, else all things are little worth, and the round world itself but an empty cipher, except to sell by the cartload, as they do hills about Boston, to fill up some morass in the Milky Way."[6] Nothing means just one thing, but neither is anything finally or merely subjective: instead, every object, person, and event in the novel is imbued with layers upon layers of meanings that different humans intuit in different ways and at different times, showing their own essence and purpose more than that of the object they analyze. So the book is not ultimately about the White Whale or God so much as it is about why men would want to hunt the White Whale, or why they all have some unique complaint with the Deity: "so the wretched infidel gazes himself blind at the monumental white shroud that wraps all the prospect around him. And of all these things the Albino whale was the symbol. Wonder ye then at the fiery hunt?"[7] Indeed, we do not, for as Melville has created his microcosm of "Isolatoes" on board the *Pequod*, his "Anarchasis Clootz deputation from all the isles of the sea, and all the ends of the earth," there was no human reaction imaginable for them, other than to lay on and pursue that maddest and most human of goals, to "lay the world's grievances before that bar from which not very many of them ever came back."[8] And although Ahab's philosophy should not be taken as identical to Melville's own, it is one that he granted "a full and proper hearing,'"[9] and with which he is (and wishes us to be) sympathetic.[10] Ahab's obsession is extreme, but it is utterly typical of the human condition, and that is why it can become the quest of everyone on board the *Pequod*, all of the "mongrel renegades, castaways, and cannibals,"[11] every Christian, pagan, atheist, pantheist, black, white, drunk, madman, blasphemer, buffoon, innocent, or virtuous dreamer among them.[12]

So from the general similarities of melancholy, morbidity, and anthropocentrism, we will proceed in this essay to consider more specific points of similarity in Pascal and Melville's idea of how humans encounter God. Two main points will be considered: human nature as it is depicted in Pascal and Melville and their use of scripture, as they show which scriptural passages and characters best illustrate the human nature they have described. As will be shown, both writers owe much of their thought and their similarity to one another to the biblical Wisdom tradition, which each modulates and elaborates in his own unique way.

Human Nature in Pascal and Melville

It may be well to start out with Pascal's most succinct and categorical statement on human nature: "How empty, yet full of filth is the human heart!"[13] But what is really interesting is what leads Pascal to this sobering and dismal conclusion. Unlike many others (Dostoevsky comes to mind), Pascal does not arrive at this idea of human depravity by accumulating examples of moral failings or atrocities. Indeed, when he does mention immoral actions, his objection to them is more often wonder at the stupidity of such actions than outrage at their immorality: "When it is a question of deciding whether one should go to war and kill so many people, or condemn so many Spaniards to death, it is one person who decides, and he is even an interested party: it should be an impartial third party."[14] Pascal is here very much in accord with the biblical Wisdom tradition that sees evil and folly as synonymous.[15] Pascal shows this vividly in his repeated mention of "Cleopatra's nose," the beautiful shape of which senselessly caused thousands of deaths.[16] And although, as we will see later, Pascal elaborates on the physical and mental shortcomings that go along with this human wretchedness, they do not seem to be his primary evidence for it. Rather, what he points to repeatedly is an emotional or psychological problem at the center of every human being: the inability to be happy.

For Pascal, our inability to be happy is shown most clearly (and ironically) in our constant attempts to make ourselves happy, for if we were capable of true happiness, all of this activity would be unnecessary, and would even lessen our happiness:

> If our condition were truly happy, we would not need to divert ourselves from thinking about it. . . . If humanity were happy, then they would be more so, the less they were diverted, like the saints and God. Yes: but isn't someone happy who enjoys diversion? No: because it comes from elsewhere, from outside, and therefore one is made dependent, and is always liable to be troubled by a thousand accidents, and such disturbances are inevitable.[17]

Incapable of true happiness, we therefore settle for distraction from our unhappiness.[18] But besides its dependence on outside influences, which make it a fragile and vulnerable kind of happiness, a further problem with distraction is that it must inevitably end. Eventually we will win whatever game or sport we are playing, or get a great job or promotion or book contract, or have sex with the person whom we have been pursuing, or capture the animal we have been hunting, and then we will realize that what we thought we wanted doesn't make us happy at all: "We do not long for an easy, peaceful state that would allow us to think about our unhappy condition . . . but rather for the turmoil that keeps us from thinking about it and diverts us. This is the reason we like the chase better than the capture."[19] But more frightening even than this would be the possibility that our distractions would succeed in distracting us forever:

> The only thing that consoles us for our miseries is diversion, but it is also the greatest of our miseries. It is the main thing that keeps us from contemplating ourselves, and it imperceptibly makes us lose ourselves. Without it we would be bored, and

boredom would push us to look for a more secure way of escape. But diversion amuses us and imperceptibly takes us to our death. [20]

The fact that we constantly distract ourselves proves to Pascal our wretchedness, our inability to be happy. But we might be so successful at distracting ourselves that we remain unhappy (but distracted) forever: "Since our true good has been lost, everything appears equally good to us, even our own destruction, even though it is simultaneously so contrary to God, to reason, and to nature. . . . Thus we never live, but only hope to live; and since we are always preparing to be happy, it is inevitable that we should never be so."[21] Pascal here envisages an oblivion of losing ourselves in our distractions, which we should not think of as limited to such obviously self-destructive activities as drugs or gambling. What makes them more dangerous and insidious is that they might be the most normal, even necessary or admirable parts of our lives: it is our careers, relationships, and goals that threaten us the most, for they may make us so busy at becoming something that we forget to be anything at all, until it is too late.[22] (On the other hand, entertainments may not destroy us, so long as they are recognized for the occasional, temporary, and trivial things that they really are, rather than permanent distractions from who we really are.)[23]

So Pascal believes that humans are irredeemable wretches, incapable of goodness or happiness. Actually, it is not so simple as that at all. For just as our unhappiness is ironically shown by our constantly trying to make ourselves happy, so too a certain kind of nobility and greatness are shown precisely in our wretchedness:

> All of these miseries prove humanity's greatness. They are the miseries of a great lord, the miseries of a dispossessed king. . . . Humanity's greatness is so obvious that it can even be deduced from their misery. What is nature in animals, we label as misery in humans, because we recognize that, although human nature today is like that of the animals, it is because humans have fallen from a better nature which was once their own. . . . To summarize: if humanity had never been corrupted, they would innocently and with assurance enjoy both truth and happiness; but if humanity had always been only corrupt, they would have no idea either of truth or of blessedness.[24]

For Pascal, human wretchedness and greatness are inextricably related: they immediately and unambiguously imply one another. We would not be wretched if we did not have some concept of a higher purpose and meaning for our lives, a concept of which our present life falls miserably short. On the other hand, we would not be great if we were not conscious of our wretchedness, for then our present life would satisfy us and it would never occur to us to call it imperfect, unhappy, or fallen: "Thus it is miserable to know that one is miserable, but it is great to know that one is miserable."[25] Without consciousness of our wretchedness, we would accept and enjoy our mortal lives for what they are, just as (as far as we can tell) animals do. Instead, we constantly hope and strive for things we cannot achieve on our own, and fail to accomplish the things we should: only humans are capable of being less than they ought, precisely because they long to be more than they are.

If any literary character summons up the image of humanity's greatness as that of the wretchedness of a "dispossessed king," it surely would be Melville's Ahab, who is "a Khan of the plank, and a king of the sea, and a great Lord of Leviathans,"[26] while at the same time he is "a poor pegging lubber,"[27] a "mutilated,"[28] crippled, "helpless, sad . . . insane old man."[29] Ahab himself diagnoses his condition:

> Oh, Life! Here I am, proud as a Greek god, and yet standing debtor to this blockhead for a bone to stand on! Cursed be that mortal inter-indebtedness which will not do away with ledgers. I would be as free as air; and I'm down in the whole world's books. I am so rich, I would have given bid for bid with the wealthiest Praetorian at the auction of the Roman empire (which was the world's); and yet I owe for the flesh in the tongue I brag with. By heavens! I'll get a crucible, and into it, and dissolve myself down to one small, compendious vertebra.[30]

Ahab encapsulates here all that it is to be human: mortal, yet with a tantalizing concept of immortality; yearning to be free, yet utterly bound (an image much elaborated in Chapter 89, "Fast Fish and Loose Fish," and generalized there to include the whole human species); knowing what physical, mental, and spiritual glory are, and yet painfully aware of his lack of them. And exactly as Pascal focused on how humans pursue happiness, but are unable to hold on to it, we see Ahab's final expression before his fatal confrontation with Moby Dick:

> But the lovely aromas in that enchanted air did at last seem to dispel, for a moment, the cankerous thing in his soul. That glad,

happy air, that winsome sky, did at last stroke and caress him; the step-mother world, so long cruel—forbidding—now threw affectionate arms round his stubborn neck, and did seem to joyously sob over him, as if over one, that however wilful and erring, she could yet find it in her heart to save and bless. From beneath his slouched hat Ahab dropped a tear into the sea; nor did all the Pacific contain such wealth as that one wee drop.[31]

As Peleg had exclaimed earlier, "Ahab has his humanities!"[32] and one human tear is worth more than all the deadly, powerful, soulless waters of the Earth. Here is a creature who is truly and completely superior to the physical world that destroys him.

The number of classical, biblical, and renaissance archetypes Ahab's character simultaneously recollects is staggering, and they further reveal his dual nature and the dual nature of humanity that he epitomizes: Prometheus, Narcissus,[33] Osiris,[34] Satan, Adam, Cain,[35] the evil Israelite king Ahab, Jonah, Job, Faust, Don Quixote,[36] King Lear, Edmund.[37] All of these characters share the image of overstepping some boundary, reaching for something more than they ought, of disobeying a "natural" or God-given command, and suffering for it. But what makes Ahab the clearest illustration of Pascal's anthropology is the timing and causality of his condition: for most of the other literary antecedents, their dispossession, their fall from grace, happens following and as a result of their overreaching hubris and defiance of boundaries. But Ahab begins the novel as "branded,"[38] "dismasted,"[39] "dismembered,"[40] "stricken, blasted,"[41] "mutilated,"[42] an "ungodly, god-like man,"[43] presented with a universe that he cannot understand or accept: it is therefore not a question of how or why he got that way,[44] but how he will react to his condition. He is therefore more like Job and Edmund than the others, though he is a great deal more appealing than either of these two. If we admire Job for his courage, then his submission in the end seems a little disappointing, at least when considered dramatically or aesthetically, if not morally or theologically. (On the other hand, if we admire him for his patience and piety, then what is the point of the rather lengthy and repetitious middle of the book?)[45] And while we certainly sympathize with the unfairness of the world's treatment of Edmund, his murderous treachery against the people who have done their best to minimize the harm to him seems ungrateful and spiteful, not heroic. Job and Edmund border on the "unnatural" or inhuman—one heavenly so, the other diabolically so. But Ahab is utterly "natural" and human in his situation and his reaction: he lashes out at precisely the being who harmed him, the White Whale / God, and he never relents. He is as appealing and dogged in his outward directed quest as Lear is in his inner one, but while we sympathize with Lear because we all make similarly foolish mistakes and reap the terrible rewards of our actions, we admire Ahab because we are all trapped in a world that we didn't make, don't understand, and can't accept, but he actually takes up a harpoon and hobbles off to do something about it, as mad and futile as that may be: "[Ahab] realizes that the Whale cannot be destroyed, that chaos and evil can never be eliminated. [But] despite this realization, Ahab continues his struggle. Value and truth cannot be achieved in any absolute sense, but in his pursuit of them, man finds salvation."[46] We are different from him only in our lesser consciousness of life and our more craven reaction to it: most of us are content to sip "the tepid tears of orphans,"[47] or ignore "all the horrors of the half known life,"[48] while Ahab has drunk deeply of "all nature's sweet or savage impressions fresh from her own virgin, voluntary, and confiding breast," making him "one in a whole nation's census—a mighty pageant creature, formed for noble tragedies."[49] The captain of the *Pequod* clearly is wretched in his greatness, and great precisely because he is wretched.

Besides being applied to Ahab, Melville also generalizes the image of a "dispossessed king" to apply to all of humanity:

> But vain to popularize profundities, and all truth is profound. Winding far down from within the very heart of this spiked hotel de Cluny where we here stand—however grand and wonderful, now quit it;—and take your way, ye nobler, sadder souls, to those vast Roman halls of Thermes; where far beneath the fantastic towers of man's upper earth, his root of grandeur, his whole awful essence sits in bearded state; an antique buried beneath antiquities, and throned on torsoes! So with a broken throne, the great gods mock that captive king; so like a Caryatid, he patient sits, upholding on his frozen brow the piled entablatures of ages. Wind ye down there, ye prouder, sadder souls! question that proud, sad king! A family likeness! aye, he did beget ye, ye young exiled royalties; and from your grim sire only will the old State-secret come.[50]

Ahab is just the extreme, heroic, and much more insightful version of all of us: through him we now realize that we are a race of broken, conquered people, and this realization makes us even more wretched, because we now have some memory and longing for our homeland.[51]

But just as wretchedness is most clearly seen by both Pascal and Melville among the great, Melville finds human greatness most clearly displayed among the humble:

> Men may seem detestable as joint stock-companies and nations; knaves, fools, and murderers there may be; men may have mean and meager faces; but man, in the ideal, is so noble and so sparkling, such a grand and glowing creature. . . . This august dignity I treat of, is not the dignity of kings and robes, but that abounding dignity which has no robed investiture. Thou shalt see it shining in the arm that wields a pick or drives a spike; that democratic dignity which, on all hands, radiates without end from God; Himself! . . . thou just Spirit of Equality, which hast spread one royal mantle of humanity over all my kind! . . . Thou who, in all Thy mighty earthly marchings, ever cullest Thy selectest champions from the kingly commons; bear me out in it, O God![52]

This is probably the closest the book will come to conventional piety or optimism, and it comes as Ishmael is contemplating human equality and humility. Ahab has only focused on the unfairness of his life, and his reaction is blinding and self-destructive anger, an attitude typified in his mad statement, "I'd strike the sun if it insulted me,"[53] and one that cuts him off from other people, whom he now only regards as "wheels"[54] or "tools."[55] It is this inhuman treatment of others, epitomized in his refusal to help the captain of the *Rachel* search for his missing son, that is Ahab's evil side, not his challenging of the Deity: indeed, with further irony, Ahab has made himself into the very image of the cold, unfeeling, arbitrary tyrant that he accuses God of being.[56] Ishmael, on the other hand, focuses on the common lot of all humanity, as painful and meager as this might be, and it fills him with a feeling of compassionate pride in his race, so that "over any ignominious blemish in [a man] all his fellows should run to throw their costliest robes."[57] This pride in humanity, despite their seeming undeservingness, is shown also in his description of the carpenter. Right after writing that "mankind in mass . . . seem[s] a mob of unnecessary duplicates," Ishmael immediately and categorically asserts that the carpenter "was no duplicate."[58] While Ahab fits everyone interchangeably into his quest and treats them in a way that ignores their humanity and individuality, Ishmael is completely aware of everyone's uniqueness as well as their participation in a common human nature, and analyzing both of these qualities in everyone on board the *Pequod* is his quest, regarding everyone with "Stoic endurance, New Testament and democratic equality in suffering and slavery, fellow-feeling and mutual help," thereby opening him up to "the emollient effect of shared suffering, of mankind full of sweet things of love and gratitude."[59]

Pascal explains why he thinks that humans are wretched and great, and how their greatness shows their wretchedness, just as their wretchedness shows their greatness. Both he and Melville show this as the greatness of a lost state that tantalizes and plagues us with its memory, and will not leave us in the relative peace of distractions that would allow us some relief from our wretchedness: "Ahab's effort, then, is to reclaim something that man knows he has lost."[60] This concept of human nature is repeatedly shown in Melville's novel, with Ahab's consciousness of his wretchedness, and the generalization of this realization to all humanity; Ahab's superiority to the physical world, even though it can (and does) easily destroy him; and in Ishmael's discovery of the human dignity placed by God equally in all, but especially noticed in the most humble.

Pascal and Melville's Use of Scripture

Pascal uses scripture constantly, and for many different purposes. It is a frequent part of his attacks on Judaism and Islam,[61] and it is a large part of his discussion of the problematic nature of miracles, which serve both to save and to condemn.[62] But what we are interested in here is an examination of which scriptural passages and characters Pascal focuses on to illustrate and elaborate his idea of the dual nature of human beings as both great and wretched.

Pascal significantly pairs the two greatest figures of the biblical Wisdom tradition—Job and Solomon—to illustrate the dichotomy he sees at the center of human nature: "Solomon and Job have known and spoken best about human misery: one was the happiest person, the other the unhappiest; one knew by experience the vanity of pleasures, and the other the reality of pain."[63] These two men typify for Pascal the extremes of human experience—extreme and lasting pleasure and pain—and they show how at either extreme, one comes to the same conclusion about human nature: it is wretched because of its greatness, it is great because of its wretchedness.

Although he only mentions "misery" or "wretchedness" directly, it is clear from his other comments about these two figures that he thinks they show us both sides of human nature. Here Pascal has directly mentioned Solomon's realization of the vanity or emptiness of pleasure, but elsewhere he comments on the futility of great knowledge, the other quality for which David's son was known. Knowledge is vain because we only pursue it for our own pride, not to help or educate others, but only to belittle them: "Curiosity is only vanity. Usually one only wants to know something in order to talk about it."[64] It is usually vain in its object as well, pursuing knowledge of creatures rather than Creator, but this is a misguided object that Solomon was able to overcome: "David [and] Solomon never said, 'There is no vacuum, therefore there is a God.' They must have been cleverer than the cleverest of those who came after them, for all of those use such proofs."[65] Solomon realized the wretched inadequacy of human knowledge, but this is also proof of human greatness: imperfect knowledge makes one unhappy only because one retains some idea of what perfect knowledge would be. Ignorance is not bliss: "Ecclesiastes shows that humanity without God is in total ignorance and inevitable unhappiness. For one is unhappy who wills, but cannot do. Now one wants to be happy and assured of some truth, but one can neither know, nor can one stop wanting to know."[66] But Pascal believes that finally even this ignorance can be useful:

> Knowledge has two extremes which meet. The first is the pure, natural ignorance in which all people are born. The other extreme is reached by great souls who, having run through everything that humans can know, find that they know nothing, and they return to that same ignorance from which they departed; but it is a wise ignorance which knows itself.[67]

This no longer vain curiosity or knowledge that seeks to dominate others or believes that it can know everything, but a "wise ignorance," a humbled and self-reflective knowledge that knows and accepts the truths that it cannot change or ignore. It cannot finally fix the human mind, but it can take a large step in diagnosing its illness.

Likewise, in considering Job's condition, we also see how Pascal would think of him as illustrating human greatness as well as wretchedness. Twice Pascal uses the image of a reed to describe the physical frailty of humans and the enormous and fatal advantage that the physical universe has over us:

Through space, the universe grasps me and swallows me up like a speck; through thought I grasp it. . . . Humanity is only a reed, the weakest in nature, but a thinking reed. It is not necessary for the whole universe to mobilize in order to crush us: a mist, a drop of water is enough to kill us. But even if the universe were to crush us, humanity would still be more noble than their killer, because we know that we are dying, and the advantage the universe has over us. The universe knows none of this.[68]

Job was crushed by the universe, but he achieves his nobility by knowing he is being crushed, and by questioning and challenging this situation. Suffering in itself is not meaningful, but the consciousness of suffering can be, and it is where humans find their greatness, in the very teeth of physical wretchedness: "Humanity's greatness comes from knowing we are miserable. A tree does not know it is miserable. . . . One cannot be miserable without consciousness: a ruined house is not miserable. Only a human being can be miserable."[69] Job's physical suffering results in an intellectual enlightenment that is very similar to what Solomon achieved, for it results in the same kind of realization of human weakness and limitation: in the end, Job knows that he cannot know why he is suffering. As with Solomon, this results in humility, but also in hope: "For I know that my Redeemer lives."[70] Solomon and Job together show for Pascal how from totally different experiences, humans can come to the same conclusions about human greatness and wretchedness. They can realize that physical pain and pleasure are irrelevant in and of themselves, and usually outside of our control; meanwhile, the mind is usually (but not always) under our control, but it is incapable of understanding the questions of meaning and purpose in which we are so desperately interested. The human mind gives us superiority over the physical world, and it gives us a glimpse of something higher, but it cannot take us to that higher realm. Again, its function is only to diagnose our illness, as crucial a role as that might be, but not to cure it.

Pascal finds the cure in the Pauline pairing of Adam and Christ: "Adam the figure of the one that was to come."[71] Pascal will even present it as the totality of all Christian belief: "All of faith consists in Jesus Christ and Adam."[72] But what is interesting is that while we can intellectually accept this solution, we cannot understand it:

It is, however, an astonishing thing that the mystery furthest from our understanding, that of the transmission of sin, is that thing without which we can have no knowledge of ourselves. . . . We can conceive neither Adam's state of glory, nor the nature of his sin, nor the manner of its transmission to us. These are things which happened in a state of nature completely different from our own, and which go beyond our present capacities. Knowing all this is useless to our escape; all that it is important for us to know is that we are miserable, corrupt, separated from God, but redeemed by Jesus Christ.[73]

Pascal uses the scriptural pairs Job/Solomon and Adam/Christ in a way similar to how he uses the contrast between our knowledge of our own nature, on the one hand, and our knowledge of and longing for God, on the other. Pascal believes we can understand and describe our own nature, which will then point us to a knowledge of God and a longing to be with God that we will never fully understand or realize in this life. Likewise, we can understand Job and Solomon all too well, for their experiences and reflections on their experiences are all too familiar to us as humans; and their pain and inadequacy point us to the other pair of Adam and Christ as the cause and solution of this human condition, but in a way that cannot be fully understood or appreciated by us in this life. For Pascal, the human mind cannot object to Adam's sin or Christ's redemption as illogical or nonsensical, but it also cannot explain or understand these concepts. It is enough for him if it can reason inductively from particular experiences of human wretchedness and greatness—such as Job and Solomon—to the general "rule" that would explain those experiences as the result of Adam's sin, and would hope for a resolution of those experiences with Christ's redemption.[74]

Like everything else in his masterpiece, Melville's use of scripture in *Moby-Dick* is blatant and overwhelming, at the same time as it is elusive: "Melville was a great biblical unscriptural writer. Anything may be, indeed the rule of the reader's road is to expect it, inverted, pulled inside out, torn down, and reconstructed into its mirror opposite. In Melville's hands anything may happen to the biblical—almost certainly will."[75] This is perhaps best illustrated by the continuing debate over the most explicit use of scripture in the novel, Father Mapple's sermon: does Melville present it only in order to use it as "a sarcastic and sneering burlesque of Christian doctrine,"[76] or is Melville in fact expressing the "essence" of his work "through the lips of Father Mapple,"[77] and if he is, is his teaching Christian, or utterly "pagan"?[78] But while the most explicit and ambiguous instance of his use of scripture is Father Mapple's sermon on Jonah, Melville's use of the biblical Wisdom literature — especially the book of Job and to a lesser degree that of Ecclesiastes — more clearly coincides with his own anthropological and theological reflections.[79]

Melville evokes the Book of Job in the critical chapter that bears the same name as the entire novel: "Here, then, was this grey-headed, ungodly old man, chasing with curses a Job's whale round the world."[80] He signals thereby that we are to think of Moby Dick as the Leviathan from the Book of Job. He is anything but "a dumb brute,"[81] as Starbuck's sincere but inadequate piety labels him. He is the evil that God allows (or perhaps even creates), and Moby Dick/Leviathan's existence implicates God in all the evil and suffering of the world.[82] Everything that Ahab says about Moby Dick is accurate, if incomplete: "I see in him outrageous strength, with an inscrutable malice sinewing it. That inscrutable thing is chiefly what I hate; and be the white whale agent, or be the white whale principal, I will wreak that hate upon him."[83] Job could finally accept the existence of awesome, unexplainable evil and pain in the world, but Ahab cannot. Nor can he destroy it, but in the end even this goal is abandoned. At the height of his power, Ahab gives his own theology its clearest expression: "I now know thee, thou clear spirit, and I now know that thy right worship is defiance. . . . I own thy speechless, placeless power; but to the last gasp of my earthquake life will dispute its unconditional, unintegral mastery in me."[84] Ahab cannot worship God, nor does he expect an answer from God, nor does he think he can destroy either God or God's "agent," evil. He simply defies God to do anything to him other than kill him, a prospect that in no way frightens him.[85]

Equally defiant but much less insightful is the version of Job given by Stubb, who is as indifferent and carefree as ever. After giving his retelling of the biblical story, Stubb responds to Flask's ever-practical objections that Stubb could not hope to toss the devil overboard:

Damn the devil, Flask; do you suppose I'm afraid of the devil? Who's afraid of him, except the old governor who daresn't catch him and put him in double-darbies, as he deserves, but lets him go about kidnapping people; aye, and signed a bond with him, that all the people the devil kidnapped, he'd roast for him? There's a governor![86]

Stubb has neither respect nor fear for God, the devil, the whale, or anything else in creation: everything is equally irrelevant and empty for him. He cannot even bend things to his own materialistic view, the way the less intelligent Flask can, for Stubb senses there is something more there, but chooses to dismiss it with a shrug: his ignorance is willful. After one of Ishmael's deepest reflections on human meaning, he characterizes this dismissive outlook of Stubb's as less than human, "fish-like . . . always . . . jolly."[87] As we will see in his evaluation of Ecclesiastes, Melville has little sympathy for those who are "always jolly," and he cannot be presenting Stubb's viewpoint for anything other than ridicule as part of the pathetic absurdity of human pride and folly.[88] Shortly after Stubb's retelling of Job, however, Melville does present Stubb's prosaic or debased estimation of the whale's power as partially correct by quoting Job 41:7, 26–29, "Canst thou fill his skin with barbed irons? or his head with fish-spears?"[89] Even nineteenth-century technology had rendered these questions rhetorical in the opposite way than they had been to the author of Job, for men now did just these things to whales every day. But in the overall context of the novel, such an estimation of God's creation is completely inaccurate, and Melville never foresees a time when it will not be so: "however baby man may brag of his science and skill . . . yet for ever and for ever, to the crack of doom, the sea will insult and murder him."[90] Even in the body of the slain whale itself there is a reminder of the awful wonder of the world, and how pathetic are human attempts to destroy, control, or understand it. Within the whale's carcass they find a spearhead that Ishmael speculates is over four hundred years old, meaning that generations of men have died trying to kill just this one whale, a sobering testimony to how much the "governor" of this world demands respect and fear, if not love: "*Moby-Dick*, like Job, affirms the mystery of the sacred, beyond the human capacity to comprehend."[91] It is beyond our ability to comprehend, but nothing is beyond human ignorance and disrespect, capacities epitomized in Stubb.

Closer to Job's acceptance is the position of Queequeg, who by no means overlooks or approves of the brutality of God's world, but also does not question or defy it, but simply describes it in his matter-of-fact way: "Queequeg no care what god made him shark . . . wedder Fejee god or Nantucket god; but de god what made shark must be one dam Injin."[92] This admission of divine malice and inscrutability never keeps Queequeg from devoutly and innocently worshiping his own little god Yojo, nor does it keep him from calmly listening to the preaching of the "Nantucket god" at the Whaleman's Chapel, nor does it keep him from being a permanent member of "the great and everlasting First Congregation of this whole worshipping world."[93] In fact, it never troubles him in the least, for he is always "entirely at his ease; preserving the utmost serenity."[94] He is "always serene in a furious world," possessed of a "wisdom . . . that saves the innocence of Ishmael."[95] Again, this is neither naivete nor pious rationalization of God's silent brutality, but a calm and vitalizing acceptance and wonder at it.

Job is evoked again at the very end of the novel, as Ishmael refers to himself with the same verses that the four messengers give after they each report their respective disasters: "And I only am escaped alone to tell thee."[96] The encounter with God in the Book of Job very nearly destroys Job, physically and spiritually, but he can finally confront the voice in the whirlwind with "wise ignorance" and withdraw his demand for a divine accounting and responsibility. This does not, I think, deny the legitimacy of such a request (again, the middle of the book seems a colossal waste of time if this is the message), but only brackets it as a question whose necessity and inevitability we must accept, but whose unanswerability we also must accept if we are to remain either faithful or sane: like Queequeg's tattoos, which supposedly reveal the meaning of the universe, such a question captivates everyone, but remains forever undecipherable, a "tantalization of the gods."[97] But the encounter with the White Whale / God is fatal to the captain and crew of the *Pequod*, for they continue to demand an answer up to their final breath, up to the final, spiteful swing of Tashtego's hammer that smashes and pins the taunting sea hawk to the mast and so "sink[s] to hell . . . dragg[ing] a living part of heaven along with her."[98] Significantly, Ahab's final confrontation is not with a whirlwind descending from above, but with the diabolical inversion of it, as the *Pequod* and all aboard are dragged down by a silent, "sullen" whirlpool,[99] a "closing vortex"[100] that silences their protest forever. In a way, Melville outdoes the author of Job in his depiction of the outrageousness of faith: not only must one accept a God who cannot offer an account of himself and his violent, cruel creation, but one must also accept a God who remains utterly silent, and who jealously guards his silence by destroying those who dare to question him.[101] Significantly, though, Melville does offer us one character who can survive the encounter the way Job did, for Ishmael is preserved to learn something from the terrible voyage of the *Pequod*: "This unique salvation of Ishmael is essential to the theme of the novel. He alone of those on the *Pequod* has faced with the courage of humility the facts of his universe; he alone has learned to know woe without becoming mad."[102] In Melville's theology, suicidal defiance is certainly an understandable reaction to the pain of existence, but it is not the only or necessary reaction.

Let us now consider Melville's evaluation of Ecclesiastes. As he stands at the tiller, Ishmael gazes too long at the flames that consume the slaughtered whale on board the *Pequod*, and he becomes so mesmerized that he almost capsizes the ship by turning it into the wind. But this brush with death leads Ishmael to ruminate on all things mortal and empty:

> The truest of all men was the Man of Sorrows, and the truest of all books is Solomon's, and Ecclesiastes is the fine hammered steel of woe. "All is vanity." ALL. This wilful world hath not got hold of un-christian Solomon's wisdom yet. . . . But even Solomon, he says, "the man that wandereth out of the way of understanding shall remain" (i.e. even while living) "in the congregation of the dead." [Prov. 21:16] Give not thyself up, then, to fire, lest it invert thee, deaden thee; as for the time it did me. There is a wisdom that is woe; but there is a woe that is madness.[103]

Exactly as in Pascal's evocation of Solomon, Ishmael realizes that humans cannot find the solution to their mortality and wretchedness by ignoring them, but only by facing them squarely, honestly, dangerously. The danger is that this confrontation with human wretchedness will lead to madness and death, as it has with Ahab.[104] But with Ishmael, he is able to incorporate all the "vanity" and "woe" of God's world into a life that finds meaning and fulfillment in both the most joyous and the most painful of experiences: "And there is a Catskill eagle in some souls that can alike dive down into the blackest gorges, and soar out of them again and become invisible in the sunny spaces."[105] Ahab clearly has an eagle in his soul, but he has plunged forever into the gorge, or perhaps, Icarus-like, has soared too high and destroyed himself. Ishmael has the wisdom to accept the "woe" of life without anger or judgment, and he can serenely sit with Solomon, just as at the end of the novel he "float[s] on a soft and dirge-like main,"[106] the murderous ocean harmlessly surrounding him and buoying him up.

Without forcing Melville into orthodoxy with Pascal, even the Adam/Christ typology is not wholly absent from *Moby-Dick* in the figure of Queequeg. Clearly he is the antithesis to the industrialized, white characters and their rationalizing madness that is typified in

Ahab: "Opposite to Queequeg, [Ahab] is a gigantic symbol of the sickness of the self, the disease of the egoist-absolutist of Christendom. If immortal health shines in the dying Queequeg, then mortal illness festers in Ahab."[107] Queequeg possesses a "simple honest heart,"[108] and bears within himself the remnants of an innocent and more vital physical and spiritual state, from which the other characters have fallen much farther than he:[109] he is more like Adam, more like God's original creation, than anyone else on board the ship, which is itself a microcosm of the world. And without forcing Queequeg into the role of a Christ figure, it is clear that he is Christ-like in many ways: "It is Queequeg, the nonwhite, non-Christian South Sea islander, who embodies Jesus' message of love when he offers to die for Ishmael if need be and divides his 'thirty dollars in silver' with him, reversing Judas' betrayal."[110] Throughout the book, his presence is redemptive to the receptive acolyte Ishmael (who refers to himself as Queequeg's "attendant or page,"[111] as well as his "wife"[112]), starting with their first encounter: "I felt a melting in me. No more my splintered heart and maddened hand were turned against the wolfish world. This soothing savage had redeemed it."[113] By defying society and making Queequeg his friend, Ishmael is forever less of an "Isolato," for he has joined Queequeg's more wholesome and healthy state of love and acceptance.[114] Queequeg's redemption of Ishmael continues to the end of the book, as his coffin saves the narrator: "Here in the broad water-courses, the illimitable solitudes traversed by Ahab, where God's predatory sharks and menacing hawks could have ripped this lone survivor in pieces, it is the sustaining influence of Queequeg that protects Ishmael. . . . Now in his loneliest hour Ishmael is redeemed again with the peace of that same Queequeg."[115] And as Adam and Christ remain forever incomprehensible for Pascal, so does Queequeg remain for Ishmael, who can only gaze at him in "awe,"[116] just as he gazes in amazement at the stupefied predators of God's deep at the end of the book, held at bay by some vital force still emanating from Queequeg's "immortality preserver."[117] Ishmael has learned quite vividly the lessons of Job and Ecclesiastes, and he can only gratefully accept, but not comprehend, the redemption that the Christ-like Queequeg has brought to him.

Wisdom in the Encounter with God for Pascal and Melville

We have shown how the anthropology and the use of scripture to illustrate human nature are similar in *Pensées* and in *Moby-Dick*. When the simultaneously wretched and great humans in these works finally encounter God, is this encounter also similar? Allowing for the rather enormous differences in genre and style, I think it is more similar than different. For Pascal, what constitutes a true, complete, and beneficial encounter with God? "It is the heart that perceives God, and not reason. That is what faith is: God perceived by the heart, not by reason."[118] So the heart is the only organ that can truly perceive and relate to God, and Pascal says that people who understand through the heart are "wise," and see "with the eyes of the heart."[119] It is also the heart that determines the object(s) of love, and these decisions are neither reasonable nor unreasonable, they are simply of a different order or kind:

> The heart has its reasons, that reason cannot comprehend: one knows this from thousands of examples. I say that the heart naturally loves the universal being and itself, as it has accustomed itself to do so; but it can choose to harden itself against either one of these. You have rejected one and kept the other: is it according to reason that you love yourself?[120]

Self-love is therefore not unreasonable (or reasonable), but it can be unwise, for it can render one incapable of loving God or other people, and it turns one instead inward to the self, which is only partially and very provisionally worthy of love. Wisdom, on the other hand, would turn one from self-love and open one up to the proper set of valuations: "All bodies together with all minds and all their products are not worth the least impulse of charity, which is of an infinitely higher order."[121] So, having used reason to understand certain realities of human nature, Pascal believes that one should then use a different faculty of the heart to will oneself to love God and others rather than oneself. "Know thyself" is the function of reason, and is the foundation for the more important command, "Love the Lord your God, and love your neighbor as yourself,"[122] which is an act of the heart. It is also the beginning and goal of all wisdom, which perceives that connectedness to God and others is the path of true, ultimate self-preservation, as foolish and difficult as it may seem at the time.[123]

For the final word on Ishmael's experience of wisdom and God, I think we should look elsewhere than his physical redemption at the end of the book, since, after all, his life is not very much redeemed if he has only been physically saved from the marine variety of sharks to return to the terrestrial world of the bipedal variety.[124] Ishmael shows his mental and spiritual redemption much earlier, as the whole boat gazes down through the water at the deepest, most life-giving secrets of God's creation:

> Some of the subtlest secrets of the seas seemed divulged to us in this enchanted pond. . . . And thus, though surrounded by circle upon circle of consternations and affrights, did these inscrutable creatures at the centre freely and fearlessly indulge in all peaceful concernments; yea, serenely revelled in dalliance and delight. But even so, amid the tornadoed Atlantic of my being, do I myself still for ever centrally disport in mute calm; and while ponderous planets of unwaning woe revolve round me, deep down and deep inland there I still bathe me in eternal mildness of joy.[125]

Significantly, neither the monomaniac Ahab (though even he receives a similar revelation in Chapter 132, "The Symphony"), nor the unconcerned Stubb, nor the shallow Flask are privy to this revelation, but only the pious Starbuck, the virtuous Queequeg, and the curious and open Ishmael. Approached with the defiance of Ahab's egoism, God's world is a silencing and annihilating vortex that drags one into its center, which is oblivion, nothingness;[126] approached with Ishmael's innocent receptivity, his "insatiable wonder at his world,"[127] together with the simple, loving, and redemptive wisdom of his friend Queequeg, the "unwaning woe" of life becomes the storm that forever revolves around one, but can never harm or change a secret, impervious center of "eternal joy."[128] Ishmael has overcome the land/sea dichotomy that drove him to sea on the first page of the novel, for he is now and forevermore both in an "enchanted pool," and "deep inland": it is surely this joyous equanimity that has allowed him to return repeatedly to the sea and its "unwaning woe" even after his experience on board the *Pequod*.[129] Furthermore, he has also overcome and inverted the potential self-centeredness of all knowledge that he mentioned in the first chapter, the tendency to see only the self reflected everywhere, for he no longer sees "that same image [of himself] . . . in all rivers and oceans,"[130] but he now sees the ocean within himself. And for one of the few times in the novel, removed from the influence of Ahab's madness and the industrialized brutality of the whaling industry, the ocean (within or without) is not a cannibalistic hell that would vie with the horrors of Dante, but an aquatic vision of heaven that overwhelms these men with a combination of maternal and sexual love that can never be forgotten, no matter what atrocities they go on to witness or perpetrate. The "wisdom that is woe" has been neither forgotten nor ignored, but it has become a wisdom that allows Ishmael finally to be redeemed by and reconciled to God and God's creation: "he has seen that, although the whale and the creation must remain unsolved to the last, the creation is plenteous, that it contains those radiant moments, abundant with spirit, which are redemptive. . . . This response issues in the deepest kind of reconciliation with the terms of experience."[131] While this reconciliation may not be uniquely or necessarily Christian, it is nonetheless compatible with, and indeed, essential to Christianity as Pascal has defined and defended it: "To become a Christian will involve not so much acceptance by the intellect . . . of a certain set of beliefs, as a surrender of the whole personality to something . . . greater than the personality itself. It will be . . . proved by the reality of the experience which the surrender will involve."[132] Ishmael's experience seems profoundly real, for he finally has the happiness, the anchoring centeredness and rest that Pascal knew all people desperately longed for, but could never achieve through self-centered and self-destructive activity, but only through the wisdom of acceptance, humility, and love: "With wisdom comes inner peace, and with peace, true happiness."[133]

Notes

Notes to Introduction

1. See Thomas Nagel, *The View from Nowhere* (New York: Oxford University Press, 1986).

2. Valentin Weigel, *The Classics of Western Spirituality*, trans. Andrew Weeks (New York: Paulist Press, 2003), 113.

3. Augustine offers the injunction, "Do not go abroad. Return within yourself. In the inward man dwells truth," "Of True Religion," xxix. 72, *Augustine: Earlier Writings*, ed. and trans. John H. S. Burleigh (London: SCM Press, 1953), 262. In *Enneads* I.6.8, Plotinus declares, "Shut your eyes, and change to and wake another way of seeing, which everyone has but few use," *Plotinus*, 7 vols., trans. A. H. Armstrong, Loeb Classical Library, rev. ed. (Cambridge, Mass.: Harvard University Press, 1989), 1:259.

4. See, for example, August Tholuck's comments on experience in his *The Lesson Learned*, partly included in *The Spirituality of the German Awakening*, ed. and trans. David Crowner and Gerald Christianson (New York: Paulist Press, 2003), 60.

5. John Henry Newman, *Sermons, Bearing on Subjects of the Day* (London: Rivington, 1843), 135.

6. Specifically condemned by the Vatican was Edouard LeRoy's *Dogme et critique* (Paris: Bloud, 1907). The book reprinted "Qu'est-ce qu'un dogme?" which had appeared in *La Quinzaine* for April 16, 1905.

7. Karl Barth, *The Göttingen Dogmatics: Instruction in the Christian Religion*, ed. Hannelotte Reiffen, trans. Geoffrey W. Bromiley (Grand Rapids, Mich.: Eerdmans, 1991), 1:67.

8. For Barth's comments on Tholuck, see his *Protestant Theology in the Nineteenth Century: Its Background and History* (Valley Forge, Pa.: Judson Press, 1973), 511, 515. These remarks should be kept in tension with Barth's view, proclaimed in 1929, that "faith is experience, experience of life, of heart, of feeling," *The Holy Spirit and the Christian Life: The Theological Basis of Ethics*, trans. R. Birch Hoyle (Louisville, Ky.: Westminster John Knox Press, 1993), 29.

9. The point is nicely made by David Tracy in his foreword to Jean-Luc Marion's *God Without Being: Hors Texte*, trans. Thomas A. Carlson (Chicago: University of Chicago Press, 1991), ix–x.

10. The classic statement of this position is Paul Tillich, *Systematic Theology*, combined volume (Welwyn, Herts.: James Nisbet, 1968), 52. Tillich outlines the method of correlation on pages 67–73 of the same volume.

11. See Jean-Luc Marion, *God Without Being*, and John Milbank, *Theology and Social Theory: Beyond Secular Reason* (Oxford: Basil Blackwell, 1990). To the extent that it seeks to secure the possibility of revelation rather than respond to Revelation, Marion's later thought, especially in *Being Given*, has established a dialogue with correlational theology. See Marion, *Being Given: Toward a Phenomenology of Givenness*, trans. Jeffrey L. Kosky (Stanford, Calif.: Stanford University Press, 2002), Book V. For a preliminary discussion of Marion and Milbank, see Kevin Hart, *Postmodernism: A Beginner's Guide* (Oxford: Oneworld, 2004), chap. 7.

12. Eberhard Jüngel, *God as the Mystery of the World: On the Foundation of the Theology of the Crucified One in the Dispute Between Theism and Atheism*, trans. Darrell L. Guder (Grand Rapids, Mich.: Eerdmans, 1983), xiv.

13. See Barth, "The Christian's Place in Society," *The Word of God and the Word of Man*, trans. Douglas Horton (Gloucester, Mass.: Peter Smith, 1978 [1928]), 285, 274.

14. Kieran Kavanaugh and Otilo Rodriguez, trans., *The Collected Works of St. John of the Cross* (Washington, D.C.: ICS Publications, 1979), 420. Denys Turner develops a general argument against experience as a central category of western mysticism in his *The Darkness of God: Negativity in Christian Mysticism* (Cambridge: Cambridge University Press, 1995). Also see, with respect to the issue and to Turner's argument in particular, Kevin Hart, "The Experience of Non-Experience," in *Mystics: Presence and Aporia*, ed. Michael Kessler and Christian Shephard (Chicago: University of Chicago Press, 2003), 188–206.

15. T. S. Eliot, "The Dry Salvages," *Collected Poems, 1909–1962* (London: Faber & Faber, 1963), 208, 212–213.

16. Karl Rahner, "New Year Meditation," *The Great Church Year: The Best of Karl Rahner's Homilies, Sermons, and Meditations*, ed. Albert Raffelt and Harvey D. Egan (New York: Crossroad, 1994), 86.

17. See, for example, Karl Rahner, "Experience of the Holy Spirit," *Theological Investigations, XVIII: God and Revelation*, trans. Edward Quinn (New York: Crossroad, 1983).

18. Jean Moureaux, *The Christian Experience: An Introduction to a Theology*, trans. George Lamb (New York: Sheed and Ward, 1954), 370.

19. Martin Heidegger, "Phenomenology and Theology," *Pathmarks*, ed. William McNeill (Cambridge: Cambridge University Press, 1998), 45–46.

20. A particularly forceful exposition of this point is made by Karl Barth in his early essay "Fate and Idea in Theology," in H.-M. Rumscheidt, ed., *The Way of Theology in Karl Barth: Essays and Comments* (Allison Park, Pa.: Pickwick, 1986), 39f.

21. One of Moureaux's warmest admirers, Hans Urs von Balthasar, argues that the subjective and the objective evidence for God converge exactly: the experience of faith and theological realism are not, for him, at variance. See his *The Glory of the Lord, 1: Seeing the Form*, ed. Joseph Fessio, S.J., and John Riches (San Francisco: Ignatius Press, 1982).

22. G. M. Hopkins, "The Principle or Foundation," in *The Note-Books and Papers of Gerard Manley Hopkins*, ed. Humphrey House (London: Oxford University Press, 1937), 304–305.

23. Von Balthasar, *Seeing the Form*, 475.

24. Ibid., 222. He refers to Jean Moureaux's study in a note to this sentence.

25. Edmund Husserl, *Logical Investigations*, 2 vols., trans. J. N. Findlay (London: Routledge and Kegan Paul, 1970), 11, 540.

26. These are the translations offered by Macquarrie and Robinson and then by Richardson. See Heidegger, *Being and Time*, trans. John Macquarrie and Edward Robinson (Oxford: Basil Blackwell, 1973), 172, and William J. Richardson, S.J., *Heidegger: Through Phenomenology to Thought* (The Hague: Martinus Nijhoff, 1974), 64.

27. Augustine, *On the Trinity*, trans. Arthur West Haddan, in *The Works of Aurelius Augustine*, 15 vols., ed. Marcus Dods (Edinburgh: T & T Clark, 1873), 7:378.

Notes to Chapter 1

1. A phenomenology is always concerned with the precise sense of appearing, with the structure of phenomenality, rather than the objective reality of an appearance. Minimally, it would bracket a causal or realist account of experience and adhere closely to a descriptive account, without being in principle committed to a Husserlian theory of "consciousness" and the primacy of the cognitive, as the history of phenomenology after Husserl testifies. In the case of the scriptures, it would concentrate on the "sense" of a faith that can move mountains rather than worrying about its objective physical or metaphysical possibility, on the sense of the angel Gabriel's "Annunciation to the Virgin Mary" rather than whether the evangelist records an actual historical episode.

2. Given the plurivocity of the word "impossible," it would be arbitrary to restrict the notion of the impossible to the objectivistic sense of a simple

logical contradiction, which is but one of its many meanings. Some things, for example, are possible for women that are impossible for men, possible for the wealthy or strong that are impossible for the poor or weak, or possible for God that are impossible for human beings; this last sense plays an important role in this paper.

3. *Kierkegaard's Writings, VII, Philosophical Fragments, or A Fragment of Philosophy and Johannes Climacus, or De Omnibus dubitandum est*, trans. and ed. Howard and Edna Hong (Princeton: Princeton University Press, 1985), 37. Kierkegaard's pseudonyms constitute clear antecedent figures in the history of phenomenology: what else are their descriptions of freedom, possibility, anxiety, despair, etc. than phenomenologies *avant la lettre*?

4. Joseph T. Shipley, *The Origins of English Words* (Baltimore: Johns Hopkins University Press, 1984), "per III," 304.

5. The name of God is not primarily a matter for philosophical or theological speculation but an historical expression in which a community articulates how "God" has entered into the structure of its everyday life—its births and deaths, joys and sorrows. Its primary sense is found in its use, in a greeting—"God be with you"—or a prayer—"O God"—before its occurrence in any philosophical treatise. The name of God will flourish as long as there are such communities, and the speculations of the philosophers and theologians about this name will always be parasitic upon these practices. Philosophers have neither the means nor the authority to ban its use; their main role is to respond to the learned despisers of this name. As William F. Nietmann says, in a religious language, the name of God is not something requiring justification or explanation, but something that is invoked in the face of the meaninglessness of life. See his *The Unmaking of God* (Lanham, Md.: University Press of America, 1994).

6. *De possest*, No. 59; see the translation of *De possest* in Jasper Hopkins, *A Concise Introduction to the Philosophy of Nicholas of Cusa*, 3rd edition (Minneapolis: Arthur J. Banning Press, 1986). In *De possest*, Nicholas of Cusa is content to show the coincidence of possibility and actuality in God: *posse est, posse / esse, possest*, where God is the actuality of every possibility. But in *On the Vision of God (De visione dei)*, he ventures further to show that God is also the coincidence of necessity and impossibility, since God by the necessity of his infinite being is capable of what is impossible for us. There he writes, "I thank You, my God, for disclosing to me that there is no other way of approaching You than this way which seems to all men, including the most learned philosophers, altogether inaccessible and impossible. For You have shown me that You cannot be seen elsewhere than where impossibility appears and stands in the way. And You, O Lord, who are the Nourishment of the full-grown, have encouraged me to do violence to myself, because impossibility coincides with necessity." See Jasper Hopkins, *Nicholas of Cusa's Dialectical Mysticism, Text, Translation, and Interpretive Study of De Visione Dei*, 3rd ed. (Minneapolis: Arthur J. Banning Press, 1988), no. 39.

7. I do not think that Ricoeur's attempt to distinguish a phenomenology of essences from a hermeneutic of historical texts and cultures can stand up; see Paul Ricoeur, "Experience and Language in Religious Discourse," *Phenomenology and the Theological Turn: The French Debate*, ed. Dominique Janicaud et al. (New York: Fordham University Press, 2000), 127–146.

8. One can say this without a trace of supercessionism, for in stressing love the New Testament is just being as Jewish as possible, despite the polemics of the new "Way" against the older Jewish traditions. See E. P. Sanders, *Jesus and Judaism* (Philadelphia: Fortress, 1985).

9. The *phronimos*, for example, knows as well as any reader of scripture that not everything is under his control and that he can only be praised or blamed for the things that are up to him. As for the rest, he leaves that up to *moira* or "the gods," which are an essential element (over and above his own virtue) in what he calls *eudaimonia*. *Eudaimonia*, which we usually translate as "happiness," means have a "good spirit," like a "guardian angel," accompany you through life and protect you from fortune's more outrageous turns. You need the good fortune not to be born stupid, ugly, poor, or dispositionally unlovable, or all of these at once, and to enjoy good luck as life goes on. A good *daimon* bears a resemblance to the loving hand of what the Scriptures call "God" watching out for the least among us, or what Jesus called his *abba* keeping a loving care over us, but within a framework governed not by love but by luck, by the shifting tides of happenstance, catching a break in the cosmic twists and turns.

Notes to Chapter 2

1. The divine Dynamis (Power) is the Holy Spirit. "For Paul grace means power, an otherly power at work in and through the believer's life, the experience of God's Spirit." James D. G. Dunn, *Jesus and the Spirit* (Philadelphia: Westminster, 1975), 202–203.

2. Cf. Augustine, *On Grace and Original Sin* and Letter 186 for his teaching on the *posse*, the *velle*, and the *agere*.

3. The title of one of Ernst Bloch's works, *Man on His Own* (New York: Herder & Herder, 1970) captures the Promethean spirit of "modern man" who relies only on his own resources.

4. The Acta of Orange II were unfortunately not available to theologians for centuries, a loss that was a factor in Luther's claim that whole areas of Christendom had become infected with what might be called "Neo-Semipelagianism!" It seems that Aquinas became aware of this issue when he read the later works of Augustine, *De dono perseverantiae* and *De praedestinatione sanctorum*.

5. Mircea Eliade, *Cosmos and History: The Myth of the Eternal Return* (New York: Harper Torchbooks, 1959), 160.

6. Joseph Rickaby, *Of God and His Creatures: An Annotated Translation of the Summa Contra Gentiles of Saint Thomas Aquinas* (Westminster, Md.: Carroll Press, 1950), 239–240.

7. For Aquinas, if we want to throw compliments God's way, we should begin with God's creatures. If taken, this sage advice might have helped later theologians to avoid their excessive celebrations of God's "arbitrary omnipotence."

8. Cf. Josef Pieper, *Guide to Thomas Aquinas* (Notre Dame, Ind.: University of Notre Dame Press, 1962).

9. Karl Rahner, "The Experience of a Catholic Theologian," *Communio: International Catholic Review* 11, no. 4 (1984), 409. English translation by Peter Verhalen.

10. Cf. R. R. Reno, *The Ordinary Transformed: Karl Rahner and the Christian Vision of Transcendence* (Grand Rapids, Mich.: Eerdmans, 1995).

11. Cf. Johannes Baptist Metz, *Christliche Anthropozentrik: Ober die Denkform des Thomas von Aquin* (Munich: Kosel-Verlag, 1962).

12. Karl Rahner, *Theological Investigations* (New York: Seabury, 1975), 13:4.

Notes to Chapter 3

1. "What would happen if one woman told the truth about her life?" Muriel Rukeyser asked in an essay about the German artist Käthe Kollwitz. "The world would split open," she answered. Kollwitz, who was among the first visual artists ostracized by the Nazis, was known for her intimate depictions of dignity, endurance, suffering, and death. Muriel Rukeyser, "Käthe Kollwitz," in *In Her Own Image: Women Working in the Arts*, ed. Elaine Hedges and Ingrid Wendt (Old Westbury, N.Y.: Feminist Press), 266, as quoted in Bettina Aptheker, *Tapestries of Life: Women's Work, Women's Consciousness, and the Meaning of Daily Experience* (Amherst: University of Massachusetts Press, 1989). Compare Adrienne Rich's similar depiction of "the truths we are salvaging from / the splitting-open of our lives" in her oft-cited poem, "Transcendental Etude [1977]" in Adrienne Rich, *The Fact of a Doorframe: Poems Selected and New, 1950–1984* (New York: Norton, 1984), 266. Note that both Rukeyser's and Rich's phrases tacitly contrast the agency of women who "tell" or "salvage" world-splitting truths to depictions of women whose consciousnesses or subjectivities have been split—passive, that is, partially muted, elided, or not represented—under oppression and gender-stratified cultures.

2. Mary Daly, *Beyond God the Father: Toward a Philosophy of Women's Liberation* (Boston: Beacon Press, 1973), 33.

3. "i found god in myself & i loved her / i loved her fiercely" in Ntozake Shange, *for colored girls who have considered suicide / when the rainbow is enuf* (New York: Macmillan, 1977; Bantam Books ed., 1980), 67.

4. See Rebecca S. Chopp's argument that feminist theological discourses must be construed, in part, "as attempts to rend and renew the social-symbolic order" in *The Power to Speak: Feminism, Language, God* (New York: Crossroad, 1989), 116.

5. Rosemary Radford Ruether explains, "The use of women's experience in feminist theology, therefore, explodes as a critical force, exposing classical theology, including its codified traditions, as based on male experience rather than on universal human experience." *Sexism and God-Talk: Toward a Feminist Theology* (Boston: Beacon Press, 1983), 13.

6. See, for example, Nelle Morton, "The Rising Woman Consciousness in a Male Language Structure [1971]," in her *The Journey Is Home* (Boston: Beacon Press, 1985), 11–39.

7. See, for example, Beverly Wildung Harrison, "Theological Reflection in the Struggle for Liberation," in *Making the Connections: Essays in Feminist Social Ethics*, ed. Carol S. Robb (Boston: Beacon Press, 1985), 235–263.

8. On difference in feminist theologies, see, for example, part 1 of *The Power of Naming: A Concilium Reader in Feminist Liberation Theology*, ed. Elisabeth Schissler Fiorenza (Maryknoll, N.Y.: Orbis Books, 1996).

9. For example, Mary McClintock Fulkerson argues, "When it relies upon appeals to women's experience as the origin or evidence for its claims, feminist theology cannot account for the systems of meaning and power that produce that experience," *Changing the Subject: Women's Discourse and Feminist Theology* (Minneapolis: Fortress Press, 1994), vii. Her critique is not directed toward the use of experience "in consciousness-raising groups, domestic shelters, or other settings where subjectivities of self-confidence are being formed." Rather, she directs her critique to academic settings, specifically challenging the appeal to experience in the "production of knowledge." "Experience," she contends, "is not the origin of theology in the sense of the evidence for our claims, but the reality that needs to be explained. I call upon feminists and all theologians to do the work of explaining by connecting their claims with the systems of discourse and social relations that produce them" (vii).

10. Beverly Wildung Harrison makes this argument in "Feminist Thea(o)logies at the Millennium: 'Messy' Continued Resistance or Surrender to Post-Modern Academic Culture?" in *Liberating Eschatology: Essays in Honor of Letty M. Russell*, ed. Margaret A. Farley and Serene Jones (Louisville, Ky.: Westminster John Knox Press, 1999), 156–171.

11. This remove is especially true of later generations of white U.S. and European feminists, less of womanist and mujerista theologians, and least of theologians working in most other global contexts.

12. William James made a similar point in his classic *Varieties of Religious Experience* (1902). For James, focusing on religious experience was a way to eschew religious dogmatism and authoritarianism. He excluded from his study "second-hand religious life," namely pieties that were merely imitated and dogma that had simply been inculcated. He assumed the complexity of a blooming, buzzing, aching, and exalting universe and the capacity of humans to engage it in diverse and profound ways. As James construed it, religious experience properly understood is the most complex of engage-

ments with the universe, demanding that one go beyond mere received conventions of belief and morality, beyond mass preferences to reach a profoundly individual response. This response entails apprehending an ambiguous universe as nevertheless to be reverenced, feared, awed, and consented to at the core of one's person. For James, religious experience is a profoundly individual matter that yet opens up to the widest realms of existence, and requires consenting to the universe on terms other than the individual's own. See especially pp. 21–58 in James, *The Varieties of Religious Experience: A Study in Human Nature*, introduction by Reinhold Niebuhr (New York: Collier Books, 1961). To look beyond mere imitation and mass preference is, of course, more than a matter of method; it is a matter of life. If we fail to attend to experience, we not only risk supplanting communion with imitation, thereby dulling down human life, as James recognized, we also risk severing the root of protest. We who live on the other side of the twentieth century's genocide and totalitarianisms from James ought to be especially mindful of this danger. Moreover, a techno-consumer globalizing culture presents new dangers for supplanting a rich engagement with the world with consumption and imitation, and for dulling our iconoclastic sensitivity. James himself remained focused on individual experience to the exclusion of questions about how to situate ourselves meaningfully and responsibly in history and cultures and before God. (Reinhold Niebuhr made this point in his 1961 introduction to James's book.) He was neither particularly suspicious of possible distortions nor curious about how "individual" experiences were also social ones—that is, shaped and located culturally, politically, historically, economically, and so forth.

13. The treatment of the circulation of experience offers a sort of rough and ready phenomenology. It is influenced by William James and other American thinkers who have described the varieties of religious experience and also somewhat by feminist "phenomenological" strands that can be traced to Simone de Beauvoir's *The Second Sex* (note her use of Merleau-Ponty), rather than by the phenomenologies of Heidegger, Husserl, and later followers. Phenomenologically speaking, my approach is descriptive, not constitutive. That is, I am interested in lived experiences and what appears in them rather than trying to give a transcendental account of the structure of consciousness. Moreover, my approach has decided hermeneutical and materialist bents (i.e., experience as entailing an interaction with what I have referred to as the "stuff" of life).

14. When early feminist theologians used experience, they mainly referred to the latter kind, the clotted kind, experiences that could be scrutinized. They often referred to experiences that had been raised to consciousness, and as such were able to reveal how women's lives were constrained and distorted by assumptions about gender, race, sex, culture, religion, and so forth. A famous *Ms.* magazine article of the 1970s described the phenomenon of women coming to critical consciousness about what they had under-

gone as the "click" of experience. In a sense, their own experiences didn't click, that is, they didn't really "have" their own experiences until they came to a meaningful interpretation of what they had undergone with the help of gender, race, and cultural critiques. By contrast, many classic treatments of religious experience have focused on experience as a flow, as the immediacy of undergoing. I think of Rudolf Otto's *The Idea of the Holy: An Inquiry into the Non-Rational Factor in the Idea of the Divine and Its Relation to the Rational,* trans. John W. Harvey (London: Oxford University Press, 1923), as well as James's *Varieties of Religious Experience.* James treated the varieties of religious experience he studied as evidence of human psychological functioning and of a complex universe. He looked to the accounts of religious "geniuses" to provide the best evidence, the most original interactions with the universe and the divine. The first generation of feminist theologians looked for commonalities in women's experiences and used these as testimonies against dominant assumptions. Whereas James assumed the most individual experiences to be the most original and the most corporate experiences to be the most derivative, feminists have assumed a complex interaction between "personal" and "political," as the now famous aphorism goes. They implicitly assumed a complex interaction of individual and social-cultural even at the level of what we undergo. Note that my essay has narrated an experience of the sort to which James might typically have turned—rather than giving an account of consciousness-raising, the sort of experience to which feminists often turned—but I am now turning to a social interpretation of it.

15. Note that the reason for marking the edges of "an experience" is not to isolate it from the flow of experiencing, but rather to better describe its relations with this flow of experience—including perhaps other demarcated "experiences"—and the stuff of life. The point of marking off "experiences" is not to somehow segregate pure, unambiguous touchpoints of the holy, but rather, as I suggest below, to enable one to sift through the ambiguity of what we undergo.

16. In other words, the intense center itself is not so much extracted from memory, as it is reconstructed from images, tenors, sensibilities, insights, and convictions—rudimentary interpretations, as it were—that memory holds. The interactions that gave rise to the images, sensibilities, etc., are not themselves retained, a point that mystics and existentialists alike have made in relation to the ecstatic or event-character of experience. And yet, by reconstructing "experience" from the rudimentary interpretations left in its wake in the memory, one does again approach the relations with the stuff of life that gave rise to the original experience, although these relations will always already have been changed by virtue of having already been interpreted.

17. Patricia Hampl, *I Could Tell You Stories: Sojourns in the Land of Memory* (New York: Norton, 1999), 18.

18. Although Hampl explores more conventional written autobiographies, her observation that to tell a true story about one's experience is to

wrestle with more expansive questions can be extended to what might be referred to as "autobiographical" religious practices. Augustine's *Confession* and the practice of confession in Christian churches through the ages (at its best) involve the admission of personal and corporate failures and inabilities in light of promises of abundant mercy and trustworthiness. In Black churches' practice of testimony, to tell one's experience true is to speak at once of one's struggles and / or triumphs and also of God's sustenance.

19. Saint Augustine, *Confessions*, trans. by R. S. Pine-Coffin (New York: Penguin Books, 1961), Book X, Chapter 16, 222–223. See also Hampl, "The Invention of Autobiography: Augustine's Confessions," 166–183.

20. Ruth Harris, *Lourdes: Body and Spirit in the Secular Age* (New York: Viking Penguin, 1999), 162.

21. Ibid., 164.

22. Ibid., 365.

23. Ibid., 366.

24. Bernadette's simplicity was conveyed—articulated, if you will—by her comportment, her limited but insistent messages to the priests, and images of her kneeling in ecstasy in the grotto.

25. Franz Werfel, *The Song of Bernadette* (London: Hamish Hamilton, 1942), 6, as quoted in Harris, *Lourdes*, 366.

26. Harris, *Lourdes*, 366.

27. Ibid., 286.

28. Ibid., 356.

29. Ibid., 287.

30. Ibid., 366.

31. Émile Zola, *Lourdes*, trans. Ernest A. Vizetelly (London: Chatto & Windus, 1894; reprint ed., Amherst, N.Y.: Prometheus Books, 2000), x. See Harris's discussion of Zola's novel in her chapter 10, especially 331–339.

Notes to Chapter 4

1. Womanist, a named coined by Alice Walker in *In Search of Our Mothers' Garden: Womanist Prose* (San Diego: Harcourt Brace Jovanovich, 1983), has been embraced by black female scholars in the United States and other countries. Among religious scholars it signifies a concern for black women and their entire community.

2. bell hooks, *Yearning: Race, Gender, and Cultural Politics* (Boston: South End Press, 1990), 28.

Notes to Chapter 5

1. See William James, *The Varieties of Religious Experience: A Study in Human Nature* (London: Collins, 1960), esp. lectures XVI and XVII.

2. Friedrich Schleiermacher, *On Religion: Speeches to Its Cultured Despisers*, trans. John Oman (New York: Harper & Row, 1958), 43.

3. Karl Rahner, *The Great Church Year: The Best of Karl Rahner's Homilies, Sermons, and Meditations*, ed. Albert Raffelt and Harvey D. Egan (New York:

Crossroad, 1994), 86. Also see "The Experience of God Today," *Theological Investigations*, XI, trans. David Bourke (London: Darton, Longman and Todd, 1974), 153.

4. Karl Rahner, *Foundations of Christian Faith: An Introduction to the Idea of Christianity*, trans. William V. Dych (New York: Crossroad, 1982), 20. See also "The Experience of God Today," 153.

5. I. A. Richards, *How to Read a Page: A Course in Effective Reading with an Introduction to a Hundred Great Words* (London: Routledge and Kegan Paul, 1943), 21–22.

6. St. Augustine, *The Confessions*, trans. Henry Chadwick (Oxford: Oxford University Press, 1991), IX. x. 25. Cf. Plotinus, *Enneads*, 1.6.7–9. Augustine speaks of ascent to the "unchangeable truth" as late as *The Trinity*, XII.5.

7. John M. Quinn, O.S.A., "Mysticism in the *Confessiones*: Four Passages Reconsidered," *Augustine: Mystic and Mystagogue*, ed. Frederick van Fletchen, Joseph C. Schnaubelt, O.S.A., and Joseph Reino (New York: Peter Lang, 1994), 269.

8. G. W. F. Hegel, *Lectures on the Philosophy of Religion*, 3 vols., ed. Peter C. Hodgson, trans. R. F. Brown et al. (Los Angeles: University of California Press, 1984–85), 1:227. In 1824 Hegel speaks instead of a "counterthrust," 1:322.

9. Ibid., 1:258. Also see *Phenomenology*, 800.

10. Karl Barth, *Church Dogmatics*, II.i, trans. T. H. L. Parker et al. (Edinburgh: T & T Clark, 1957), 178.

11. Karl Barth, "Biblical Questions, Insights, and Vistas," *The Word of God and the Word of Man* (London: Hodder and Staughton, 1935), 94.

12. Karl Barth, *The Göttingen Dogmatics: Instruction in the Christian Religion*, ed. Hannelotte Reiffen, trans. Geoffrey W. Bromiley (Grand Rapids, Mich.: Eerdmans, 1991), 1:67. Much later Barth observes, "A confession of faith, religious experience as such, is good. There is no faith without experience. But a candidate for the ministry speaks of faith, not of experience as such. He gives an answer to what he has heard of the Word of God," *Karl Barth's Table Talk*, ed. John D. Godsey (Edinburgh: Oliver and Boyd, 1963), 38.

13. Also see in this regard an essay by Barth's Catholic admirer, Hans Urs von Balthasar, "Experience God?" *New Elucidations*, trans. Mary Theresilde Skerry (San Francisco: Ignatius Press, 1986).

14. Eugene Ionesco's play contains a very funny stretch of dialogue about a man ringing the doorbell and not appearing when the door is opened. See Ionesco, "The Bald Soprano," in *Four Plays*, trans. Donald M. Allen (New York: Grove Press, 1958). Emmanuel Levinas invests the dialogue with philosophical seriousness in his "Phenomenon and Enigma," *Collected Philosophical Papers*, trans. Alphonso Lingis (The Hague: Martinus Nijhoff, 1987).

15. Anselm, "On the Incarnation of the Word," in *Trinity, Incarnation and Redemption: Theological Treatises*, ed. Jasper Hopkins and Herbert Richard-

son, rev. ed. (New York: Harper & Row, 1970), 10. Schleiermacher quotes from Anselm in the epigraph to his *Der christlich Glaube* (1821–22): "Neque enim quaero intelligere ut credam, sed credo ut intelligam. Nam qui crediderit, non experietur, et qui expertus no fuerit, non intelliget."

16. George P. Schner argues that "experience" assumes methodological significance in theology only in the twentieth century. I think this overlooks the influence of Schleiermacher. However, Schner is quite correct to underline the importance of "experience" in twentieth-century theology and his taxonomy of different appeals to experience is useful. See his "The Appeal to Experience," *Theological Studies* 53 (1992): 40–59.

17. Marcus Borg argues that the basileia bespeaks Jesus' spiritual experience. See his *Conflict, Holiness and Politics in the Teaching of Jesus* (New York: Mellen, 1984), 261. As will become clear, I find his position unconvincing.

18. On the importance of open commensality as a sign of the basileia, see John Dominic Crossan, *Jesus: A Revolutionary Biography* (San Francisco: HarperSanFrancisco, 1994), 66–74.

19. The second edition of the OED lists sixty-three senses of the preposition "of." Also see John Hollander, "Of of—The Poetics of a Preposition," *The Work of Poetry* (New York: Columbia University Press, 1997), 96–110.

20. In his eighteenth homily on Luke, Origen observes that "the word 'answer' does not mean the give and take of ordinary conversation, but the teaching found in the Scriptures," Origen, *Homilies on Luke, Fragments on Luke*, trans. Joseph T. Lienhard (Washington, D.C.: Catholic University of America Press, 1996), 78.

21. Filip Müller, *Eyewitness Auschwitz: Three Years in the Gas Chambers*, literary collaboration by Helmut Freitag, ed. and trans. Susanne Flatauer (New York: Stein and Day, 1979), 29.

22. See Jean Louis Chrétien, "The Wounded Word: Phenomenology of Prayer," in *Phenomenology and the "Theological Turn": The French Debate*, ed. Dominique Janicaud et al. (New York: Fordham University Press, 2000), 158.

23. Simone Weil, *The Notebooks of Simone Weil*, 2 vols., trans. Arthur Wills (London: Routledge and Kegan Paul, 1956), 1:205. Later she observes, "Attention: non-active action of the divine part of the soul upon the other part," 1:262. In the second volume she adds, "The highest ecstasy is the attention at its fullest," 2:515.

24. Kieran Kavanaugh and Otilo Rodriguez, trans., *The Collected Works of St. John of the Cross* (Washington, D.C.: ICS Publications, 1979), 534.

25. Eberhard Jüngel, *God as the Mystery of the World: On the Foundation of the Theology of the Crucified One in the Dispute between Theism and Atheism*, trans. Darrell L. Guder (Grand Rapids, Mich.: Eerdmans, 1983), 32.

26. My expression "counterexperience" needs to be distinguished from Jean-Luc Marion's use of the word. For Marion, the counter experience

suspends the constituting "I" and turns it into a "me" that can only stand as a witness to bedazzlement. I agree with this general movement, though I do not posit a "saturated phenomenon": the counterexperience, as I understand it, is not a preamble to faith but is conducted by faith. On Marion's understanding, the counterexperience is strictly phenomenological, not theological. See his *Etant donné* (Paris: Presses Universitaires de France, 1997), 296–303.

27. See Francis Ponge, "Le verre d'eau," *Le Grand Recueil*, 3 vols (Paris: Gallimard, 1961), 2:114–167.

28. Augustine, *The Trinity*, trans. Stephen McKenna (Washington, D.C.: Catholic University of America Press, 1963), 12:5.5. Weil notes, "The way of ascent, in the *Republic*, is that of degrees of attention," *Notebooks* 2:527.

29. Weil, *Notebooks* 2:527. She adds, "The Spirit is attention," 2:628.

30. Maurice Blanchot, "Affirmation (desire, affliction)," *The Infinite Conversation*, trans. Susan Hanson (Minneapolis: University of Minnesota Press, 1993), 121.

31. The most thorough account of chiliasm in the patristic age is Charles E. Hill, *Regnum Caelorum: Patterns of Millennial Thought in Early Christianity*, 2nd ed. (Grand Rapids, Mich.: Eerdmans, 2001).

32. See H. A. Drake, ed., *In Praise of Constantine: A Historical Study and New Translation of Eusebius' Tricennial Orations*, University of California Publications: Classical Studies, vol. 15 (Los Angeles: University of California Press, 1976), 3:5; and Augustine, *City of God*, 20.9; 18.29.

33. I discuss Kant's account of the basileia in detail in "Kingdoms of God," in *Kant after Derrida*, ed. Philip Rothfield (Manchester: Clinamen Press, 2003).

34. Friedrich Schleiermacher, *The Life of Jesus*, ed. Jack C. Verheyden, trans. S. Maclean Gilmour (Mifflintown, Pa.: Sigler Press, 1997 [1975]), 234.

35. See David Friedrich Strauss's criticisms of this aspect of Schleiermacher in *The Christ of Faith and the Jesus of History: A Critique of Schleiermacher's The Life of Jesus*, trans. Leander E. Keck (Philadelphia: Fortress Press, 1977), 103–106.

36. Godsey, ed., *Karl Barth's Table Talk*, 47.

37. Augustine, *The Trinity*, VIII.8.12. Augustine returns to the theme in XV.3.

38. See my essay, "Forgotten Sociality," in *Discerning the Australian Social Conscience*, ed. Frank Brennan (Sydney: Jesuit Publications, 1999), 53–71, 368–372.

Notes to Chapter 6

1. See Jean-Luc Marion, "The Saturated Phenomenon," in *Phenomenology and the "Theological Turn,"* ed. Dominique Janicaud et al. (New York: Fordham University Press, 2000), 176–179. I have considered this in some

detail in my "Respect and Donation: A Critique of Marion's Critique of Husserl," *American Catholic Philosophical Quarterly* 71, no. 4 (1997): 523–538.

2. So again, at stake here is phenomenality per se (see previous note).

3. All of the same issues are analyzed in Marion's "The Saturated Phenomenon."

4. I have critically analyzed this in much more detail in my *Speech and Theology: Language and the Logic of Incarnation* (New York: Routledge, 2002), chaps. 2 and 5.

5. Cf. Derrida's discussion of "prayer" precisely in relation to the question of predication in "How to Avoid Not Speaking: Denials," in *Derrida and Negative Theology*, ed. Toby Foshay and Harold Coward (Albany: SUNY Press, 1992), 73–142. For further discussion, see my "Between Predication and Silence: Augustine on How (Not) to Speak of God," *Heythrop Journal* 41 (2000): 66–86.

6. This is a curious position, since it seemed to be precisely the "mediated" character of "experience" (proper) which led Hart to conclude that God could not be the "object" of experience. And yet here, he is happy to posit a different "medium"—what Marion might call a "screen"—which somehow does not compromise the alterity of God. If God can be "revealed" through a medium (in this case, faith), then must we not reconsider the rejection of "experience" simply because it involves "mediation?" I hope to return to this below.

7. This is related to what Alvin Plantinga and others, following Calvin, describe as the noetic effects of sin, which undergirds the reformational critique of natural theology. See, for instance, Alvin Plantinga, "Reason and Belief in God," in *Faith and Rationality*, ed. Alvin Plantinga and Nicholas Wolterstorff (Notre Dame: University of Notre Dame Press, 1983), 34ff., and more recently, *Warranted Christian Belief* (Oxford: Oxford University Press, 2000), chap. 7. What I am suggesting here is that there is a phenomenological correlate to this, what we might describe as the "perceptual" effects of sin. I hope to pursue this further elsewhere.

8. Kevin Hart, *Trespass of the Sign* (Cambridge: Cambridge University Press, 1989). Hart's book was one of the first I read in the field and remains one of the first that I recommend to my students.

9. I have considered this in more detail in my "Taking Husserl at His Word: Towards a 'New' Phenomenology with the Young Heidegger," *Symposium: Journal of the Canadian Society for Hermeneutics and Postmodern Thought* 4 (2000): 89–115.

10. I provide a much fuller consideration of this in chapter 2 of *Speech and Theology*, in a section on "Phenomenology as Respect."

11. My thinking on this is informed by the work of Herman Dooyeweerd, who argues that part of the structure of human being is what he calls the "pistic aspect" or faith mode, which is integral to being human. See, for instance, Dooyeweerd, *In the Twilight of Western Thought: Studies in the Pre-*

tended Autonomy of Philosophical Thought, ed. James K. A. Smith (Lewiston, N.Y.: Edwin Mellen, 1999).

12. Edmund Husserl, *Cartesian Meditations*, trans. Dorion Cairns (Boston: Kluwer, 1993), 122. This is characteristic of every external perception (ibid.; cf. I §44). Husserl then "applies" this to "the case of experiencing someone else."

13. Ibid., 129.

14. I have catalogued a number of passages from *Ideen I* that suggest this in my "Respect and Donation," 535–536 (see esp. 190).

15. I am alluding here to Derrida's analyses of intuition in *Memoirs of the Blind*.

Notes to Chapter 7

1. Translator's note: Throughout this translation, I have rendered the French *autrui*, the personal other, as "the Other" and the French *autre*, the generic other, as "other."

2. Translator's note: See "The Thing" in *Poetry, Language, Thought*, trans. Albert Hofstadter (New York: Harper & Row, 1971).

3. Translator's note: The French *sentir* has been rendered with the English "sensibility." Another possible translation would be "feeling," which has the advantage of being more grammatically ambiguous as to its transitive or intransitive status. I decided ultimately against "feeling" because in ordinary English usage "feeling" is in fact less ambiguous and lacks cognitive or significative content. It is additionally strongly associated with Schleiermacher's notion of "religious feeling"—a notion that Lacoste criticizes forcefully in his *Expérience et Absolu*. I do however use the phrase "God felt in the heart" to render the French "Dieu sensible au coeur," since in this case Lacoste appears to invoke the notion he criticizes.

Notes to Chapter 8

1. Lacoste rarely uses this word "secular," seeming to prefer terms better suited for discussion with phenomenology. One finds this, for instance, in the initial pages of his *Expérience et Absolu* (Paris: PUF, 1994), where the ego is defined by a deep "inherence" anchoring us in the world, which we tend to accept as the essential environment of all meaning. The text goes on to argue for a more originary non-inherence hidden or buried behind the ego and its trappings.

2. The terms "intrinsicist" and "extrinsicist" come from Maurice Blondel. The former designates the view that desire for the triune God is natural, whereas the latter designates the view that we are possessed of a distinctly natural end and a distinctly supernatural end.

3. M. Heidegger, "Phänomenologie und Theologie" (1927), in *Wegmarken* (Frankfurt: Klostermann, 1967), 32. Needless to say, one may attempt to answer such questions in the affirmative, holding the theology can remain

entirely free of such contaminations. According to Hart and Maraldo, Heidegger himself flirts with this view, perhaps under the influence of Bultmann, but also Barth. See M. Heidegger, *The Piety of Thinking*, trans. and ed. J. Hart and J. C. Maraldo (Bloomington: Indiana University Press, 1976), Part II, § 6 of the *Commentary*, 108–112.

4. Cf. M. Heidegger, *History of the Concept of Time: Prolegomena*, § 11, trans. T. Kisiel (Bloomington: Indiana University Press, 1992), 102–107.

5. As it happens, for Lacoste himself, early Heidegger and late Heidegger are separated only by a hiatus in a single pathway. For close discussion, see §§ 2–5 of *Expérience et Absolu*.

6. Perhaps this use of the Heideggerian *Gefahr* is not evident in the published text of "Liturgy and Coaffection." It was an explicit feature of the oral presentation, as well as in discussion afterward.

7. The argument is not absent from "Liturgy and Coaffection," but stated more explicitly in *Expérience et Absolu*, § 29, 92–93.

Notes to Chapter 9

1. Samuel E. Balentine, *The Hidden God* (Oxford: Oxford University Press, 1984), 117.

2. Ibid., 120.

3. Ibid., 153.

4. Ibid., 155.

5. Paul Moyaert, "On Faith and the Experience of Transcendence," in *Flight of the Gods*, ed. I. L. Bulhof and L. ten Kate (New York: Fordham University Press, 2000), 381.

6. Balentine, *The Hidden God*, 123.

7. Ibid.

8. Ibid., 124.

9. Ibid.

10. Ibid.

11. Ibid., 135.

12. Ibid., 164; cf. Samuel Terrien, *The Elusive Presence: Toward a New Biblical Theology* (New York: Harper & Row, 1978), 262.

13. Ibid., 165.

14. Leora Batnitsky, "On the Suffering of God's Chosen," in *Christianity in Jewish Terms*, ed. T. Frymer-Kensky, David Novak, Peter Ochs, David Fox Sandmel, and Michael A. Signer (Boulder: Westview Press, 2000), 205.

15. E. Levinas, "Useless Suffering," in *The Provocation of Levinas: Rethinking the Other*, ed. R. Bernasconi and D. Wood (London: Routledge, 1988), 160.

16. Ibid., 161.

17. Ibid., 159.

18. Ibid.

19. Balentine, *The Hidden God*, 175.

20. The translation loses it somewhat. In "talking to God" there is no direct object, and reflexive verbs take no direct object. *On s'adresse a,* "one addresses oneself to . . ."—it is as if the one who speaks becomes the one who is placed in question by that very speaking.

21. Zvi Kolitz, *Yosl Rakover Talks to God* (London: Jonathan Cape, 1999), 3–4.

22. E. Levinas, "Loving the Torah More Than God," in Kolitz, *Yosl Rakover Talks to God,* 80. See G. Agamben, *Remnants of Auschwitz* (Cambridge, Mass.: Zone Books, 1999).

23. E. Berkovits, *Faith After the Holocaust* (New York: Ktav, 1973), 136. Howard Wettstein gives a worthwhile account of the attendant difficulties in "Against Theodicy," *Judaism* 50, no. 3 (Summer 2001): 341–350.

24. Kolitz, *Yosl Rakover Talks to God,* 9–10.

25. Ibid., 9.

26. Berkovits, *Faith After the Holocaust,* 136.

27. Kolitz, *Yosl Rakover Talks to God,* 18.

28. Ibid., 24.

29. Moyaert, "On Faith and the Experience of Transcendence," 381–382.

30. Ibid., 382.

31. Ibid., 383.

32. Kolitz, *Yosl Rakover Talks to God,* 18.

33. Levinas, "Useless Suffering," 163.

34. Levinas, "Loving the Torah," 80.

35. Ibid., 81.

36. Ibid.

37. Ibid.

38. Ibid., 82.

39. E. Levinas, *Totality and Infinity* (The Hague: Martinus Nijhoff, 1979), 58.

40. Ibid.

41. Ibid.

42. Ibid., 78.

43. Ibid.

44. Ibid., 79.

45. Ibid.

46. Ibid., 54.

47. For a fuller and detailed treatment of this, see F. Ciaramelli, "The Posteriority of the Anterior," in *Graduate Faculty Philosophy Journal* 20, no. 2, and 21, no. 1 (1997): 409ff.

48. Levinas, *Totality,* 153.

49. Ibid., 171.

50. Ibid., 169–170.

51. Levinas, "Loving the Torah," 82.

52. See E. Levinas, "The Temptation of Temptation," in *Nine Talmudic Readings*, (Bloomington: Indiana University Press, 1994), 30–50.

53. Levinas, "Loving the Torah," 81.

54. Levinas, *Totality*, 58–59.

55. Levinas, "Loving the Torah," 82–83.

56. Ibid.

57. Ibid., 82.

58. Ibid., 83.

59. Ibid.

60. Ibid.

61. Ibid., 85.

62. Ibid., 81.

63. Batnitsky, "On the Suffering of God's Chosen," 215.

64. Ibid., 216, quoting R. Rubenstein, *After Auschwitz: Radical Theology and Contemporary Judaism* (New York: Bobbs-Merrill, 1966), 153.

65. Ibid., 218.

66. Ibid.

67. Ibid.

68. I consider that there is much purchase here with the Pauline notion of suffering somehow "making up what is lacking in the suffering of Christ."

69. Levinas, "Useless Suffering," 159.

Notes to Chapter 10

1. Gershom Scholem, *On the Kabbalah and Its Symbolism*, trans. Ralph Manheim (New York: Schocken Books, 1965), 117.

2. Levinas, it seems, resigns "incarnation" to the dustbin of sentimentality.

3. Johannes-Baptist Metz, *Faith, History, and Society: Towards a Practical Fundamental Theology.*

4. Such an idea has been variously construed by von Balthasar and Moltmann as an intratrinitarian event—the alienation of God from God.

5. Julian of Norwich, *Revelations of Divine Love*, trans. Elizabeth Spearing (New York: Penguin Books, 1998), 67.

6. Julian, *Revelations*, 71.

7. Cornel West, "Restoring Hope," Public Address to Villanova University, January 2000.

8. Julian, *Revelations*, 69.

Notes to Chapter 11

1. Edith Stein was born into a Jewish family in Breslau, the old capital of Silesia, in 1891, and later studied phenomenology and wrote her dissertation (*On the Problem of Empathy*, 1916) under Edmund Husserl's direction. From 1917 to 1919 she served as Husserl's "Lady Assistant" and edited a number of important works, including *Ideas II* and his lectures on internal

time consciousness. In 1922 her habilitation thesis was published in Husserl's famous *Jahrbuch*. Following her conversion to Christianity, Edith Stein was baptized and confirmed into the Catholic Church in early 1922; she taught German language and literature for eight years at St. Magdalena College, a small Dominican Sisters training institute for women teachers, in Speyer. In 1932 she was able to procure a teaching position in Munster, where she developed an outline for "Catholic education" at the German Institute for Scientific Pedagogy. Two semesters later she was forced to resign when the anti-Semitic laws of Hitler's National Socialist Party went into effect in January 1933. On October 14, 1933, Stein entered the Order of Discalced Carmelites in Cologne. She professed perpetual vows as Sister Benedicta of the Cross on April 21, 1938.

2. Following the terrible events of Kristallnacht, Edith Stein crossed the German border under the cloak of darkness on December 31, 1939 and sought refuge at a Carmelite convent in Echt, Holland. There she wrote the final redactions to her most mature theological and philosophical works, including *Finite and Eternal Being*, *The Science of the Cross*, her autobiography, *Life in a Jewish Family*, and the essay that is the subject of this article, "The Symbolic Theology of Dionysius the Areopagite and Its Objective Presuppositions." On August 2, 1942, Edith Stein and her sister, Rosa, were forcibly taken from their convent in Echt and transported to the Drente-Westerbork Camp, barracks 36. She was sent by train to Auschwitz, where she and Rosa died in a gas chamber on August 9, 1942. On October 11, 1998, Edith Stein was canonized a saint by Pope John Paul II.

3. See Steven Payne's notes on the discovery and reconstruction of Stein's correspondence with Marvin Faber regarding the *Journal of Philosophy and Phenomenological Research* in "Ways to Know God," *Knowledge and Faith: The Works of Edith Stein* (Washington, D.C.: ICS Publications, 2000), 8:xiii–xiv.

4. This was the title of Stein's article published in *The Thomist* in 1946.

5. Edith Stein studied phenomenology with Husserl, first at Göttingen and later at Freiburg, and was a vibrant member of the Göttingen circle of friends who gathered around Husserl.

6. The implications to Stein's rejection of what she believed was Husserl's Idealist position will be explored later. For now, I wish only to alert the reader to Edith Stein's rejection of Idealism. See Edith Stein, *Self Portrait in Letters*, trans. Josephine Koeppel, O.C.D. (Washington, D.C.: ICS Publications, 1993), 5. The original letter was published by Ingarden in *Philosophy and Phenomenological Research* 23 (1962).

7. For a "reversal" of Husserl's position, as opposed to a model of "modification," I would point to Emmanuel Levinas's rejection of the very principle of intentionality, as presented in *Totality and Infinity*.

8. For this line of argument, I am indebted to Carol Gilligan, *In a Different Voice: Psychological Theory and Women's Development* (Cambridge, Mass.: Harvard University Press, 1996).

9. The words "numinous" and "mysterium tremendum" come to mind here. Of course, concerning what is genuinely other we must "bear always in mind that these expressions do not hit with precision, but merely hint at what is really meant." See Rudolf Otto, *The Idea of the Holy* (London: Oxford University Press, 1958), 50ff.

10. Following Husserl, Edith Stein agrees that my knowledge of the Other as other is constituted in the order of cognition. But she would disagree with Husserl by arguing, along with Scheler, that the order of experience is even more primordial than that of cognition.

11. Edith Stein hints at this important modification of Husserl's position in section three of the last chapter of her dissertation, "The Constitution of the Person in Emotional Experiences." She does not, however, draw out its consequences.

12. Of course, even for Kierkegaard the human person is a synthesis of the finite and the infinite, just as for Sartre the Self is always in some sense constituted as a for-itself by "the look" of the Other. Here, Stein is following a Schelerian model.

13. Edith Stein, *On the Problem of Empathy*, trans. Waltraut Stein, *The Collected Works of Edith Stein* (Washington, D.C.: ICS Publications, 1989), 3:18.

14. Manfred Frings, *Max Scheler: A Concise Introduction into the World of a Great Thinker* (Pittsburgh: Duquesne University Press, 1965), 136.

15. It should be noted, however, that the thematic of "reciprocity" is a theme that Husserl also explores to a great extent in his own writings on intersubjective constitution.

16. Catherine Baseheart, who wrote the first serious critical exposition of Stein's work in English, in fact chose "person-in-the-world" for her title. While it is beyond the limits of this paper, I think a worthwhile comparison between Edith Stein and Karl Rahner would be in order, precisely on this theme of the prethematic in Stein's philosophical anthropology. These two authors share much in common.

17. Edith Stein, "Ways to Know God," from *Knowledge and Faith* (Washington, D.C.: ICS Publications, 2000), 104.

18. In traditional existential psychoanalysis, the therapist offers a "master-student" model in which feelings and actions can be properly evaluated by the patient. This does not present an empathic I-Thou relationship of co-equality, but may instead emphasize such issues as dependency, fear, and anxiety.

19. The parallel to Levinas's critique of Husserl's theory of constitution is striking.

20. Stein, "Ways to Know God," 104.

21. The other great Spanish mystic of the sixteenth century, St. Ignatius of Loyola, called this experience of God "desolation."

22. Pseudo-Dionysius, *Celestial Hierarchy* III.1.

23. Karl Rahner, *Foundations of Christian Faith* (New York: Crossroads, 1985), 81.

24. Stein, "Ways to Know God," 87.

25. See Pseudo-Dionysius's discussion of this topic in "Mystical Theology," in *Patrologia Graeca*, ed. Migne, 1033–1034.

26. Stein, "Ways to Know God," 88.

27. This is an important distinction to make, though a full defense of this statement is beyond the limits of this paper. My argument is that Emmanuel Levinas offers a more radical reversal—even a rejection—of the very principle of intentionality, whereas Edith Stein remains in agreement with Husserl as to the general significance of constitution.

28. Stein, "Ways to Know God," 114.

29. Although Stein uses the imagery of the person being "seized" by God, it does not *necessarily* carry with it the same sense of violence that accompanies Levinas's image of being seized by the *tout autre*.

30. Soren Kierkegaard, *The Sickness Unto Death*, ed. Howard and Edna Hong (Princeton: Princeton University Press, 1980), 131.

31. Stein, "Ways to Know God," 116–117.

32. Ibid., 130.

33. Ibid., 125.

34. As Levinas and Derrida demonstrate so well, the experience of *tout autre* violates Husserl's phenomenological description of inner time consciousness. Thus, the "wholly Other" is impossible to constitute. It is my contention that Edith Stein offers a somewhat similar critique of Husserl on precisely this same point.

35. I am here offering my own terminology by use of the word "mineness." What I mean to infer is that, either the Other comes from outside the sphere of ownness, or the Other is constituted by the sphere of ownness. If the latter, then the Other cannot be said to be "wholly" other; if the former, then we again arrive at Husserl's conclusion that radical alterity cannot be constituted. Stein points us to a third possibility, namely, that foreign experience is not constituted, but constitutive, that the "person" (in Stein's rich sense of the word), is fundamentally and essentially oriented toward transcendence.

36. Stein, "Ways to Know God," 89.

37. Ibid., 125.

38. Ibid., 124.

39. This line of argument is presently under consideration by several leading Catholic phenomenologists (including Jean-Luc Marion). See his *God Beyond Being* for a more thorough analysis.

40. Stein, "Ways to Know God," 124.

41. Ibid., 127.

42. Ibid., 98–99.

43. Stein, *On the Problem of Empathy*, 96.

44. Stein, "Ways to Know God," 125.

45. Ibid., 124.

46. Ibid., 127.
47. Ibid., 106–107.
48. Ibid., 108.
49. Ibid., 114.

Notes to Chapter 12

1. *Physics* B III, 194b.

2. E. Husserl, *Ideas Pertaining to a Pure Phenomenology and a Phenomenological Philosophy*, First Book, § 103.

3. Needless to say, this reaction to idolatry does not originate in Christianity but Judaism, which moreover furnishes the evident substance of that reaction in Paul's own thinking. The invisible God worshipped in the Jewish Shema (Deut 6:4) implies a critique of worldly reason that cuts much more deeply than any Greek discomfort with anthropomorphism. To be sure, both of these elements are present in Paul's thinking, but it is the Shema that he would recite daily, already in his youth.

4. See L. Feuerbach, *The Essence of Christianity*, trans. G. Eliot (Amherst, N.Y.: Prometheus, 1989), 120.

5. P. Berger, *The Sacred Canopy: Elements of a Sociological Theory of Religion* (New York: Doubleday, 1967), 25–27.

6. E. Fromm, *Psychoanalysis and Religion* (New Haven: Yale University Press, 1950), 21ff.

7. John of the Cross, "The Ascent of Mount Carmel," III, in *The Collected Works of John of the Cross*, trans. K. Kavanaugh and O. Rodriguez (Washington, D.C.: Institute of Carmelite Studies, 1979), 217ff.; and F. Nietzsche, *Twilight of the Idols*, VII, in *Twilight of the Idols and the Antichrist*, trans. R. J. Hollingsdale (New York: Penguin Books, 1968), 47–54.

8. Recall Nietzsche's famous remark, "We are not rid of God because we still believe in grammar," *Twilight of the Idols*, 35.

9. Nietzsche, *Sämtliche Werke: Kritische Ausgabe* (KA), ed. G. Colli and M. Montinari, 7:126.

10. Developed as a defining insight in M. Merleau-Ponty, *Eloge de la philosophie* (Paris: Gallimard, 1953).

11. J.-L. Marion, *The Idol and the Distance*, trans. T. Carlson (New York: Fordham University Press, 2001), 72–73. Cf. J.-L. Marion, *God Without Being*, trans. T. Carlson (Chicago: University of Chicago Press, 1991), 38. In both instances Marion's crucial reference is KA VIII / 3, 323, 17, §5. These are the preferred moments in Marion's reading of Nietzsche. Near the end of *God Without Being* (p. 183), he returns to defining idolatry by "the assurance of an object that is defined precisely by the preeminence of a subject" in a manner that seems to suddenly forget the lessons of his encounter with Nietzsche.

12. It was this that interested Heidegger, Marion's authority for reading Nietzsche. In an interpretation that resembles Nietzsche's position as much

as it "corrects" it, Heidegger's own meditation on chaos leads him increasingly away from any theological inflection in his work. Cf. E. Brito, "Connaissance du chaos. Heidegger et Nietzsche, "in *Revue théologique de Louvain* 29 (1998): 457–483, esp. 475ff.

13. This theme lies at the heart of J.-L. Chrétien, *The Unforgettable and the Unhoped For*, trans. J. Bloechl (New York: Fordham University Press, 2002).

14. M. Huot de Longchamp, *Lectures de Jean de la Croix. Essai d'anthropologie mystique* (Paris: Beauchesne, 1984), 476.

15. John of the Cross, "The Ascent of Mount Carmel," II, 26, 8; in *The Collected Works*, 195. The following citation comes a section later, and at the bottom of the same page of the translation.

16. Ibid., II, 8, 11, 124–125.

17. The theme of the passion of Jesus Christ as exemplar of humility recurs throughout Christian mysticism, but seems to have faded from view without our having noticed it. A different, moral exemplarity is certainly more familiar to many people, even if they do not grasp its proper root in the mystical notion. It is tempting to blame this phenomenon on Nietzsche, who does not hide his contempt for the imitation of Christ (cf. *Twilight of the Idols*, X, 4, 69), but the reduction of religion to morality underway at least since Kant is already enough to explain this phenomenon.

18. Cf., e.g., Nietzsche, *Ecce Homo: How One Becomes What One Is*, II, 7–8 trans. W. Kaufmann, in *On the Genealogy of Morals / Ecce Homo* (New York: Random House, 1967), 251–253.

19. Heidegger's interpretation of conscience and singularization exploits the semantic link between *Stimme* (voice) and *Stimmung* (mood). The fundamental mood (*Grundstimmung*) of anxiety is at once an affect that permeates Dasein and the voice that calls it to itself. M. Heidegger, *Being and Time*, §§ 57–58, trans. J. Stambaugh (Albany, N.Y.: SUNY Press, 1996), 253–258.

20. Cf. E. Levinas, *Otherwise Than Being or Beyond Essence*, trans. A. Lingis (The Hague: Martinus Nijhoff, 1981), 163–165.

21. Cf. Marion, *God Without Being*, 132–138.

22. J.-L. Chrétien, *L'antiphonaire de la nuit* (Paris: L'Herne, 1989).

23. For commentary, cf. G. Morel, *Le sens de l'existence de après Saint Jean de la Croix* (Paris: Aubier, 1960), 2:176ff.

Notes to Chapter 13

1. Joel 2:28. All biblical references are to the King James Version.

2. Lee's text was first published in 1836, establishing hers as the first autobiography written and published by a black woman in the United States. William Andrews, ed., *Sisters of the Spirit: Three Black Women's Autobiographies of the Nineteenth Century* (Bloomington: Indiana University Press, 1986), 27–48. She later published *Religious Experience and Journal of Mrs. Jarena Lee, Giving an Account of Her Call to Preach the Gospel in 1849*. Henry Louis

Gates Jr., ed., *Spiritual Narratives* (New York: Oxford University Press, 1988).

3. 2 Corinthians 3:5.

4. Zechariah 3:2.

5. 1 Samuel 7:12.

6. For a fuller discussion of the literary conventions of spiritual autobiography, see Daniel Shea, *Spiritual Autobiography in Early America* (Princeton, N.J.: Princeton University Press, 1968).

7. Toni Morrison, *Beloved* (New York: Penguin Books, 1987), 89.

8. Hortense Spillers, "Moving on Down the Line," *American Quarterly* 40, no. 1 (1988): 84.

9. Ibid., 86.

10. Carla Peterson, *Doers of the Word: African-American Women Speakers and Writers in the North (1830–1880)* (New York: Oxford University Press, 1995).

11. Dolan Hubbard, *The Sermon and the African American Literary Imagination* (Columbia: University of Missouri Press, 1994), 6.

12. James Forbes, *The Holy Spirit and Preaching* (Nashville, Tenn.: Abingdon, 1989), 19.

13. William Andrews, *To Tell A Free Story* (Urbana: University of Illinois Press, 1988), 64, my emphasis.

14. Peterson, *Doers of the Word*, 80.

15. It should be noted that I use spirit-writing as Holy Spirit–led writing to define homiletics as opposed to spiritualist automatic writing.

16. White seminary-style preaching differs in that the sermon begins with a pronouncement of the biblical text, moves to an exposition of the text, and culminates with "the inevitable trinity-of-points-plus-climax." Henry Mitchell, 178.

17. My characterization of black church worship comes from over thirty years' experience as an active member of two black Baptist churches and a predominantly black Pentecostal church. In an unpublished paper titled "The Preaching/Singing Voice: When Watching Religious Television Is Not Like Attending a Black Church" (December 1987), I observed and recorded the components of several black worship services, which typically include the choir's processional, opening prayer, morning hymn, scripture reading, choir selection(s), altar prayer, announcements and welcome to the visitors, the sermon, the invitation to salvation, closing remarks, and benediction. I have also spoken extensively with Rev. James Stawlings of the Board of National Ministries of the American Baptist Churches U.S.A., Inc.

18. Crawford attributes this term to Jon Spenser, who uses it to describe black preaching as a legacy of West African sensibilities in *The Hum: Call and Response in African American Preaching* (Nashville, Tenn.: Abingdon, 1995). See also Jon Spenser, *Sacred Symphony: the Chanted Sermon of the Black Preacher* (New York: Greenwood Press, 1987).

19. Warren H. Stewart Sr., *Interpreting God's Word in Black Preaching* (Valley Forge, Pa.: Judson Press, 1984), 71–72.

20. Julia Foote, *A Brand Plucked From the Fire*, 164.

21. Ibid., 163.

22. Like the A.M.E. Church, the A.M.E. Zion Church originated as a dissenting body from the John Street Methodist Episcopal Church in New York City. Also like their counterparts in Philadelphia, the black population of the predominantly white church had risen to over 40 percent, but the members were consistently devalued and discriminated against. Historian C. Eric Lincoln notes that in 1796, at the urging of Peter Williams, a former slave employed by the church, several members decided to create their own separate church. By 1800, the black dissenters had built their own building. It was not until twenty years later, however, that the A.M.E. Zion Church established its own Discipline and became an independent denomination, choosing not to affiliate themselves under Bishop Allen and the A.M.E. Church because of a dispute over Allen's exercising too much jurisdictional latitude in their area.

23. C. Eric Lincoln and Lawrence H. Mamiya, *The Black Church in the African American Experience* (Durham, N.C.: Duke University Press, 1990), 58.

24. Foote, *A Brand Plucked From the Fire*, 167.

25. Ibid., 178.

26. Andrews, *Sisters of the Spirit*, 12.

27. Foote, *A Brand Plucked From the Fire*, 180.

28. Established in 1817 as the Philadelphia Sunday and Adult School Union and renamed in 1824, the American Sunday School Union was one of many unions established during the nineteenth century to reach out to abandoned and disadvantaged youth throughout the country. The Union's publications fell in three categories: tracts and presentation or reward books; periodical literature; and textbooks and curricular materials. The publications shared four commonalties, to relate the purpose of the Sunday School and to establish the relation of the Sunday School to the local church, to the broader denomination (where relevant) and to the changing society. The Free Library of Philadelphia Rare Book Department has the most extensive collection of the American Sunday School Union's holdings. Also, for the history of nineteenth-century Sunday schools, see Rev. Galbraith Hall Todd, *The Torch and the Flag* (Philadelphia: American Sunday School Union, 1966) and Anne M. Boylan, *Sunday School: The Formation of an American Institution, 1790–1880* (New Haven: Yale University Press, 1988).

29. Foote, *A Brand Plucked From the Fire*, 172.

30. Quoted in Hubbard, *The Sermon and the African American Literary Imagination*, 8.

31. Ibid.

32. Crawford has created a sermon evaluation form that documents phrases drawn from the repertoire of congregational responses to the preacher. He says that "the aim is to encourage a constructive response, with a bit of playfulness and freedom of the black church heritage." Ultimately, the preacher wishes to move the congregation from praying "Help 'em Lord" to shouting "Glory Hallelujah!" 15–23.

33. Foote, *A Brand Plucked From the Fire*, 168.

34. Ibid., 170.

35. Ibid., 178, emphasis added.

36. Ibid., 207.

37. Ibid., 197.

38. Ibid., 227.

39. Ibid., 231.

40. Ibid., 232.

Notes to Chapter 14

1. Herman Melville, *Moby-Dick*, ed. H. Hayford and H. Parker (New York: Norton, 1967), Chapter 16, "The Ship," 68. All page references are to this edition.

2. Ibid., Chapter 96, "The Try-Works," 355.

3. Cf. L. Kolakowski, *God Owes Us Nothing* (Chicago: University of Chicago Press, 1995), 124, who finds the most prominent proofs in the *Pensées* are those "we come across when we turn our attention, not to stars and plants, not even to prophecies and miracles, but to ourselves, to our spiritual constitution."

4. Pascal, *Pensées* (Garden City, N.Y.: Doubleday, 1961), fragment 556 (449), my translation. All quotations from Pascal are my translation. The first number refers to the fragment number (hereafter abbreviated "fr.") in the Brunschvicg edition, and the number in parentheses refers to the fragment number in the popular English translation of A. J. Krailsheimer (New York: Penguin Books, 1966), based on the edition of M. Lafuma. For a discussion of the various editions, see R. J. Nelson, *Pascal: Adversary and Advocate* (Cambridge, Mass.: Harvard University Press, 1981), 229–234.

5. Melville, *Moby-Dick*, Chapter 133, "The Chase—First Day," 448.

6. Ibid., Chapter 99, "The Doubloon," 358.

7. Ibid., Chapter 42, "The Whiteness of the Whale," 170.

8. Ibid., Chapter 27, "Knights and Squires," 108.

9. P. H. Reardon, "Captain Ahab's Rebellion," *Touchstone* 8 (1995): 15–18, where he continues, "Melville is not really convinced that the old sea captain is altogether wrong."

10. Cf. W. Braswell, *Melville's Religious Thought: An Essay in Interpretation* (New York: Pageant Books, 1959), 68, who believes Ahab "sounds very much like Melville."

11. Melville, *Moby-Dick*, Chapter 41, "Moby Dick," 162.

12. Cf. E. M. Behnken, "The Joban Theme in Moby Dick," *The Iliff Review* 33 (1976): 37–48, esp. 42, "Melville makes the ship into a microcosm of the world. Ahab as its captain is not different in kind but only in degree from the rest of mankind. Ahab, then, provides a magnified case of the reality that is man."

13. Pascal, *Pensées*, fr. 143 (139). Krailsheimer's rendering is less literal but wonderfully succinct: "How hollow and foul is the heart of man!" T. V. Morris, *Making Sense of It All: Pascal and the Meaning of Life* (Grand Rapids, Mich.: Eerdmans, 1992), 32, gives it even more pithily as, "We are . . . full of crap."

14. Pascal, *Pensées*, fr. 296 (59).

15. See J. L. Crenshaw, *Old Testament Wisdom: An Introduction* (Atlanta: John Knox Press, 1981), 80–91.

16. Pascal, *Pensées*, fr. 162 (413), fr. 163 (46), fr. 163b (197).

17. Ibid., fr. 165b (70), fr. 170 (132).

18. Cf. Kolakowski, *God Owes Us Nothing*, 133: "The goal is not to show us that we tend to embellish our image for our own comfort as well as for the eyes of others, but to make us realize that, whatever we might think, we are really unhappy, and only pretend not to feel our pain . . . we come to see that we spend most of our time seeking an illusory escape from reality into all sorts of 'divertissements.'"

19. Pascal, *Pensées*, fr. 139 (136).

20. Ibid., fr. 171 (414).

21. Ibid., fr. 425 (148), fr. 172 (47).

22. Cf. Kolakowski, *God Owes Us Nothing*, 134–135: "anything we do — useful or not, necessary or otherwise — is at the service of the devil if it is not done for God's sake; if it is not, in people's minds, an act of obedience to the divine commandments and of praising the Lord. Any other goal — not only pleasure or gain but the sheer necessity of sustaining one's own life — is illicit if it is the goal in itself."

23. Cf. Morris, *Making Sense of It All*, 34: "What is wrong is our *always* using such activities as diversions in such a way as to keep us from *ever* having to grapple with the big issues of life" (emphasis in original).

24. Pascal, *Pensées*, fr. 398 (116), fr. 409 (117), fr. 434 (131); on human greatness in Pascal, cf. R. H. Soltau, *Pascal: The Man and the Message* (Westport, Conn.: Greenwood Press, 1970; originally published 1927), 119–121.

25. Pascal, *Pensées*, fr. 397 (114).

26. Melville, *Moby-Dick*, Chapter 30, "The Pipe," 114.

27. Ibid., Chapter 36, "The Quarter-deck," 143.

28. Ibid., Chapter 41, "Moby Dick," 160.

29. Ibid., Chapter 52, "The Albatross," 203.

30. Ibid., Chapter 108, "Ahab and the Carpenter," 392.

31. Ibid., Chapter 132, "The Symphony," 443.

32. Ibid., Chapter 16, "The Ship," 77.

33. The identification of J. F. Gardner, "Ishmael on Watch," *Parabola* 2 (1977): 30–39, and T. Woodson, "Ahab's Greatness: Prometheus as Narcissus," in *Critical Essays on Herman Melville's Moby-Dick*, ed. B. Higgins and H. Parker (New York: G. K. Hall, 1992), 440–455.

34. The primary identification of H. B. Franklin, *The Wake of the Gods: Melville's Mythology* (Stanford, Calif.: Stanford University Press, 1963), 72–98.

35. One of the points made by J. Stampfer, "Reply to 'The Modern Job,'" *Judaism* 13 (1964): 361–363.

36. W. H. Auden, "Ahab," in *The Enchafed Flood; or, the Romantic Iconography of the Sea* (Charlottesville: University Press of Virginia, 1950), 133–140; reprinted in *Ahab*, ed. H. Bloom (New York: Chelsea House, 1991), 15–19.

37. See, from the preceding note, the excellent collection of essays *Ahab*. On the parallels with Edmund, see J. Markels, *Melville and the Politics of Identity: From King Lear to Moby-Dick* (Urbana: University of Illinois Press, 1993).

38. Melville, *Moby-Dick*, Chapter 28, "Ahab," 110.

39. Ibid.; also Chapter 36, "The Quarter-deck," 143.

40. Ibid., Chapter 37, "Sunset," 147.

41. Ibid., Chapter 16, "The Ship," 77.

42. Ibid., Chapter 41, "Moby Dick," 160.

43. Ibid., Chapter 16, "The Ship," 76.

44. Ahab's past is left deliberately ominous, meaningful, but mysterious, by the crew's conflicting speculations on Ahab's scar. Ibid., Chapter 28, "Ahab," 110.

45. Cf. the description of Job by M. Friedman, "The Modern Job: On Melville, Dostoevsky, and Kafka," *Judaism* 12 (1963): 436–455: "Job is wrong not because he has witnessed for himself and contended with God but because he could not justify himself without condemning God. . . . This image includes the existential situation of a man who suffers and despairs, the question about man and about the meaning of his own existence that this situation produces, and the courage and strength of the Biblical rebel who both trusts and contends."

46. J. Bernstein, "Herman Melville's Concept of Ultimate Reality and Meaning in *Moby-Dick*," *Ultimate Reality and Meaning* 5 (1982): 104–117.

47. Melville, *Moby-Dick*, Chapter 2, "The Carpet-Bag," 19.

48. Ibid., Chapter 58, "Brit," 236.

49. Ibid., Chapter 16, "The Ship," 71.

50. Ibid., Chapter 41, "Moby Dick," 161.

51. Cf. B. Cowan, "Reading Ahab," in *Ahab*, 116–123: "This something, roughly phrased, consists of the realization that man in his present state not only is alienated from his original kingly image but has even forgotten this alienation. The reason for both alienation and forgetting is the too great suffering attendant on the dethronement of original man."

52. Melville, *Moby-Dick*, Chapter 26, "Knights and Squires," 104–105; cf. the analysis of the passage in W. Hamilton, *Melville and the Gods* (Chico, Calif.: Scholars Press, 1985), 12–13. On Pascal's compatibility with democracy, see Morris, *Making Sense of It All*, 147: "On the contrary, many people have argued that the case for democracy can be made most strongly from the perspective of a worldview in accordance with which all human beings are created with equal, eternal, and infinite value in the image of God."

53. Melville, *Moby-Dick*, Chapter 36, "The Quarter-Deck," 144.

54. Ibid., Chapter 37, "Sunset," 147.

55. Ibid., Chapter 46, "Surmises," 183.

56. Cf. W. A. Young, "Leviathan in the Book of Job and *Moby-Dick*," *Soundings* 65 (1982): 388–401: "His downfall is not his metaphysical challenge, but a moral deterioration which destroys the innate human tendency to act justly and with compassion. . . . In the final analysis, 'Ahab becomes an accomplice of the divine malice to which he offers the worship of defiance'" (quoting T. W. Herbert Jr., *Moby-Dick and Calvinism: A World Dismantled* [New Brunswick, N.J.: Rutgers University Press, 1977], 157).

57. Melville, *Moby-Dick*, Chapter 26, "Knights and Squires," 104.

58. Ibid., Chapter 107, "The Carpenter," 387.

59. H. Hayford, " 'Loomings' : Yarns and Figures in the Fabric," in *Critical Essays on Herman Melville's Moby-Dick*, ed. B. Higgins and H. Parker (New York: G. K. Hall, 1992), 456–469. On this theme, see also N. K. Hill, "Following Ahab to Doom or 'Goberning de Shark': *Moby-Dick* as Democratic Reflection," *Cross Currents* 40 (1990): 256–264; and Markels, *Melville and the Politics of Identity*, esp. 86–104, for the Hobbesian and Lockean influences on the contrast between Ahab and Ishmael. Through strange numerological manipulations, V. Sachs, "Moby Dick; or The Wale [*sic*] et l'écriture biblique," *Foi et Vie* 90 (1991): 81–92, arrives at the similar conclusion that the novel is an allegory for Melville's America.

60. A. Kazin, "Ishmael and Ahab," *Atlantic Monthly* 198, no. 5 (November 1956): 83, reprinted in *Ahab*, 28–30.

61. For example, Pascal, *Pensées*, fr. 446 (278), fr. 592 (204), fr. 730 (324), fr. 774 (221). See also D. Wetsel, *Pascal and Disbelief: Catechesis and Conversion in the Pensées* (Washington, D.C.: Catholic University of America Press, 1994), 177–242.

62. For example, Pascal, *Pensées*, fr. 564 (835), fr. 808 (846), fr. 839 (854), fr. 843 (840). Cf. Nelson, *Adversary and Advocate*, 186: "In Pascal's theology, miracles do not convince and they are far from converting. As Pascal will maintain in his projected Apology for the Christian Religion, miracles may even confound belief." This position opposes the more simplistic view that Pascal considers miracles as unambiguous "proof": e.g. D. Adamson, *Blaise Pascal: Mathematician, Physicist and Thinker About God* (New York: St. Martin's Press, 1995), 78–81, 183–185.

63. Pascal, *Pensées*, fr. 174 (403).

64. Ibid., fr. 152 (77).

65. Ibid., fr. 243 (463).

66. Ibid., fr. 389 (75). The relevance to Solomon is greater since Pascal probably accepted the attribution of Ecclesiastes to him: see the discussion of authorship by R. N. Whybray, *Ecclesiastes* (Grand Rapids, Mich.: Eerdmans, 1989), 3–14.

67. Pascal, *Pensées*, fr. 327 (83).

68. Ibid., fr. 348 (113), fr. 347 (200).

69. Ibid., fr. 397 (114), fr. 399 (437).

70. Ibid., fr. 741 (811), quoting Job 19:25.

71. Ibid., fr. 656 (590), quoting Rom 5:14.

72. Ibid., fr. 523 (226).

73. Ibid., fr. 434 (131), fr. 560 (431).

74. Cf. H. M. Davidson, *The Origins of Certainty: Means and Meaning in Pascal's Pensées* (Chicago: University of Chicago Press, 1979), 47: "At the end of this process, in the fact of our incomprehensibility—for we are in the midst of a discussion of reason and what it can understand of our condition—we look for some principle of explanation. Pascal tells us that it is the mystery of original sin. That represents one degree of intelligibility, one step in the pacifying of the mind and the removal of obstacles."

75. Edwin Cady, "'As Through a Glass Eye, Darkly': The Bible in the Nineteenth-Century American Novel," in *The Bible and American Arts and Letters*, ed. G. Gunn (Philadelphia: Fortress Press, 1983), 33–55. The classic work on Melville's overall use of scripture is N. Wright, *Melville's Use of the Bible* (Durham, N.C.: Duke University Press, 1949).

76. L. Thompson, *Melville's Quarrel with God* (Princeton: Princeton University Press, 1952), 163.

77. D. B. Lockerbie, "The Greatest Sermon in Fiction," *Christianity Today* 8 (November 8, 1963): 9–12.

78. The opinion of J. A. Holstein, "Melville's Inversion of Jonah in *Moby-Dick*," *Iliff Review* 42 (1985): 13–20.

79. Cf. J. Stout, "Melville's Use of the Book of Job," *Nineteenth-Century Fiction* 25 (1970): 69–83, esp. 69–70, "Both Job and Ecclesiastes . . . held special appeal for the speculative and unorthodox Melville."

80. Melville, *Moby-Dick*, Chapter 41, "Moby Dick," 162.

81. Ibid., Chapter 36, "The Quarter-deck," 144.

82. Cf. Reardon, "Captain Ahab's Rebellion," 17: "So God is as responsible for evil as for good. In this line of reasoning, damnation is not a divine afterthought. God himself must be held to account for the metaphysical injustice of man's plight. Of this, Captain Ahab entertains no doubts."

83. Melville, *Moby-Dick*, Chapter 36, "The Quarter-deck," 144.

84. Ibid., Chapter 119, "The Candles," 416, 417. Again, this position is at least in part Melville's own, as Stout, "Melville's Use of Job," 78, points out: "it appears likely enough that he meant as his own Ahab's 'I now know thy right worship is defiance.'"

85. Cf. Behnken, "Joban Theme," 43–44: "Ahab and Job were asserting their natural right to know, to receive answers, and when they were close to the Unknowable, they became even more determined and insistent. . . . His complaints cannot be ignored until he is dead because as long as he is living, he will raise the taboo questions of existence."

86. Melville, *Moby-Dick*, Chapter 73, "Stubb and Flask Kill a Right Whale," 277.

87. Ibid., Chapter 114, "The Gilder," 406.

88. But cf. J. A. Holstein, "Melville's Inversion of Job in *Moby-Dick*," 13–19, esp. 14–15, who regards Stubb's interpretation as simply a less sophisticated version of Melville's own.

89. Melville, *Moby-Dick*, Chapter 81, "The Pequod Meets the Virgin," 300.

90. Ibid., Chapter 58, "Brit," 235; cf. Friedman, "Modern Job," 440: "If *Moby-Dick* is, indeed, a celebration of the American whaling industry and of expanding American civilization, it is also, at a profounder level, a deep recognition of the tragedy of such expansion—the inevitable, tragic limitations that are encountered by the American frontiersman, the giant industrialist, or, for that matter, modern man in all his forms since the Renaissance. These are the limits of existence, the limits of creation with which God 'taunts' Job."

91. Young, "Leviathan in the Book of Job and *Moby-Dick*," 398.

92. Melville, *Moby-Dick*, Chapter 66, "The Shark Massacre," 257.

93. Ibid., Chapter 18, "His Mark," 83.

94. Ibid., Chapter 10, "A Bosom Friend," 52.

95. J. Baird, *Ishmael* (Baltimore: Johns Hopkins University Press, 1956), 247.

96. Melville, *Moby-Dick*, "Epilogue," 470, quoting Job 1:14–19.

97. Ibid., Chapter 110, "Queequeg in His Coffin," 399.

98. Ibid., Chapter 135, "The Chase—Third Day," 469.

99. Ibid.

100. Ibid., "Epilogue," 470. On the image of the vortex in *Moby-Dick*, see Baird, *Ishmael*, 266–273; R. Zoellner, "Ahab's Entropism and Ishmael's Cyclicism," in *Ahab*, 104–115, esp. 112–114.

101. Though possibly even the end of Job could be read this way, as done by Behnken, "Joban Theme," 46: "God has put eternity in men's minds, and then He punishes the person who reaches out to grasp it. Both Job and Ahab know in the end that they *must* take destiny into their own hands because no loving God will take care of them" (emphasis in original). On the contrast between Ahab and Job, see Friedman, "Modern Job," 440: "Ahab contends with existence but can have no real dialogue with it. Ahab has stood his ground before Moby Dick as Job before God Who created Leviathan together with him. But Ahab lacks that experience of an answering response to his cry that gives Job back his humanity and gives meaning to his suffering."

102. C. H. Holmain, "The Reconciliation of Ishmael: *Moby-Dick* and the Book of Job," *South Atlantic Quarterly* 57 (1958): 477–490.

103. Melville, *Moby-Dick*, Chapter 96, "The Try-Works," 355.

104. See the similar analyses of Hamilton, *Melville and the Gods*, 14–15; M. M. Sealts Jr., "Melville and the Platonic Tradition," in *Critical Essays on Herman Melville's Moby-Dick*, 355–376, esp. 370–371; but cf. the contrary opinion of Thompson, *Melville's Quarrel with God*, 222–227, who sees Melville embracing Ahab's madness, not counseling against it.

105. Melville, *Moby-Dick*, Chapter 96, "The Try-Works," 355; cf. the analysis of D. S. Arnold, " 'But the Draught of a Draught': Reading the Wonder of Ishmael's Telling," *Semeia* 31 (1985): 171–193: "Ishmael is never completely overwhelmed by the wonders of the terrible reality he confronts. Melville does not submit to nihilism, for the self survives the voyage to tell of the ambiguities of the quest for certainty."

106. Melville, *Moby-Dick*, "Epilogue," 470.

107. Baird, *Ishmael*, 251.

108. Melville, *Moby-Dick*, Chapter 10, "A Bosom Friend," 52.

109. This is true, even if Queequeg is "only" a "well-governed shark," as per R. Zoellner, "Queequeg: The Well-Governed Shark," in *Twentieth Century Interpretations of Moby-Dick: A Collection of Critical Essays*, ed. M. T. Gilmore (Englewood Cliffs, N.J.: Prentice-Hall, 1977), 87–93, for he does not participate in the hypocrisy and subtle viciousness of the white characters, his "sharkishness" is frank, acknowledged, and always under control.

110. M. L. Taylor, "Ishmael's (m)Other: Gender, Jesus, and God in Melville's *Moby-Dick*," *Journal of Religion* 72 (1992): 325–350.

111. Melville, *Moby-Dick*, Chapter 47, "The Mat-Maker," 185.

112. Ibid., Chapter 10, "A Bosom Friend," 54.

113. Ibid., 53.

114. Cf. Holmain, "Reconciliation of Ishmael," 488: "Queequeg, the cannibal harpooner, gives him the first lesson in acceptance, and he doubles his world by pledging eternal friendship with this heathen seller of shrunken heads."

115. Baird, *Ishmael*, 246–247.

116. Melville, *Moby-Dick*, Chapter 110, "Queequeg in His Coffin," 395.

117. Ibid., Chapter 127, "The Deck," 433.

118. Pascal, *Pensées*, fr. 278 (424).

119. Ibid., fr. 793 (308).

120. Ibid., fr. 277 (423).

121. Ibid., fr. 793 (308). In the parallelism of this fragment, people are either carnal, intellectual, or wise, according to whether they value bodies, minds, or charity.

122. Matt 22:37–39; Mark 12:30–31; Luke 10:27; Deut 6:5; Lev 19:18.

123. Cf. Morris, *Making Sense of It All*, 191: "The heart is the deepest point of contact for emotions, attitudes, and beliefs. It is also the deepest source

for human actions. . . . It may involve connectedness that is mental (intellectual), attitudinal (emotional), and volitional (involved with will and action) and thus, in its completeness, spiritual."

124. Though Melville most frequently contrasts the land and sea, on the image of sharks he sees both realms as full of them: *Moby-Dick*, Chapter 64, "Stubb's Supper," 249, and Chapter 65, "The Whale as a Dish," 255–256. He performs the same undoing of the land-sea dichotomy with Chapter 89, "Fast Fish and Loose Fish."

125. Melville, *Moby-Dick*, Chapter 87, "The Grand Armada," 326.

126. On the contrast between Ahab and Ishmael, cf. Young, "Leviathan in the Book of Job and *Moby-Dick*," 394: "The lack of interaction between Ahab and Ishmael suggests that Melville intends to separate their journeys and exploit the resultant ambiguity of meaning."

127. Holmain, "Reconciliation of Ishmael," 482.

128. Cf. the similar conclusion of Zoellner, "Ahab's Entropism and Ishmael's Cyclicism," 113–114: "The Grand Armada is a partial, essentially cetological resolution for Ishmael's hypo concerning the void. . . . The 'Epilogue' is the ultimate statement of the redemptive cyclicism of *Moby-Dick*, and the final repudiation of Ahab's entropism."

129. Cf. J. Stampfer, "Reply," 361, "The paradoxes remain, the awesome mystery and power of the whale, but however Biblical Melville's drama, his point of view is that of Ishmael, rather than of Isaac. Men are redeemed not by encounter, but by its avoidance." This last sentence cannot be correct: Ishmael has continued his encounter with the sea and God, but it is with a much different outlook and goal than Ahab.

130. Melville, *Moby-Dick*, Chapter 1, "Loomings," 14; cf. R. A. Sherrill, "The Career of Ishmael's Self-Transcendence," in *Herman Melville's Moby-Dick*, ed. H. Bloom (New York: Chelsea House, 1986), 73–95: "When all meaning appears to be relative, when the possibility of objective knowledge seems lost, it is not surprising that knowledge, for Ishmael, comes to be understood as self-projection onto what is essentially indeterminate ground. His gazing into the water reflects only his self-image: he can become Narcissus."

131. Sherrill, "Ishmael's Self-Transcendence," 94–95; cf. Stout, "Melville's Use of Job," 78: "But like Job Ishmael regains his serenity; he learns reconciliation to the world, though not an answer to the riddle of why evil and suffering exist."

132. Soltau, *Pascal*, 115.

133. From the last page of Morris, *Making Sense of It All*, 212.

Contributors

Michael F. Andrews is Assistant Professor of Philosophy at Seattle University, where he also directs the Faith and the Great Ideas Program. He has published in *Analecta Husserliana* and *The Husserl Circle* and has contributed to *The Phenomenology of Prayer*, ed. Bruce Benson and Norman Wirzba (Fordham University Press). He is currently working on a study of Edith Stein's phenomenology of empathy.

Jeffrey Bloechl is Edward Bennett Williams Fellow and Assistant Professor in the Department of Philosophy at the College of the Holy Cross. He is the author of *Liturgy of the Neighbor: Emmanuel Levinas and the Religion of Responsibility* (Duquesne University Press), and the editor of *The Face of the Other and the Trace of God: Essays on the Philosophy of Emmanuel Levinas* (Fordham University Press) and *Religious Experience and the End of Metaphysics* (Indiana University Press). He is also the translator of Roger Burggraeve's *The Wisdom of Love in the Service of Love* (Marquette University Press) and of Jean-Louis Chrétien's *The Unforgettable and the Unhoped For* (Fordham University Press).

John D. Caputo is the Thomas J. Watson Professor of Religion and Humanities at Syracuse University. His newest books are *The Weakness of God: A Theology of the Event* (Indiana University Press, forthcoming) and *Augustine and Postmodernism: Confessions and*

Circumfession, coedited with Michael Scanlon (Indiana University Press). His recent publications include *On Religion* (Routledge), *More Radical Hermeneutics: On Not Knowing Who We Are* (Indiana University Press), *The Prayers and Tears of Jacques Derrida: Religion without Religion* (Indiana University Press), *Deconstruction in a Nutshell: A Conversation with Jacques Derrida* (Fordham University Press). He also serves as editor of the Fordham University Press book series "Perspectives in Continental Philosophy" and as Chairman of the Board of Editors of *Journal of Cultural and Religious Theory*.

Kristine A. Culp is Dean of the Disciples Divinity House of the University of Chicago and Senior Lecturer in Theology at the Divinity School of the University of Chicago. She has written on feminist and womanist theologies, on Christian community, on protest and resistance as theological themes, and on the use of fiction in theological construction. She is currently completing a book entitled *Ambiguity, Community, Salvation: A Theology of Life Together before God*.

Kevin Hart is Notre Dame Professor of English at the University of Notre Dame, where he directs the Program in Religion and Literature and edits *Religion and Literature*. He is the author of *The Trespass of the Sign* (Cambridge University Press; rev. ed. Fordham University Press), *A.D. Hope* (Oxford University Press), *Samuel Johnson and the Culture of Property* (Cambridge University Press), *Postmodernism: A Beginner's Guide* (Oneworld), and *The Dark Gaze: Maurice Blanchot and the Sacred* (Chicago University Press). He is the coeditor, with Geoffrey Hartman, of *The Power of Contestation: Perspectives on Maurice Blanchot* (Johns Hopkins University Press) and, with Yvonne Sherwood, of *Derrida and Religion: Other Testaments* (Routledge). The author of several collections of poetry, Kevin Hart's most recent collection is *Flame Tree: Selected Poems* (Bloodaxe).

Kevin L. Hughes is Associate Professor of Theology and Religious Studies at Villanova University. He is the author of *Constructing Antichrist* (Catholic University of America Press), and has published articles in *Modern Theology*, *Heythrop Journal*, and *Augustinian Studies*. He is currently working on a study of St. Bonaventure.

Jean-Yves Lacoste is Fellow of Clare College, Cambridge, and a parish priest in Paris. His publications include *Experience and the Absolute* (Fordham University Press), *Note sur le temps: essai sur les raisons* *de la mémoire et l'espérance* (Presses Universitaire de France) and *Le Monde et l'absense de l'oevre, et autre etudes* (Presses Universitaire de France). He is the editor of the *Encyclopedia of Christian Theology* (Routledge).

Crystal J. Lucky is Associate Professor of English, Africana Studies, and Women's Studies at Villanova University, where she teaches nineteenth- and twentieth-century African-American literature. She is currently working on a critical edition of the autobiography of Charlotte Riley, a nineteenth-century preaching woman from South Carolina (forthcoming from the University of Wisconsin Press). She is also an ordained elder in the Church of the Living God International.

Renee McKenzie is the Rector of Calvary Episcopal Church, NL, in Philadelphia. She recently completed her doctorate at Temple University with a dissertation entitled, "A Womanist Social Ontology: An Exploration of the Self / Other Relationship in Womanist Religious Scholarship."

Kim Paffenroth is Associate Professor of Religious Studies at Iona College. His most recent publications include *The Heart Set Free: Sin and Redemption in the Gospels, Augustine Dante and Flannery O'Connor* (Continuum), *In Praise of Wisdom: Literary and Theological Reflections on Faith and Reason* (Continuum) and, coedited with Robert Kennedy, *A Reader's Companion to Augustine's Confessions* (John Knox Press).

Michael Purcell is Senior Lecturer in Systemic Theology in the Divinity School of the University of Edinburgh. He is the author of *Method and Mystery: The Other in Rahner and Levinas* (Marquette University Press) and *Emmanuel Levinas and Theology* (Cambridge University Press).

Michael J. Scanlon, O.S.A., holds the Josephine C. Connelly Chair in Christian Theology at Villanova University. He has coedited with John D. Caputo *God, the Gift, and Postmodernism* (Indiana University Press), *Augustine and Postmodernism* (Indiana University Press) and *Questioning God* (Indiana University Press). He has also published articles recently in *New Theology Review* and *The Ecumenist*.

James K. A. Smith is Associate Professor of Philosophy and Director of Seminars in Christian Scholarship at Calvin College. He is the author of *The Fall of Interpretation: Philosophical Foundations for a Creational Hermeneutic* (Inter Varsity Press), *Speech and Theology: Language and the Logic of Incarnation* (Routledge), *Introducing Radical Orthodoxy: Mapping a Post-Secular Theology* (Baker Academic), and, with Kelly James Clark and Richard Lints, *101 Key Terms in Philosophy and their Importance for Theology* (John Knox Press).

Index

objectivity, 111, 124
reflections, 73–74
Divine Names, The (Pseudo-Dionysius), 141
Divisions, in experience, 3–4
Doty, Thomas K., 181–82

Economic Trinity, 11
Ecstasy, 224n23
Edge of experience, 221n15
Ego
    alter, 141, 150–52
    as consciousness, 95–96
    displaced, 16
    intention of, 107
    perception of, 91–92, 93
Égoïsme á deux, 9
Egology, 158–61
Eliot, T. S., 8–10
Emotional empathy, 152–53
Emotional feelings, 4–5
Emotional life, 101
Empathy, 138, 140–41, 144–45, 150–53
Empiricism, absolute, 20
Empiricist, 23
Empty experience, 141, 205–6
Encyclopedia (Hegel), 74–75
Epiphany, 69
Ethical humanity, 124–25
Ethical relations, 122–23
Ethics
    of suffering, 127–28
    in Torah, 119–20
Evaluation, of sermon, 238n32
Excellence, of human nature, 26, 196–97
Existence, 94–96, 106–8
    liturgy and, 98
    question about, 243n85
Expectation, living with, 166
Experience
    of human nature, 3, 6
    tradition v., 3–4
Experiential clot, 55–57, 67–68
Experiential flow, 57, 221n15
Experiential risk, 23–24, 30–31
Extremes, in human nature, 201–9
Extremis, limit point in, 37
Extrinsicist, 227–28n2

Facere veritatem, 23–24, 41, 45
Faith
    concentration on, 82
    before experience, 76–77
    during holocaust, 118–20
    life of, 106–7
    of mediocre fellow, 29–31
    in phenomenological structure, 40
    potentiation of, 30
    recognition of, 81–82
    structure of, 91–92
    test of, 119–20, 207
    in Torah, 119–20
    transformation from, 81–83, 89–90
Faithfulness itself, 10
Feelings, 4–5
Female sermons, black, 173–74, 176–81, 236n16, 238n32. *See also* Foote, Julia
Feminist theology, 13
    accountability in, 60–64
    challenges in, 48–49
    critique in, 219n9
    disjunction in, 58–60, 64–66
    history of, 47–48, 220–21n14
    iconoclasm in, 58–59
    sympathy in, 58–59, 64
    truth in, 59–60, 69, 218n1
    universalizing, 66
    use of, 49–50
Feminist women, community of, 47–48
Feminized piety, 61–62
Fetishized experiences, 49–50
Finite being, 74–75
Foote, Julia, 174, 181–83, 186–91
Foreign experience, 139, 145–46
Foretaste, 109–12
Four Quartets (Eliot), 8–10
Frage-Antwort-Modell (Jüngel), 6–7
Fragility
    of experience, 109–10
    of Job, 202–3
Freedom, in human nature, 197–98
"The Freedom Church," 182–83
Fulkerson, Mary McClintock, 219n9
Future, absolute, 33–34
Future-present, hope in, 31–34

Perspectives in
Continental Philosophy Series
John D. Caputo, series editor

14. Mark C. Taylor, *Journeys to Selfhood: Hegel and Kierkegaard*. Second edition.

15. Dominique Janicaud, Jean-François Courtine, Jean-Louis Chrétien, Michel Henry, Jean-Luc Marion, and Paul Ricœur, *Phenomenology and the "Theological Turn": The French Debate*.

16. Karl Jaspers, *The Question of German Guilt*. Introduction by Joseph W. Koterski, S.J.

17. Jean-Luc Marion, *The Idol and Distance: Five Studies*. Translated with an introduction by Thomas A. Carlson.

18. Jeffrey Dudiak, *The Intrigue of Ethics: A Reading of the Idea of Discourse in the Thought of Emmanuel Levinas*.

19. Robyn Horner, *Rethinking God As Gift: Marion, Derrida, and the Limits of Phenomenology*.

20. Mark Dooley, *The Politics of Exodus: Søren Keirkegaard's Ethics of Responsibility*.

21. Merold Westphal, *Toward a Postmodern Christian Faith: Overcoming Onto-Theology*.

22. Edith Wyschogrod, Jean-Joseph Goux and Eric Boynton, eds., *The Enigma of Gift and Sacrifice*.

23. Stanislas Breton, *The Word and the Cross*. Translated with an introduction by Jacquelyn Porter.

24. Jean-Luc Marion, *Prolegomena to Charity*. Translated by Stephen E. Lewis.

25. Peter H. Spader, *Scheler's Ethical Personalism: Its Logic, Development, and Promise*.

26. Jean-Louis Chrétien, *The Unforgettable and the Unhoped For*. Translated by Jeffrey Bloechl.

27. Don Cupitt, *Is Nothing Sacred? The Non-Realist Philosophy of Religion: Selected Essays*.

28. Jean-Luc Marion, *In Excess: Studies of Saturated Phenomena*. Translated by Robyn Horner and Vincent Berraud.

29. Phillip Goodchild, *Rethinking Philosophy of Religion: Approaches from Continental Philosophy*.

30. William J. Richardson, S.J., *Heidegger: Through Phenomenology to Thought*.

31. Jeffrey Andrew Barash, *Martin Heidegger and the Problem of Historical Meaning*.

32. Jean-Louis Chrétien, *Hand to Hand: Listening to the Work of Art*. Translated by Stephen E. Lewis.

33. Jean-Louis Chrétien, *The Call and the Response*. Translated with an introduction by Anne Davenport.

34. D. C. Schindler, *Han Urs von Balthasar and the Dramatic Structure of Truth: A Philosophical Investigation*.

35. Julian Wolfreys, ed., *Thinking Difference: Critics in Conversation*.

LaVergne, TN USA
19 August 2009
155101LV00006B/199/P